Praise for *Ghosts of the Farm*

'Nicola Chester is the John Clare of our time.'

GUY SHRUBSOLE, author of *The Lost Rainforests of Britain*

'This is a rich and riveting book, and I didn't want it to end. Interweaving the fascinating story of a woman farmer in the Second World War with the author's own story as she attempts to advocate for a nature-depleted countryside, it's a gentle battle cry – heartwarming, melancholy and vital.'

LISSA EVANS, author of *Small Bomb at Dimperley*

'A wonderfully evocative account of a fascinating and until now untold story, uniting two women's passions for farming and the English countryside.'

STEPHEN MOSS, author of *Ten Birds That Changed the World*

'Nicola's evocation of Miss White truly haunts me. Energetic, enigmatic and with one foot poised over a chasm of change, *Ghosts of the Farm* brings joy and thoughtfulness, litanies of horses' names, and Land Girls hoeing in their underwear. The woman farmer from wartime and the woman writer from the present, whose stories haunt this book, share a practicality, frustrations, hopes and fears for the future of the landscape they love.

'You are drawn, in the green sweet breath of hay, into these women's worlds.'

ALISON BRACKENBURY, poet and broadcaster

'This captivating dual-stranded memoir puts rural women firmly in their place: right at the heart of the farm. Nicola Chester and her indomitable predecessor Miss Julia White are unforgettable guides to a changed and changing countryside.'

MELISSA HARRISON, author of *All Among the Barley*

'Nicola Chester will come to be seen as a Nan Shepherd of our time. She knows the land, and its lives, with a knowing that can only come from a million barefoot steps across it. She loves the land with a tenacity that stems only from having fought and cried hot tears for it. And she writes with a clarity that aches on the page. *Ghosts of the Farm* is devastatingly good. Hairs-on-the-back-of-my-neck good.'

NICK ACHESON, author of *The Meaning of Geese*

'No one, but no one, writes like Nicola Chester. Her blend of grit, sensitivity, integrity, wisdom and artistry is unique. *Ghosts of the Farm* is a clear-eyed view of the social and ecological thinning of English rural life, but it's also a breath of oxygen to its resilient embers of sustainability and equitability. A bittersweet and timely tonic for the soul of British farming.'

AMY-JANE BEER, author of *The Flow*

'A heartening, haunted and beautifully written book that is a powerful paean to rural life and working the land.'

ROB COWEN, author of *The North Road*

'Through Nicola's experiences, the heartbeats of ghosts are revived and woven into the present and future, reminding us that we are all rooted to the earth we share, live and eventually become. Nicola is a special writer: her words the tips of her consciousness and the core of her bones. *Ghosts of the Farm* transports me through time while inviting me to embrace every single moment and the wild and tame lives we share our territories with.'

HANNAH BOURNE-TAYLOR, author of *Nature Needs You*

'*Ghosts of the Farm* is much more than a tale of two women struggling to become farmers while battling prejudice against their gender. Written in exquisite prose, it is a story celebrating the glory of the countryside and country living, a story of struggles and triumphs, in times of war and peace. I found myself rooting for both heroines.'

RHYS BOWEN, internationally best-selling author of *The Tuscan Child*, *The Venice Sketchbook* and other historical novels, as well as the Royal Spyness and Molly Murphy mystery series

GHOSTS OF THE FARM

Also by Nicola Chester

On Gallows Down

GHOSTS OF THE FARM

Two Women's Journeys Through Time, Land and Community

Nicola Chester

Chelsea Green Publishing
White River Junction, Vermont
London, UK

First published in 2025 by Chelsea Green Publishing | PO Box 4529 | White River Junction, VT 05001 | West Wing, Somerset House, Strand | London, WC2R 1LA, UK | www.chelseagreen.com
A Division of Rizzoli International Publications, Inc. | 49 West 27th Street | New York, NY 10001 | www.rizzoliusa.com

Cover art, *Day Begins Again*, by Kris Mercer, www.krismercerart.co.uk.

Publisher: Charles Miers
Deputy Publisher: Matthew Derr
Commissioning Editor: Muna Reyal
Project Manager: Susan Pegg
Copy Editor: Susan Pegg
Proofreader: Jacqui Lewis
Designer: Jenna Richardson

ISBN 978-1-915294-67-8 (hardcover) | ISBN 978-1-915294-68-5 (ebook) | ISBN 978-1-915294-69-2 (audiobook)
Library of Congress Control Number: 2025020976 (print)
A CIP catalogue record for this book is available from the British Library.

Our Commitment to Green Publishing
Chelsea Green sees publishing as a tool for cultural change and ecological stewardship. We strive to align our book manufacturing practices with our editorial mission and to reduce the impact of our business enterprise in the environment. We print our books using vegetable-based inks whenever possible. This book may cost slightly more because it was printed on paper that contains recycled fiber, and we hope you'll agree that it's worth it. *Ghosts of the Farm* was printed on paper supplied by Lake Book Manufacturing that is made of recycled materials and other controlled sources.

Authorized EU representative for product safety and compliance
Mondadori Libri S.p.A. | www.mondadori.it
via Gian Battista Vico 42 | Milan, Italy 20123

Printed in the United States of America.
10 9 8 7 6 5 4 3 2 1 25 26 27 28 29

This account of Julia Maud White is based upon her diary, *The Inkpen Saga*. Both her story, and mine, are true.

For my ghosts – imperfect, unknowable, incorruptible saints: Julia, Doris, Marguerite and Honor.

And for community leaders and engagers everywhere, in common unity, kindness and care.

Velvet cantered down the chalk road to the village. She ran on her own slender legs, making horse-noises and chirrups and occasionally striking her thigh with a switch, holding at the same time something very small before her as she ran.

Enid Bagnold, *National Velvet*

This is a female text, written in the twenty-first century. How late it is. How much has changed. How little.

Doireann Ní Ghríofa, *A Ghost in the Throat*

CONTENTS

PART II
INKPEN

PREFACE

The Bedroom Carpet Farm

I am eight years old.

I am a horse.

But. I am also its rider.

As my legs gallop faster along the road, my hands are raised to hold the reins (sometimes a thin dog lead), the leather passing correctly between ring and little finger of both hands, crossing my palms to be held, softly, sensitively on top by each thumb. I put my reins in one hand to reach down to pat my good horse's neck-of-air and shake my own mane in response.

In my imagination, all-consuming and utterly convincing to me, I am riding out to inspect my cows in the water meadows. From the old watermill, where Lytton Strachey and some of the bohemian Bloomsbury set lived before moving close to the village I live in now, I cross a narrow bridge over a little grass-washy chalk stream, straightened during the farming efforts of the Second World War. In wet weather, the stream's original meanders return like ghosts; little floods making inverted commas around the sentence of the straight line. I pass the concrete-block houses of that era's pillboxes; guard posts built to defend against an expected invasion in 1940. Sometimes, the cows shelter inside. Behind them, a dozen lovely cows of mixed breeding are already looking at me. I dismount my horse, reach out and rub the creamy dun cow with the black nose on the soft whorls of her forehead. I call her Rebecca (of Sunnybrook Farm). Her breath smells of fermented grass, her broad wet nose makes me grin. Her pink tongue licks my hand roughly and then goes up each of her nostrils in turn. The calf at her flank is curious, and I steal a glance, but even that makes the cow raise her head a little: it would be silly of me – and a breach of trust – to even attempt to touch her baby. I wipe my hands in the grass, giving them a 'farmer's wash', before remounting. We ride around the field boundaries, checking each trough is refilling, poking at the orange ballcock with a stick, before turning for home: back through the fields, through the allotments and clattering through our edge-of-village estate, in my old brown Mary Jane school shoes. Mrs Pastern (I think of the springy, shock-absorbing part of a horse's leg, between hoof and fetlock) calls out, 'Which is it you are exercising today?'

'Emma,' I call back. 'The chestnut mare… She doesn't like waiting!' Mrs Pastern waves, and the beginnings of an awkward self-consciousness prickle into my world as soon as the words are out of my mouth. I am grateful to this neighbour who plays the game with me, pretending I am riding a horse that exists in reality, not just in my imagination. I gallop off into my embarrassment, as if I can't stop myself. 'Emma', the horse I am riding, the horse I *am*, is a spirited chestnut mare; known among 'horsey people' (whom I desperately want to be) for a bold and unpredictable sensitive horse, not best suited to checking cows and fences. Tomorrow, I must bring out the sensible and patient pony I have imagined as Jack. But for now, I am home, and I must get on with the farm work.

I am also the farmer of my own bedroom-carpet farm.

I rebuild the little plastic-cobbled, drystone walls that clip together satisfyingly, like the bobble catch on Nan's handbag. *Clip*. It's my favourite form of enclosure that goes with the rest of my Britains Farm Toys, still Europe's biggest maker of accurate, to-scale agricultural toys. I love the piece with three rails and a stile built into it, which I place in the opposite corner to where I put the metal trough (so walkers and farmworkers alike won't have to walk through mud, puddled by thirsty animals; I try to be a good farmer). I put the sheep in, that I decide are probably Hampshire Downs, and put one ram in with them, with his plastic whorled fleece. Then I hitch Boxer, the grey carthorse, with his black harness collar, blinkers and gloriously feathered legs, into the blue-and-red tip cart and fill it with hay; stems of summer-dry grass, which I've snipped and twisted into haycocks.

The beloved battered and muddy blue Land Rover that lost its top in the garden is parked beneath the plastic curved and corrugated roof of the Dutch barn, beside the blue-and-white Ford tractor. Both of these vehicles have a towing hitch and suspension. I'll need to move them somewhere else if I happen to get the red Massey Ferguson combine harvester. I like the mixture of old and new on my farm. It's how I feel the best farms should be: change, progress and modernity, yes; but not forgetting what has gone before – especially if it is still perfectly useful. The stables are full, and all the horses named: Drummer and Comet, Clover and Skylark, Starlight and Sparrow, Copper and Beechnut; Joe, the Suffolk Punch; and Marmalade and Porridge, the Shetland ponies.

I am frustrated that there aren't other animals available on my farm though: the ones that aren't enclosed by the walls and fences; the farmland wildlife. Because this means just as much to me, and I see it all around, and wonder why it isn't included in the animals I can save up for and buy. Later, I make hedgerows and trees with green scouring pads, and graduate to Humbrol model paints.

There are a few people on my farm: a tractor driver; an ancient shepherd carrying a lamb and a crook, with a hessian corn sack as an apron rolled around his middle; hatless riders of the seventies, others with caps; and women. There are a few old figures from the 1930s (possibly lead-painted) – a rosy-cheeked woman with a basket and a missing arm in a long pink frock, apron and headscarf; a farmer and a carter in grubby, worn smocks – but also, more modern women: a seventies 'daughter' feeding chickens from a broad pan of meal, dressed in wellies and a miniskirt; a daffodil-blonde figure in a blue dress; an older woman wearing a green jacket, cap and a sensible, pleated skirt. But there are two others I like the best, that I feel could be grown-up me. One is a brunette dairy girl, smiling in white overalls, with red lips and black wellies, and her more serious friend is dressed in blue overalls over a cream blouse, with green wellies and the same postbox-red lips. Both are leaning to carry a heavy silver pail, using their hips and left arms to balance its weight. Both look keen, capable and full of energy for the work required of them. Most of the figures have a clever timelessness to them, while, at the same time, being utterly modern, summing up for me the mise en scène of the farms I see on TV or peer into from the sticky leatherette seats of our passing family Cortina.

These women were farmers on my farm. Not wives or daughters, but farmworkers. It didn't occur to me then that all but the two red-lipped figures first cast in the 1940s wore dresses with their sensible boots and carried baskets of corn for the hens or eggs, and had a distinct domestic tie to the farmhouse, market and kitchen.

I've seen and known some of these women, with their headscarves and intimidating, efficient, no-nonsense practicality. They are out in the fields, driving Land Rovers, organising things in the village. One of them appears on a poster on my wall: the legendary Miss Marguerite de Beaumont of the Shalbourne Stud, pictured in breeches and jacket, holding a beribboned horse she has bred, named Shalbourne Fiesta. I have one of her books, *The Way of a Horse*, on my shelf, sandwiched between pony stories featuring adventurous, courageous girls of slender (or no) means, and fiction, no matter the genre, of deep husbandry and knowledge that examine everything through the prism of the rural. Books where beguiling, ancient magic and history sit just below the surface, constantly threatening to break through into the now, overlaying my imagined and real countryside in deep-tilled layers. But in the books, and on the posters on my wall that mingle horses and farming scenes scissored out of magazines, there is a strange gender divide and a generation of women missing. Almost all the images of horses are with women and men, but all of the images of farming are exclusively with men and boys.

Yet I know they are there, or have *been* there, these often-older women from a different age, and I wonder, where have they gone and who is coming behind them? Hovering on the margins is the presence of those indomitable farming, horsey, outdoor women, ready, surely, to take me on as some kind of apprentice. With these women, and with these red-lipped girls in my bedroom-carpet fields, I am a farmer too, on my farm that spills out from my bedroom, right outside into the village, its estate, its fields.

I am seven, eight, nine, ten – eleven, even (at this point, my mother *and* my schoolteacher are worrying about me) and THIS IS NOT A PHASE.

I live almost entirely in my own imagination. I farm the greensward and ploughed swirls of the orange, patterned carpet, and it is inconceivable that, when I am a grown-up, I will be anything other than a farmer – one that rides and trains horses too; because if I dream it, and see and read about grown-up women doing it, that job surely exists? I just have to find these women and overcome my shyness and timidity around them, before they fade from view. Because I get a sense that that's what's happening. Like them, I am not afraid of hard work. I am there for the energy represented in the cheery seriousness of those 1:36 scale figures. It's all I want to be when I grow up.

I've been trying to find and inhabit that farm ever since, in whatever way I can.

PART I

APPRENTICES

CHAPTER ONE

Julia and the Caravan

October 1940

It is just past Michaelmas, the beginning of the new agricultural year, and Miss Julia White is as old – or young – as the century itself. For the second time in just over a week, she is committing herself to a new life, making the journey again from her comfortable home in Burley, in the New Forest in Hampshire, to a village neighbouring mine, just over the border in Wiltshire. She is driving her little Rover car, fuelled with just enough petrol to get her there (she hopes; petrol rationing is *strict*, and she silently and discreetly thanks an earlier version of herself, bold enough to hide a couple of cans away in the garden). Navigating with difficulty, because a German invasion is expected and all the road signs have been removed, this is an added pressure. But she's made the journey, the mistakes and several wrong turns before, and is determined not to make them again. This time, however, she is towing a small apple-green caravan behind her. Her two Dandie Dinmont terriers, Jo and Dina, are in their baskets on the back seat and somewhere along the bleak, open expanse of Salisbury Plain, with its parallel dust ribbons of white chalk for roads, live firing and intense military manoeuvres, she becomes subsumed into an army convoy of tanks. They are horribly close. She worries about stopping: if the colossal tank in front of her halts, will *she* be able to? And then what of the one behind? She pictures the frightful monster going right over her van and car, with herself and Jo and Dina in it, without it noticing a thing. She feels a bubble of a giggle rising as distant riding-club days before the last war swim unbidden into her memory: of riding an unstoppable pony that cannoned into the back of an orderly line, spilling every rider except herself, left, right and centre. She feels ridiculous, but also, deliciously alive and full of adventure. It is four months after the taking of France in just six short weeks and the retreat of Dunkirk. Her senses are heightened. The smell of soil from fresh craters reminds her vividly of the closest German bomb yet – that just missed her house six days ago, exploding in the bog beyond the garden after a horrible, pregnant pause; splattering her full, contraband petrol cans with mud as well as the walls of the house, and dropping into her hair and the trembling mug of beef tea still clutched in her hand, as she ventured outside, afterwards.

A hare dashes from the long, whitened grass and flees in front of her car, its mouth open, ears laid flat along its back. She gasps and instinctively lifts her foot to stamp on the brake but, alert to the danger, stops herself. The hare is swallowed back up by the Plain and its grasses.

I picture her gripping the slender wheel of the little Rover car, which nevertheless has the power to pull her new caravan, bought for £200 and fitted out herself with the considerable weight of a cast-iron Valor Perfection kerosene stove, a wooden haybox to cook in and all the caravan's heavy internal fittings. I imagine her rolling her shoulders back, pushing her seat bones down firmer into the car seat to urge it forwards, but not too much (she is a horse rider, after all). I doubt she talked to herself, as I might have done, or even to the dogs, restless in their baskets, between glances at the soldiers turning round to wave or jeer in front and those she couldn't see pressing in from behind. I wonder at their reactions and hilarity, shared in a lighter moment above the pumped-up roar of excitement, war, fear and machines, and the blanched-pale dust spun out by their metal caterpillar tracks. I wonder quite how she ended up in the middle of a column of tanks, towing a caravan across Salisbury Plain as if she were going on holiday (she wasn't, but I bet that's what they thought, incredulous). It probably made the soldiers' day. But I can feel her shuddering, relieved laugh – perhaps she allowed herself a half-scream, knuckles crammed into her mouth, or a snort – when she came off the Plain and finally pulled away from them, drawing her still-intact, little round apple of a home behind her.

She passes farms she remembers from the week before and notes the progress made with ploughing, waves enthusiastically at a gang threshing a tall rick – it cheers her as they wave back. She drives on through the Wiltshire villages, her little caravan turning heads in these quiet places; is chased by a group of children, agog around the village pond at Collingbourne Ducis, where a gleaming steam engine is filling up with water, and waves to them too.

Somewhere, on the long, lonely stretch over the Downs, she feels confident and near enough, now, to pull in and stop. Looking out to Chute Causeway and the hidden hamlet of Hippenscombe, painted by Ravilious three years earlier, she lets the dogs out of their baskets and opens her green Thermos vacuum flask of thin broth and unwraps a fish paste sandwich. She is quietly jubilant – and a little exposed.

Nevertheless, half a mile from her destination, she pauses for a moment, admitting cold feet. This time, she has let her house in the New Forest, to a bombed-out family from Southampton. She simply cannot turn back now, so she bustles Jo and Dina back into their baskets, settles in her seat again, straightens her elbows to fix the direction of the steering wheel into Shalbourne village and kicks on. Minutes later, she pulls boldly into the driveway of the small, Tudor Shalbourne Manor, adjoining remote Baverstock Farm, scattering gravel. She is met with open arms by the two women who have invited her back: Miss Marguerite de Beaumont and Miss Dorothy Mason, Marguerite's romantic and business partner.

In a letter to Miss de Beaumont a few months previously, Miss White, inspired and enthused by stories of Miss Mason and the farm she runs at Baverstock alongside Miss de Beaumont's horse and pony stud, wrote to ask if she might learn to farm 'from an amiable farmer who would take me on as a kind of pupil'. She says that she does not feel tough enough to join the Women's Land Army, set up to train and deploy women to fulfil roles left vacant by farmworkers away fighting – but I wonder if this is true. Up until the war, she has spent her summers sailing and her winters riding and foxhunting (as almost all country people, except the horseless working class, did then; and many of those followed on foot); she is a Girl Guide and Boy Scout leader and has been working as a Land Girl, anyway. I suspect she didn't want to be put off her course, but also, she wanted to manage, to *run*, a farm. The advent of war brought about a change – of course it did – but it brought about a change of direction in her life. Like many women, she saw opportunity. A now or never, if Hitler was coming. She found purpose, a necessity of *doing*, of action: an open gate and an invitation – that she'd perhaps tried to pursue in her late teenage years.

In 1918, she had a job on a poultry farm at a military hospital in Kent. Hen's eggs became a potent, homely and galvanising symbol of recovery, support, sacrifice and strength during the First World War. The National Egg Collection for wounded soldiers and sailors was instigated by *Poultry World* magazine and grew to be a national occupation from 1914–1919. At least 250,000 eggs were sent weekly over the Channel to military hospitals in France and beyond, increasing to over a million at its peak, with the campaign proclaiming, 'There is no substitute for eggs in maintaining a man's vitality, hastening his convalescence or even in preserving life.' Indeed, 'In cases of gassing, spinal or facial wounds, eggs are practically the only diet that is suitable.' A health-giving, morale-boosting hen's egg reached the hospitalised wounded, even in France, within three days of being laid.

Donors and children were encouraged to write their name, address and a heartening message on the shells to the wounded as 'eggograms', and they often received replies. One story recalls a recuperating soldier receiving an eggogram from his small daughter back home.

And so, Miss White, aged eighteen, with the upper-middle-class world she was born into, and all its expectations shattered around her, found purpose and opportunity in the fresh air, which she clearly loved. All those hens mucked out, fresh straw in the nesting boxes and sharp pecks from broody hens braved; all those warm, feathered indignant bodies checked for red mite – all those eggs picked and endless baskets crooked for all those broken men to dip their soldiers into. Going to war on an egg.

I wonder if there was a beau, or two. Or three. Something in what I've read and heard about her doubts that. I can't be sure. But friends gone, certainly; the lives of her whole generation utterly shaken up together and smashed. It took another world war for Miss White to find her purpose again, and I imagine her drifting a little, unable even to vote for another ten years. Yet, she was a well-off, well-travelled, independent young woman of the jazz age. Still wealthy enough to be living alone in her own property aged thirty-nine, apparently not working, though busy sailing, riding, Scouting.

At the outbreak of the Second World War, she undertakes various jobs with the Voluntary Aid Detachment, hop-picking with the Land Army and taking in two evacuee boys ('nice little boys but being a nurse maid is not my line'). On a Girl Guide training camp, she meets Marguerite de Beaumont, and their campfire chats ignite an old spark and interest for farming. Miss de Beaumont is a year older than Julia White. Inspired by Robert Baden-Powell's 1908 book *Scouting for Boys*, she formed her own small, mixed 'pack', aged nine. The group, aided by Marguerite's mother, attended the first Boy Scout Rally at Crystal Palace a year later, having adapted a uniform and bought Scout hats. There were around one thousand girls at the eleven-thousand-strong gathering, but Miss de Beaumont's patrol, arriving late and without tickets, attracted the attention of Baden-Powell himself. Miss de Beaumont responded, 'I am the PL [pack leader] of the Wolves Patrol of the Girl Scouts and we want to do Scouting just like the boys.' A year later, the Girl Guides Association was founded. Miss de Beaumont went on to become close friends with the Baden-Powell family, writing biographies of both Lord and Lady Baden-Powell and receiving the coveted Silver Fish Award for a lifetime of effort. But while it is Girl Guiding and a love of the practical, outdoors life that brings the two women together, it is Marguerite's warm talk of her partner Doris and *her* farming that captures Julia's interest. Not long after, back at home in the New Forest, Julia blows the spark into a flame. It is possible now, perhaps, to learn to be a farmer.

She writes to Miss de Beaumont:

> *Ever since I met you at Salisbury and you told me about your farm, my longing for this kind of thing has been so thoroughly awakened that I am writing to ask if you will help me in this line ... I think I could probably make myself quite useful to a farmer to repay him for any trouble he might be put to in having a novice about the place.*

As it turns out, 'in quite a remarkable way', as Julia later observes, it is a *Miss* that is that amiable farmer – Marguerite's partner, Miss Dorothy Mason, in fact.

Once this agreement is established, an offer is made to Julia White to come and stay at the Tudor manor house and learn to farm. Miss White insists, however, on finding a room in the village, as Shalbourne Manor is teeming with evacuees, and begins her apprenticeship in September, at Michaelmas; that traditional time of new contracts and fresh beginnings in the farming calendar, when harvest was over and all safely gathered in, new staff were hired, land exchanged and debts paid. The women begin by agreeing to call each other by their first names – Marguerite, Doris and Julia – and on the first morning, a fortnight before the caravan trip, Doris begins Julia's induction with a walk around the undulating 200-acre downland farm at a most tremendous pace. She struggles to keep up.

I can see the two of them, teacher and pupil, striding out in the quickset and ready companionship of like-minded, mature women, excited at the prospect of a new project. Both women are exceptionally tall – Julia is almost six foot and Doris two or more inches taller

– but Julia is breathless, ruefully acknowledging the fate of having friends that walk very fast, while admitting to a slow temperament, accustomed (having lived much by herself) to not hurrying. She tries hard to 'be intelligent, keep up and take everything in', as Doris lopes purposefully across ploughed fields, over fences, through hedges and up and down hills, without altering pace, in that long, free-striding gait of country people. It's a gait I recognise instantly – and one my husband, our three children and I have. It looks slower than it is, but covers the ground quickly, regardless of its condition; muddy plough, wet field, ankle-twisting flint and chalk rubble. It makes me smile to picture Doris and Julia, and I am willing her to keep up. For what is better, or more infectious, than the excitement, enthusiasm and delight of a well-matched, experienced tutor and their keen, willing student? And I fall in love with them there and then – particularly with Julia; her honesty and her words. I feel I know her. I certainly knew women *like* her, Doris and Marguerite – daunting, determined, strong, slightly terrifying: women in a man's world, certainly in access, agency and ownership – but one they managed very much on their own terms. Contemporary, Hardyesque Bathsheba Everdenes, perhaps; not alone, but part of a community and older. Unmanned. And, it seems to me, there were more women farmers than we have been led to believe – successful ones, too. It seems to me also, that in those war years, and for a short time after, it might have been *easier* to become a woman farmer than it is now. Than it ever was, for me.

I didn't know Julia White, but there are those that still remember her in my village, very many years later – and I have something precious of hers: her own words, her own account of her time. Fairly perfunctory, it is a slice of farming history, written by a woman running a farm anew, having bought it, in partnership with another woman, and not in the absence of a man. And in an age when the wartime Ministry of Agriculture could take your farm off you if it felt you were not producing enough, or the right sort and quality of food it expected, it was risky and required a radical effort and belief.

Full of honesty and insight, Miss White wrote up and published her diaries as *The Inkpen Saga* years afterwards, when she was into her mid-eighties. Out of print now, I remember borrowing it from my local library several times, sometime in the late nineties, when I hadn't quite given up the dream of farming, myself. Then, when I happened to move to the village she had farmed, I came across it again in the big new library that replaced my teenage one, and which I now worked in part-time. Eventually, I searched the internet and found an ex-library copy of my own, with its dull cover, gently foxed pages and slightly puffy, tactile plastic wrapping around its dust jacket. I recognised so many parallels in this same rural village, some seventy or eighty years on: much she would have readily got involved in, as well as much she would have disagreed with and resisted. A village, emptying of its rural workers, yet still willing and able to put on a social gathering – a barn dance fundraiser, fetes and junketings, accepting refugees with open arms, chasing loose animals, dealing with water shortages, the lack and quality of genuinely affordable rural housing, and the raising and burning of beacons. I think she would have railed against the wholesale destruction of wildlife and cheered the beauty of working outdoors; the honest, hard-worked harmony of it. She humbly accepted her place in a community. She flouted rules that didn't work for the greater good; she took action. She made things better for people. She learnt. She took advice and she loved the wildflowers, the birds and her animals. Because when Julia White farmed, she did it properly – and she took the whole community with her.

That first day she walked over her apprenticed farm in a neighbouring village, trotting and stumbling over chalky clods to keep up, infused with joy, warmth, anxiety, purpose and possibility, glows off the page at me. It is infectious.

I wonder. I want to know what this deeply familiar place was like to her then. What farming might be like today – where we have continued to destroy wildlife, climate and environment, and been provided with inconsistent and homogenised grants that don't take locality, community and diversity into account – if women instead had been allowed and enabled to continue when the men came back? If women had been part of the conversation? I know it can't be and isn't as simple as that, but I have so many questions. I want to tell her forgotten story – to unearth it and bring her back to life. I would like to be *her* apprentice. I think we'd have some fun. She has got under my skin so much, over this same land, its lanes, harvests, big hill and buildings I know so well, that I can sense her ghost sometimes, as well as the ghosts of those that worked these fields. The ghosts of the horses, the old whoops and hollers, temperamental tractors and traction engines that had names – Racing Lizzie and Nightingale – the village get-togethers, meetings, so many different kinds of work, proper seasons and the birds. The birds, the birds... I want to take her book into the fields and plot its action, like I might with my childhood carpet farm. To write her back into being and celebrate this incredible sixteen-year endeavour where a single woman took a farm – *this* farm – from smocks, horses and hand tools, labour gangs, a wealth of wildlife and rural poverty, to mechanisation, productivity, the poorly managed dawn of chemical aids, and efforts in social improvement. All in such a short time of war and revolutionary social change in the countryside, with community and camaraderie.

I want to plough her words and deeds back into the same fields and see what comes up. I want to colour in the missing details of weather and character and conversation with my farming imagination, and I want to examine it all against the light of my own rural life of near, but not quite, farming.

That first day, Julia White describes the sun setting in a golden end-of-September haze behind the elm trees, full of the roaring caws of rooks and chacks of jackdaws. She describes thick, wide hawthorn hedges, rich with red waterfalls of berries, with a 'full population' of winter thrushes, blackbirds and smaller birds – tits, finches, buntings, tree and house sparrows, 'chattering and twittering away'; and I can hear their volume, the many and mass of them dialled up so loud, and I can see them, moving as a single living organism through the hedges and over the trees, fields, vanished ponds and farm. She describes them with such joy, with such profound satisfaction, it feels like a cue, a key, a reason. And I wonder – and perhaps I know – why and where it all went so very wrong and we lost our way, our connection, our wildlife and sense of our place, in the drive for efficiency and the necessity of feeding a country on its knees during and after the Second World War.

We forgot, afterwards, the fundamental workings of a planet that feeds and sustains us all; where food, farming, people, women and nature should be interlinked in close relationship. Of course, of course, it had all been (and always had been) pulling apart long, long before the latter part of the twentieth century, if it had ever been comfortably woven together in the first place. Rural living, the agricultural life, was mostly a hard, poor, difficult and sometimes brutal and isolated one; let's not be rose-tinty and nostalgic about this. Farming has always been about change, about progression and ease. But it seems somehow that here was a chance. A more reflective, thoughtful and considered way of doing things. A humility and acceptance of mistakes, of things that weren't working. Of learning, of collaboration, of leading by listening, adjusting and supporting others, and not either excluding people, business and industry outside of agriculture nor letting them off the hook in their responsibilities to the land and planet.

It haunts me. I want to go back and marry then with now and interrogate the handfasting. I want to know what might've happened if women had been allowed to farm more often and more easily than the tiny percentage of them whom did in the intervening years. I want to know if we'd still have the birds. I see them, some days, all the birds we've lost, made refugees of, evicted, almost as clearly as I might today, like a film over a film, a glitching, double-exposure of all their ghosts – and I grieve and feel their loss more keenly and more profoundly than I've ever felt it before.

After her lodgings mysteriously prove 'unsatisfactory' after just a week, Julia is forced to return home and think again. The warmth, purpose and camaraderie of the outdoor work at Baverstock Farm prove more of a draw than her lonely New Forest house and its very near miss with the bomb in the garden (the fortieth to land on her village at that point), and the sounds of machine-gunning, air battles overhead and air raids on nearby Southampton that have become a nerve-wracking fixture. She has lived through one world war, and, after the Dunkirk evacuation, the likelihood of invasion is considered inevitable. Just eighty miles from France, the New Forest has effectively been militarised and is on high alert. Shalbourne, this place of the shallow, sparkling bourne, is 'more peaceful and remote', and Julia White is galvanised. The morning after the bomb, she is seduced by the apple-green Cheltenham van at Caravan Corner in nearby Ringwood and spends the rest of the week fitting it out, resolving to live independently.

On her triumphant return, she sets up camp in the pony paddock behind the big barn, in the lee of the prevailing south-westerlies, and joins Doris and farmhand Jack Palmer after breakfast the next day. Doris pats a perch on the trailer beside her, and Julia hops up behind the straw-yellow Fordson tractor, and they sit among coal for the threshing machine, sacks for the corn and coils of baling wire. As they chug out to the ricks in the fields, the trailer sledge glides away underneath them, with a swoop that is deliciously familiar to me. Julia writes:

> *The sun was just coming behind the downs, making a golden light with streaks of light among the edges of the clouds. I sat with Doris on the front of the trailer, and she nudged me as we went along and rubbed her hands together and gave me such a twinkling look. I understood, I was feeling that way myself. Some things in life are very good.*

I think, but cannot fully know, what that feeling was. I am smiling as I read those lines again. Everything that comes next, in the fifteen years that follow, and everything after, pivots from that golden September morning of light, motion, twinkling camaraderie and purpose: hope, action and the possibility of fulfilment, all against the terrible backdrop of a country at war. Of life altering, unutterably. Of not being hit by a German bomb; of not being run over by a tank. I see them laughing. I can almost hear soaring strings over the tractor engine, a choir's voices raised in crescendo. Skylarks.

I'm there with them. Running to catch up and hotching on the edge of the trailer, on the edge of life as we know it, grinning, desperate not to be left behind.*

* A country colloquialism that may have its roots in southern county or Midlands dialect, 'hotch', or sometimes 'ootch', refers to two particular movements: it is to wiggle-hop inelegantly up onto something almost out of reach, such as a ledge, trailer or log; even a horse if there's someone already on it. Others are then compelled to 'hotch up' to make room, involving an ungainly bottom shuffle or thigh walk. Hotching is distinct from perching or hitching; it is a friendly thing involving light peril, like reaching out a helping hand to a stranger from an equally precarious position.

CHAPTER TWO

The Barn at Beech Farm

Michaelmas 1977–1981

I quickly discover that riding real horses is more than a manifestation of desire and study and belief, however hard I do these things. My Saturdays and, later, my Sundays too, begin with an early morning walk from our village fire brigade house, past the little library, shops and pubs, working men's club and rowing club, and then out of it, up over the glorious iron toll bridge, spanning the River Thames. It is a ladder to heaven; solid, confident, gleaming white against the wide glitter far below it, its gentle arch of latticework girders and supersized bolts replacing a worn wooden one in 1902. In about one hundred paces, I dig in my pocket among fuzzy Polo mints and crumbs of sugar cubes for sticky coppers to pay for my passage across, at The Tollhouse door ('built, 1792'). I like that it is a stable door. I imagine Black Bess jumping the high gate with ease, steel shoes slipping perilously on landing and sparking off the cobbles. When I look back over my shoulder, The Tollhouse frowns in mock horror, its patterned brickwork a pair of eyes above a surprised mouth of a porch. It's a house designed to stop everyone in their tracks. But not Black Bess.

The rest of the short journey is in the back of a straw-filled Land Rover, from a house with stables at the bottom of the garden near the Hardwick Estate, whose manor was the inspiration for Toad Hall. Sometimes, the trip is shared with other girls my age, shy but friendly, our grins increasing with the depth of the bumps over potholes, and the in-your-face proximity of Polar, the smiling Dalmatian, and Jet, the Labrador; our hair filling with a thick cloud of black diesel. Two older girls follow behind on the big horses, Lady and Napoleon; diverting up a bridleway and across fields, they arrive a few minutes after us. It is Carmen James that takes us to Beech Farm. It's her riding school, of just seven ponies, on a small farm with old red-brick, flint-seamed buildings: a small, walled stable yard, with a cart shed and high, blue-painted, wooden gates that open onto an old chalk track, fields and beech woods. Next to it is a very old farmhouse and two adjoining barns forming an open L-shaped interior, deep in golden straw. It's a picture-book farm. I know Carmen James doesn't own it because the farmer, I remember, Mrs Brickhill, 'lets her'. We sometimes brush and walk her dogs, a motley crew of terriers, and this is a good thing to do. ('That'll make her happy, girls; well done,' says Carmen, in a rare moment of praise.) There is some kind of pleasing that needs to be attended to, a feeling of mild but ever-present tensing; a precarity of having to keep things in good order, at all times. Something in the 'letting' of a place that seems otherwise to belong so absolutely to Carmen and the fields, the ponies, birds and ourselves.

We work, us girls, us women – we groom, curry and wisp, pick out feet, catch and turnout, heft bales and lead-rein children younger than us; we muck out, rug up, clean tack, fill haynets and water buckets, fork straw and 'square off' the muck heap so that it is a neat and stepped steaming pile of thatch, with a central plank to push the wheelbarrow up at a run to the top, and over. In freezing winter, in our rubber riding boots, this is a welcome job. By mid-afternoon, the tinfoil we have wrapped around our feet, between two pairs of socks, is crumbling and our feet are numb. We bury our boots in the hot muck and try not to stick the pitchfork through them (I still have a scar where I did). We heft great forkfuls of manure skywards, spilling worms and bugs and beetles in the pungent steam, and are attended by birds; robins, wrens, blackbirds and thrushes, wagtails – the yard rings always with their *Chiseek! Chiseek!* – swallows and martins in the summer, and once, memorably, a hoopoe, showy as a carnival queen.

In winter, on quiet mornings when we get here first, sometimes, a fox is sleeping on the warm straw hotbed of the dung heap's heat, which was once utilised to grow melons under glass.

We have lessons in the field from Carmen (no fancy arena for us), hanging on her every word; falling off, getting up and on again, bruised and besmirched with mud. We go for hacks, trotting and cantering to keep up behind the prancing, shying Lady, all flying mane, silver shoes and taut martingale, ears like shells, and nostrils crimson-flared. We work for free rides and steadily I learn how to ride; how to handle, care for and manoeuvre an animal much bigger than myself with a gentle but firm authority, while being always in awe of it. I learn to listen, watch, interpret and respond to so much subtle language. It's a constant transaction, a negotiation between individual characters: what works with one animal might not with another. An instinct for wildness, independence and flight is never very far away.

It still astonishes me, that an animal so big can be irritated and tickled by a single stray hair from your head when you are bent to their barrel-bellies, brushing mud and burrs from silky leg feathers, and yet will carry you hard, hoof-spanking miles along traffic-filled roads; or fly over thorny hedges, forgiving an accidental jab in the mouth from a bit or an unbalanced thump back in the saddle, if you get 'left behind'; or even pull creaking carts piled high with their own foodstuff and rattling machinery through heavy ploughed earth, trusting you to go wherever you ask, even into the teeth of battle.

How lucky we are to have had this; to have brokered this relationship, upon which so much is built. How heartbreaking that sometimes is.

Horses are incredibly generous creatures; but they'll not suffer fools if they can help it. They'll give you the best lessons in resilience, perseverance and humility, too: that this much hard work, this ultimate 'boot camp' must be undertaken in order to earn the right to ride, is something willingly undertaken, without complaint, in an all-consuming love. But it's a rude awakening from a dream of fair and galloping horses, that it takes this much resolve, endurance and an acute awareness of your surroundings in a deeply animal sense, to achieve the ultimate partnership between a human – essentially a predator – and another animal, a prey animal at that, to ride upon its back and be 'as one'.

It's learning to spot something like the foil of a deflated balloon in a hedge, or the white gills of a tea-plate-sized, upturned toadstool glowing in a dark woods, and thinking like a prey animal, albeit a bold and capable one, *knowing* your horse might perceive either as a veiled, spook-worthy threat: the ghost of a wolf, or wild boar, or the spirit of some other ancestral predator that could rush out. Or be an excuse to ditch your not-so-alert self and gallop home. Horses see and believe in ghosts, and their evolutionary descendants, too. But they do not always acknowledge them and are not always afraid. As a rider, or self-appointed herd leader, sitting up there, directing, it's our job to register the thing, the potential threat, and confidently dismiss it. A physical, mental and emotional communication of, 'Yes, I've seen it, but it's nothing. We can push on,' while knowing if you're not believed or not ready to correct an overactive response, you could find yourself airborne and heading for the high knuckles of the beech tree roots, with the ground coming up rapidly to meet you – and all the intensified smells; fungi, soil, tree sap and leaf mould – sharp and hard and miscalculated as a bite of a too-early apple, and the crump of bodily impact driven right through your fallible bones, as they separate from your mind's wholly committed intention and that of your mount's. Or dismounts.

That first winding. That sitting up and, if you are able, checking you are in one piece before panicking about where your steed has gone, which usually gets you up on your feet quickly. And then the whole process, of learning to go *with* the horse, to direct and control it, begins again – hard-won, bruised, tipped, thrown-off, tumble-thump-crunch – until, with fear overcome and a new resilience, you earn the best prize of all. You can ride. Someone will say, 'She's a great little rider, at one with the horse!' Yet, the most important lesson of all takes us right back to the start of your dreaming – to galloping along on your own two legs, champing at the imaginary bit in your own mouth, while you are simultaneously holding all its power in your infinitely gentle hands: imagination *is key*. That an enormous part of this wonder-fuelled contract is in believing and imagining you can do this most improbable thing. That you and the horse *are* one: both a part of nature. You have to imagine flying, sailing, or clopping along, or what fear tastes and smells like, while you are sitting astride the broad back of some beautiful, powerful creature as if you were some kind of slightly grubby goddess that serves it; ignominious at times, and necessarily humble, but, nevertheless, like a myth or a fairy tale, you have become the half-girl, half-horse you always wanted to be.

And even done on shoestring after shoestring tied together, what a deep privilege that is. I wish it were available to anyone who wanted it.

Riding is an alchemy, born of this hidden world of hard work, strength, perseverance and gentleness that doesn't seem to belong anywhere else in our girl's world. We are tough, resilient and filthy, with hayseeds and earwigs in our hair, and dirt and muck in every crevice. Our clothes are nicked by barbed wire and brambles, our fingers pinched by bolts and gate hasps, blistered, splintered and bruised by the tools of our trade: yard broom, hay rake, curry comb and dandy brush. We are unafraid of mice, rats, adders, heights in the haybarn or boys, darkness, ghosts and even, here at least, the biggest spiders. We are stronger than we look, and by Sunday evening, blissfully, bone-achingly, bodily tired.

The dreaming and the doing fill my days.

In summer, we walk to the woods for our lunch, to sit on the edge of the old bomb crater, but the rest of the year, we have our lunches above the horses in the hayloft, climbing up a worm-pocked wooden ladder, to sit on hay bales we have named after the ponies, pulling percussively and munching at their hay, below. In autumn, the bales are stacked almost to the rafters, and we have to lie on our stomachs, aware of the horrors of slipping between them, and the trip and fall hazard of loose bale strings (always, to pick them up, loop them over and over, and tie them a safe waist; like a useful, modern corn dolly). As the year wears on, the haystack becomes lower, creating steps that change weekly; the soft deep pad of loose hay on the barn floor deepens, and our ways of getting down, sliding, leaping from the top bales, sillier, and more daring.

On one of the big beams at the back of the tiled barn, a barn owl sits permanently, glowing in the gold-lit dust like a pale pilaster god. Or goddess, in this world of girls and women. We are, I think, slightly afraid of her. Deeply respectful, anyway. The Barn Owl Must Not Be Disturbed. So, we don't; and when the barn is full of the summer's new hay, and we are closer to her, we whisper, reverentially. At least for the first few minutes until we forget. Sometimes, she turns her pepper-freckled face (like a dandelion clock) towards us. She is important because she eats the mice that get in the feed bins, and ruin the rugs, and catches the rats that chew the bale strings, loosing the hay and making the stack dangerous. She is not afraid of us, and she is beautiful. When we remember, we leave her giggled offerings: a fluorescent Wotsit; half a digestive biscuit, a crust from a peanut butter sandwich.

When it's chilly, we slide down the ladder and give each other 'leg-ups' to sit on the ponies' warm backs. With the sounds of the weather outside, mote-filled beams spotlight patches of satiny yellow straw, a dappled rump here, the light through a swishing tail there, clouds of breath purling in the strawy air, or the whiskers on a velvet muzzle in the dark-brown interior of the barn: this is our church. Here is where we worship. The warm apple, wood, leather, meadow and dung smells; summer stored to the rafters even in the depths of winter. And as you come through the ankle-deep mud into the barn, all the heads are turned to you, ears pricked in greeting: chestnut Jimmy James; Pickles and Blossom; Spring and Anita; Padjo, with the little white snip on his muzzle; glorious bay Emma; dear Worcester; Abba and Babycham (both named for the era), the latter able to turn on a sixpence and whose tail you had to ease through a padded crupper to stop the saddle sliding over her neck when she put her head down.

The language, the words we used, the knowledge that outside of this environment, no one understood; kimblewick, snaffle, Weymouth;

barley straw, fetlock, sugar beet; linseed, oats, roller, surcingle; stirrup, halter, flying changes, set fair – you don't need to know what all of these words mean to recognise a poem. A spell – an incantation or prayer even – that sounds as good as it smells.

The drum of galloping hooves over turf is internalised forever. The contented pulling and munching of hay from the long wooden rack that stretches the length of the barn, a soothing and rhythmic sound, like a broom sweeping a yard. Everything about a horse is rhythmic. Percussive as a heartbeat, like writing, like typing, like poetry; I gallop, trot and canter my fingers over the keyboard, leaping over words.

One frosty Saturday, the Hunt comes through. Somebody has telephoned the farmhouse and Carmen is walking briskly: 'Untie the horses! Turn them to face the door and hang on!' It is as if a fire has broken out. We race to pull the quick release knots from their orange baler twine loops, attached to the silvered oak-and-elm chamfered planks of the barn-length hay rack. The baler twine loops are there for this very reason – if a horse panics and pulls back with all its might, the string will break first, rather than pull the rack or parts of it off the wall or harm the horse itself. We are a well-oiled machine; each holding a horse as the heads and ears go up, pricked to a sound we can't yet hear; the munching and steady breathing has stopped to listen. With one hand near the clip on the headcollar and the other holding the loose end (*never* wrapped around our hands, for fear of broken fingers or dislocated shoulders), we wait. The horses grow restless. Emma spins round, Abba snorts and Pickles paws the ground. We talk to them soothingly, though we are as nervous as our charges. The sound reaches us then – a hunting horn – we listen, nod and agree between us it is the 'gone away', so we know a fox is being hunted. In these days, to be around horses is to be aware of and supportive of foxhunting, at least outwardly. Then we hear the 'hound music'; a wave of hounds, crying in full flight. It is an awesome and unsettling sound. My stomach churns and grips, the hairs on my arms and neck stand up; I am deeply conflicted. Worcester breaks out in a sweat and stamps at the ground. The horses have grown in stature, muscles tensing, heads higher. There is a great stirring of hooves and flanks and pulling, and suddenly hounds pour through the farmyard in a sea of liver and cream, sterns waving, heads down, in full cry. Then comes the Master and hunt staff in their 'pink' jackets, cantering on the grass verge, or trotting hard and fast on the old cement track, their horses blowing, hooves ringing. The field of horses and riders follows, filling the track and pouring through the gateway past the barn. Voices call, greetings and 'thank yous' are shouted, and our horses spin and snort. Three rogue hounds come into the barn and are called away by the whipper-in: 'Ratchet, Rascal, *Posset*!' His brass buttons catching the light, his big grey horse foam-flecked. Abba neighs, Anita neighs, Pickles rears and plunges. Worcester shakes and chucks his head about, almost pulling me over. I wrap the rope around his nose to give me more leverage – all want instinctively to run with the herd.

Beautifully turned-out plaited horses in all sizes and colours clatter through, the veins standing high on their sleek, clipped necks and shoulders, blood-red nostrils flaring. Farmers' cobs and children's ponies follow, their riders in informal tweed 'ratcatcher' dress; two in bowler hats trot past, feet thrust forwards in their stirrups, mud-spattered and breathless.

There is a strange mechanical screech above it all and I look up. The barn owl, spooked by the commotion, flies out; a white ghost winging out of the dusky, dark barn, circling over the frenetic scene below, calling an urgent *Shhhhhhht*, with a sudden, chilling, churchyard eeriness, and, for a moment, everything slows. We have never seen the owl outside of the barn before. I think of the hunt, and its quarry – the fox on the muck heap, perhaps. The friendly-looking hounds and their thrilling voices, the horses, the (mostly) polite field of riders. All a direct contrast to what they are actively engaged in. It doesn't add up in my head. I look up at the owl, circling, screeching, rowing off through the frosty afternoon – She Must Not Be Disturbed.

Worcester has pulled me towards the front of the barn and a girl about my age is coming through the open gate past the farmyard last. She turns her black, plaited-up pony round with some effort and reaches to close the gate, but the pony won't stand, won't be pushed within reaching distance of the gate, wants to be going on and galloping off with the rest. She catches my eye and asks, 'Should I close the gate?'

I freeze. The hunt clatters on, and no one waits for the girl (which I know, because I've read, is against foxhunting etiquette). She turns her pony again, and he tosses his head, makes a half-rear and she clutches at the bobbles of his mane. I could say, 'No, leave it, we'll do it,' but I don't. I feel conflicted and complicit and that I must make some kind of stand. I am not comfortable with this. I break eye contact with her and watch the owl fly to the woods and hear my own small voice say, 'Yes.'

'Yes,' I say. Not 'please', no 'thank you'. Not hiding behind the fact that I am holding my own plunging desperate-to-gallop pony myself – who has gone quiet in the moment. Another of us girls steps forward then, leading her pony, and says cheerily, 'I'll do it, go on!' The girl raises a yellow string-gloved hand, says, 'Thank you very much,' stands up in her stirrups and lets her pony go like an arrow from the bow of her strained and aching arms.

I feel mean. Like I've already spoilt this memory of 'when the hunt came through' that we'll talk about for many lunchtimes to come. I think perhaps that nobody noticed; perhaps not even the girl. But I feel I have done an unkindness, either way, in being thrilled by the hunt and horses, and in my small protest against foxhunting of being deliberately unhelpful – and I *always* wish to be kind. Especially here, among these people and this environment.

I watch the owl fly towards the covert where the hounds have found the fox. The fox. The victim in all this. How am I going to be a farmer or work with horses if I need to hide some of my feelings away in this rural life, where it seems everyone else accepts foxhunting? It's a foreshadowing of what's to come, because it won't ever just be foxhunting; it will be pheasant shooting, access to the countryside, indiscriminate hedge-cutting, the chemical dousing of fields: if a woman is excluded from an industry, how can she speak up about it? How does she hear others that might feel the same? How does it change? I know, at this moment, that I will have to work, sometimes, against my feelings. I will have to internalise, keep quiet, sit on the fence, steel myself. Maybe, even look the other way sometimes. Compromise – before I even know the meaning of the word, or the complexity of these feelings. At the moment, I just feel like I've let everyone down in a small, inside way. Who's to say I'm not the only one.

This isn't a book about horses. But it is a book about the gateways they lead you through. And, from this moment on, there will always be horses, one way or another. And always, a barn owl with them.

CHAPTER THREE

Racing Lizzie and the Sheen

November 1940

Miss White's first proper week of apprenticeship begins with threshing. I had always associated threshing – the act of thrashing loosed sheaves of corn mechanically or with a hand-held flail to shake out the kernels and separate it from the straw – with a part of the late-summer harvest procedure, as it is now. But *of course* it wasn't, of course: the sheaves of corn (any grain of oats, wheat or barley, etc.) were harvested and stored in ricks – skilfully built, windowless villages of golden-yellow round houses, or square huts, built out in the fields or in sheltered rickyards and thatched against the worst of the weather – until a few dry days could be predicted in late autumn or winter, and a team of people (and a turn with the journeying thresher and steam engine) could be got together from all the other pressing jobs on a farm.

I say *of course* because threshing was a staple winter job that kept the wolves at bay for many farm-labouring families, until the eventual acceptance and need of the thresher – with the subsequent lack of rural labour. Dismantled ricks were carted into great barns, unloaded and beaten with the threshing flail (two sticks hinged together on a swinging chain). The wind blowing through opposite pairs of wide-open, wagon-sized doors winnowed and blew the lightest chaff and dust away. It was partly the advent of the threshing machines around 1830 that tipped many a labourer into intolerable poverty – and his redundant swinging flail was used to 'swing' at them instead, smashing them up, under the collective pseudonym of 'Captain Swing'. Now, threshing is done by a harvester that combines reaping, shaking and separating the grain, pouring it out as if from a cereal box on high, into the tractor-driven grain cart alongside, while spilling out thick tresses of shiny golden straw out the back – all while rolling forwards through the fields. A late-summer job, and when all the straw is baled, telehandlers, a kind of telescopic forklift, assemble huge monoliths and wheels of gold straw in place of those resting, hand-built, thatched ricks.

The threshing machine (the men call it the 'chine' or 'sheen') and its attendant steam engine, 'Nightingale', have been manoeuvred into place, and steam got up in the engine. All hands are here and take their practised places. It takes around ten people to operate the whole affair, all communicating and working together in a kind of dance around the engine and sheen; an extension of it – oiled cogs themselves, that feed the two great beasts, rocking, puffing and clanking with a rhythm between the enormous belts and their drive wheels. When I watch them, mesmerised, at our local county show, they remind me of wooden stagecoaches from the Wild West, and I love the smell of the coal-fired steam. Two or three men stand on the rick itself and stab and pitch the rustling sheaves, first down, and then up to the sheen's platform as the rick gradually lowers, with two-tined, long-handled forks. A man on the platform cuts the waist-string around the sheaf and feeds it, 'ears' first, into the feeder and down into the threshing drum. Here, it is thoroughly shaken and beaten until the corn spills out into different grades – head corn, lighter tail corn and weed seeds. Here is another man, hooking on sacks, catching and filling them, tying them off without spilling the flow, and moving them on. Meanwhile, at the rear end of the sheen, loose straw emerges and is baled. Another hand threads the baler wire in, and another stacks the bales as they are pushed out. The driver of the steam engine shovels coal and keeps Nightingale topped up and singing with water, her belts whirring away to power the sheen, and a horse and cart or two are busy supplying coal and water for the engine, and taking sacks of grain or bales of straw back to the granary at the farm. No less important, any other available hands, the oldest, youngest and least experienced, are tasked with raking the great quantity of husks and broken straw (cavings) from the underbelly of the sheen, keeping it clear and forking the broken straw back into the baling machine.

Here is Miss White, raking and forking for hours upon end. All is dirt and dust and glory, and despite broad-brimmed hats and kerchiefs and scarfs tied sometimes over mouths and noses, the shower of debris gets everywhere. The men on the rick have cord tied below the knees of their trousers, to stop mice or rats fleeing the dismantling of their home by running up their legs. There are a lot of mice, and a lot of rats – the ricks being larder and shelter for both; but they cause great damage in such quantities, and it is an *imperative* responsibility to deal with them. War work, in fact. Around the traction engine, threshing sheen, carts and workers, older boys have brought their sticks and men their terriers. There are shrieks and 'sport', but rats and mice are quickly, cleanly and methodically dispatched; the terriers ('good ratters') are particularly efficient. Dogs and children dart in and out of the circle round the pumping pistons, flywheel and drive belt, the heat and combustibility of everything, even on a winter's day, the team of people, pitchforks, horses and blinding dust – I worry about the safety of everyone.

One morning, Frances and Ralph Partridge and their small son, Burgo, walk out from their Bloomsbury set retreat at neighbouring Ham Spray to watch the threshers. As confirmed pacifists, and with Ralph a decorated survivor, twice wounded, once buried alive, from his long campaign in the First World War, they have collected an assorted household of refugees, evacuees and guests. Frances describes the 'downs iced all over with frost, standing in a deep belt of palest pink mist … smoke already rising vertically from the thresher in the field under the downs … nothing I have seen lately has given me more pleasure: steaming horses, carts laden with straw and a buzz of active figures around the sacrificial column of smoke – poking, thrusting, dragging.'

In a pause to straighten her back and swig from a clay jar of cold tea, Miss White blinks away the dust and waves at the small, indiscernible group. Around her, she notices the lovely colours of clean, new oat straw; some of it bashed flat into satin ribbons by the thresher; here is deep old gold through every shade of yellow and pale jade green, to pink, brown and almost white; all shiny, sheeny and clean. John, the farm boy, comes to relieve her.

At fourteen or fifteen, a little older than school age, John is something of an apprentice too; one of Shalbourne Manor's several evacuees, along with his younger twin siblings, he has come from East London Docks, and, like his brothers, is of mixed race. Though this is uncommon in rural Wiltshire of the time, the children are welcomed and absorbed into the community as the Londoners they are. John is much valued as part of the team, and I wonder how he and the other East End children embraced this new life. There is another evacuee boy his age at Shalbourne Manor, who works for a neighbouring farmer, plus two other school-age children, making six (and, eventually, twelve) evacuees looked after by a 'kindly village woman'. They have all become Cubs, Scouts and Guides, settling down happily together and mingling with other children in a village swelled by evacuees. I think of the tiny village school today, with its roll of twelve children. What an impact this influx of urban children must have had: what an impact such a parentless upheaval must have had on those urban children, too – and what opportunities for both, to broaden horizons and experience – though reality and individual circumstance would have varied wildly.

Apart from the bedrooms, our 'Manor Six' live chiefly between the very beautiful drawing room of the Tudor manor (given over as a playroom) and its kitchen. Miss Mason and Miss de Beaumont have their bedrooms, the library and the dining room – until the latter is turned into an official first aid post by Miss de Beaumont. The beautiful old house, its furnishings and papered walls take a battering, but neither woman bats an eye. It is simply a wartime necessity; 'People are more important than paintwork,' says Doris Mason emphatically. It does sound like the best kind of evacuee household. I hope it was.

Meanwhile, Julia White *learns*. She learns the tricks and hacks, the short cuts and the long, uneven road to skill. She learns from

Joe the cowman, how to lift sacks of grain (with a swing onto the hip and back, then midway onto the shoulder) and, wiping her sore, gritty red eyes, admires the scene of which she is now part – the rhythm, the polished brass of the engine gleaming, the purpose of the work, the smoky sparks. All on a fine, crisp autumn day.

Later, the haystacks are dismantled to go in the baling machine in a similar fashion, though tractor-powered this time, with the little, bright-yellow Fordson tractor, 'Racing Lizzie'. Jack Palmer forks the hay down to Miss White, who forks it into the baler – Jack slows his pace to Julia's and they find a pleasing, steady rhythm. But when great, strong (dear old) Charlie Tucker takes over from Jack, he continues at his usual pace. Julia tries to keep up, but the stack rises around her, then threatens to bury her until she has to admit defeat and call for quarter. She loads the trailer endlessly with heavy, newly made bales and cannot match Doris at all, until she copies her method – making steps of the bales and 'walking' each one up using her knees – a method I learnt at Beech Farm that means you can pitch and heft weights much heavier than you feel and look like you can. Though at one hundredweight (112 pounds, or 50 kilogrammes) Baverstock's new square bales are much heavier than those I heft from nearby Rolf's Farm for our own horses (at around 66 pounds, or 30 kilogrammes). I take my headscarf off to them both. When Doris leaves Julia alone for two hours, Julia loads three tons by herself, in four, tightly packed, crossed layers. She is quietly pleased with herself, grimy, exhausted.

As autumn turns to winter, a dairy apprenticeship is next. Miss White heads across the predawn farmyard from her caravan in the field every morning to the farmhouse kitchen, to drink a cup of tea with the boy John. She could go straight to the cowshed, but she enjoys their morning ritual, his cheerful, youthful company.

Across the garden in the dark, they walk to the cowshed. Despite the blackout, numerous sputnik needles of light escape between planks and through knotholes. They cut sharply through the darkness, giving the barn the impression of a circus tent. The men, head cowman Joe Eggleston and second milker Charlie Tucker, are already there, washing the cows, who are kept in the barn overnight. The clanking of pails and half-asleep talk to the animals is warming. These are cold, cold winter mornings in a succession of bitterly cold winters, but the dim lantern light inside, the rustle and gold of straw, the grassy-muck smell, and the chewing sounds and warmth from the cows is friendly, busy, cosy and comfortable-feeling.

In the relentless early mornings, before breakfast, when a relatively warm bed pulls hard before any fires are lit in unheated homes, noses run and breath comes in clouded condensation, conversation is limited. There are 'good mornings' and, other than 'git overs' and 'come along thens' spoken soothingly, there is just the sound of munching and the steady swish, swish, swish from the squirted jets of rich, creamy milk going rhythmically into the pails.

Baverstock's milkers are pedigree Jerseys. Small, gentle and butterscotch coloured with huge, dark eyes circled in white, and film star lashes. Miss White puts on her white milking smock (cleanliness is paramount), finds her pail, takes her three-legged stool from the pipes on the wall, and gets to work. She is used to it now, is proficient and enjoys it. It no longer makes her fumbling hands ache, but the cows are so small she struggles to get her long legs underneath them, sitting on the low stool. And it's back-aching. Miss White's first attempts with Emily were dispiriting. She pulled and squeezed down the long, soft teats just as Charlie and Joe showed her, but very little milk came. Her hands cramped and she had to keep stopping. By the time Miss White began to coax a decent amount of milk, Emily had stopped eating, regarded her with scorn, and stamped on her feet in impatience. Charlie had to finish milking her. She thinks how far she has come, as the milk is weighed and put into the cooler, though she takes the chance to soothe her hands over the cool dome of a chalk cobble sat in a line of others, all along a window ledge. She passes it from one hand to the other and notices the double lines of dots impressed into it like an Easter hot cross bun, and recognises it as a fossil. She goes to speak, but Charlie chips in: 'Thunderstones from the fields, Miss. You'd best keep 'em present in a milking shed. Will stop the milk souring and crudling in a thunderstorm.' Joe looks up and rolls his eyes, but Miss White gently places it back. Gives it a little pat with her fingers. The cows are turned out onto the grass for the day, their breath purling on the frosty air, and the calves are fed – the youngest animals, utterly charming and not much bigger than hares; the older ones like fawns, with preternaturally large eyes, transparent ears and merry legs. The churns are sealed and labelled to await the milk lorry, and it is time for breakfast.

A thorough mucking out of stalls and the cleaning of utensils follows, before running fencing repairs are continued, with barbed wire and stakes. It is a cold and hateful job – and the only one Charlie Tucker is irritable with; no one disagrees when he says for the umpteenth time, shaking his head, 'It must'a bin a farmer who inven'ed barbed wire 'tanglements for they trenches.'

At second milking in the afternoon, the atmosphere is jollier and chattier, as it usually is when doing outdoor work, lunch and warmth refreshed; the various accents add a diverse musicality to the proceedings. Head cowman, Joe, quick of mind and movement, inclined to impatience, though never with Miss White or the animals, has a strong Cumberland accent among the broad Wiltshire burr of methodical, thoughtful Charlie Tucker and his family. John brings a modern, playful, London freshness to the clipped, forthright, feminine cheeriness of the Misses White, Mason and de Beaumont's upper-class, BBC received pronunciation. All in a cowshed.

Now and then, I walk as close as I can to Baverstock's and Shalbourne Manor's barns. Their scant Grade-II listing under Historic England notes brick-and-flint-sills, a thatched roof on one, tiles and corrugated asbestos on the other. Clasped purlin roofs are hipped over the midstrey (allowing wagons to drive in) and there is a brick threshing floor. These dimly lit, humble, gold-moted cathedrals to rural work are supported by oak wind braces, and canted and queen struts to collars. Marguerite sings a hymn of them in her book *The Way of a Horse*: 'Wonderful buildings from Elizabethan times, lofty and full of fresh air without draughts and with a great atmosphere about them.'

I can almost hear the voices of afternoon milking time: Charlie Tucker, now positively garrulous, regales Miss White with village tales and antics, while John teases Charlie about his thunderstones; their milker's cheeks pressed against the soft butterscotch warmth of a cow's flank and udder. Charlie's own self-deprecating reminiscences of army life during the First World War make them all laugh. He demonstrates rifle drills with a hay fork, hobnailed boots scraping on the barn floor. I doubt any of them who lived through that war thought they'd be here again. Dear old Charlie, says Miss White. She doesn't think he could have been a very good soldier. But he and Joe, 'of a very different calibre', are both in the Home Guard. Joe is an NCO, a non-commissioned officer: a leader and trainer. The two men take endless trouble to teach her, and she is deeply humbled by that.

Charlie's Tucker's family, she says, are 'of the old Wiltshire breed', by which she means slow and methodical in their work, and highly skilled. Charlie lives at home at a small and 'rather dirty' neighbouring farm, with two brothers, a sister and her husband, Jack Palmer, who is 'very knowledgeable and a pleasure to work with' and works at Baverstock Farm, too. The oldest brother, also called Jack, works on the smallholding and Stan, the youngest brother, at a farm in Ham, the village between Shalbourne and my village of Inkpen. They are exempt from conscription due to age (being over forty-one), being declared unfit (some ploughman's lameness) or because they are needed to farm.

Old Harry Tucker, the patriarch, is a character if ever there was one. Conservative to a degree, Miss White describes him as a 'real martinet', prioritising discipline, etiquette and rules over all else, keeping his 'boys' in order with a firm hand and laying down the law for all and sundry. Harry is not one for progress. He loves his horses and will not have a tractor on the place. He tells Miss White, on more than one occasion, that they are the 'invention of the Devil himsef' and that, if he had his way, he would have them all taken to the top of the Downs 'and rowed over the edge, in the steepest place'. Yet Old Harry is not averse to accepting help from Miss Mason when behind with the ploughing, or haycart (the process of haymaking) or when their 'anywhen' methods have got them all behind hand. Harry is famous for his strong opinions, and his venerable bowler hat. Over many seasons, the brim has become sown with a fine crop of hayseeds and grain, and at several times in the year sports a nice greensward trimming around its ancient crown. It is Jack Tucker, Harry's eldest son, who offers and is determined to teach Miss White to plough with horses. She learns from among the very best. Whenever she has a little time and energy to spare, she walks round to the Tuckers' and finds Jack for a lesson. He has a smashing team of Suffolk Punches – big, strong, chestnut heavy horses, without the feathers around their fetlocks. Bred by Marguerite de Beaumont, they are owned, perhaps permanently on loan, by Doris Mason. The work is extraordinarily hard, particularly on the ankles, tendons, calves and wrists, but Miss White finds it fascinating and is determined to build up stamina and be a worthy student of Jack's.

At first, Jack drives the horses and walks alongside Miss White. His horses are turned out immaculately, their bits, brasses, arched necks and leather collars gleaming. He himself proudly wears a traditional clean linen ploughman's smock that Miss White admires – his initials are embroidered onto the collars and the central smocking has been done lovingly by someone (his mother?) in a practised hand. Miss White learns to walk behind the furrow horse, and to work with her gloves off at first so she can feel the movement of the plough. The knife coulter cuts through the soil and the share tip follows, the shining curved flank of the mouldboard lifting and turning the furrow slice so that it folds over to lie against the furrow cut before it, hinged over on its right side. The big wheel sits low in the furrow, and she must keep it pressed in close to the earth wall the coulter and the mouldboard have created. The smaller land wheel travels along on the unplough, behind the land horse's heels.

The gleaming furrow folds away to the right like an eternally twisting ribbon, like an Archimedes screw. The earth parts before her. She is mesmerised by it, watching worms drop onto the new smooth, narrow road under her feet. 'Don't watch the foldin!' laughs Jack.

'It'll ipnotise yer! Watch yer furrer wheel, and the stick in the 'edge, 'tween Folly's ears.' It is good advice, she finds.

The horses bend to their task and the plough bumps and scrapes over the biggest flints that slice into her bootsoles, and reveals white chalk under thin topsoil. The plough pivots on its midpoint, so driving it seems at first counter intuitive. When she wants to make the furrow wider, she ends up narrowing it. They stop the jingling horses with a 'whoa there, whoa', and the animals turn their heads to look back, snort, stamp a foot, shake a mane. Then it dawns on Miss White: 'Oh! But it's like the tiller on a boat! Then I've got it – make way, I've got the helm!' Jack is bemused; amused to see a such a sudden leap in progress that seemed to have stalled. Miss White is an accomplished yachtswoman. She must push the wheel against the furrow wall to widen the furrows, or away from it to narrow them. On the turns, or over rises, dips, slopes and softer ground, she must press down on the handles to lift the plough and raise her hands to deepen it. There is much more to learn, but she becomes proficient over her lessons, learning to adjust the angles of the draught chain connecting the plough to the horses, then taking the reins at the same time as the plough handles, watching their ears as they flick back and forth, listening and responding to her instructions. She can look up and enjoy the task. Watch the birds lift and settle as they make progress; black-and-white and sheeny-green plovers, winter thrushes, rooks. The gulls following behind her flapping coat as she sails her land yacht over the swell of the fields, tillering at clouds, working up a sweat.

One afternoon, in the kitchen after lunch, Jack presents Miss White with his treasured smock, as a 'souvenir'. She is rather moved. Wears it sometimes; values it greatly. Charlie Tucker bangs his cup and fist on the table and leads a rousing rendition of 'All Jolly Fellows That Follow the Plough'.

Then we harness our horses, our way then we go
And trip o'er the plain boys so merrily-O,
And when we come there, so jolly and bold,
To see which of us the straight furrow can hold.

Our master came to us and thus he did say,
'What have you been doing boys, all this long day?
Well you've not ploughed an acre, I'll swear and I'll vow.
And you're all idle fellows that follow the plough.'

I stepped up to him and made this reply,
'We have all ploughed an acre, so you tell a lie.
We have all ploughed an acre, I'll swear and I'll vow,
And we're all jolly fellows that follow the plough.'

He turned himself round and he laughed in a joke,
'It's past two o'clock, boys; it's time to unyoke.
Unharness your horses and rub them down well,
And I'll give you a jug of the very best ale.'

So come all you brave fellows, where e'er you be,
Take this advice and be ruled by me,
And never fear your masters, I'll swear and I'll vow,
For you're all jolly fellows that follow the plough.

Charlie finishes, saying, 'Well, I've never bin to sea, but mebe I could sail a yacht after all.' They cheer, and give the last verse a rousing go again.

Three months into her apprenticeship, and Miss White has settled into an almost-routine – though, given the great variety of work and equal urgency of multiple things needing doing, no day is the same. She enjoys the company of Doris and Marguerite, the independence of living in her van with her two dogs, and she enjoys the work, camaraderie and skill of the men on the farm.

No one can forget for a minute there is a war on. Everything has changed in that respect. The news is full of the horrors of the Blitz, of Southampton, Portsmouth, Bristol, London, Coventry. The skies often glow orange, booms and *ack-ack* from anti-aircraft guns are heard, and someone will say, *Someone is getting it tonight*. Some nights, bombers stream in over the dark fields, villages and farmsteads to bomb elsewhere. There have been air battles above them and bombs close by: ten bombs kill three cows and blow all the glass of Elcot Park inwards, and in September, three bombs fall on the nearby village of Kintbury and another ten on East and West Woodhay, damaging houses. Incendiaries fall onto neighbouring ricks, and a member of the Home Guard is killed by a bomb two days before Christmas in a village along the Downs. Only a crow-flying mile away, four bombs blow craters in the road past the Bloomsberries' Ham Spray House. Ralph and Frances Partridge's maid, Joan, is illuminated as she cycles up the tree-lined avenue and arrives to prepare the evening meal, shaken, mud-spattered, with her hair blown loose and wild. The only casualty is a skylark. And in the same village, a little boy thought killed is found asleep unharmed under his parents' garden, lifted and dropped back down, vegetables and all, on top of his bedroom. A (sometimes estranged) friend of the Partridges, Gerald Brenan, reports on the terrors of London, but remarks in defiance that 'many people are enjoying finding themselves braver than they knew'.

The threat and vigilance for invasion is very real. But Julia has found family and purpose, it seems. She relishes her walks with Doris around the farm; her clear, straightforward mind, her patience and the happy relationship Doris has nurtured with the men on the farm. Julia finds her 'a cheerful and truly delightful companion'. There is much 'running about' with the tractor, and errands to be done, on a manor farm that is also the heart of this village, and Julia delights in aiding Doris. The sunflower-yellow Fordson tractor is a joyfully bold statement, and, seemingly, available for any community eventuality. With its pneumatic tyres and temperamental disposition, modern Racing Lizzie has but two speeds: flat-out or stop. The regular sight of Doris speeding through the village, with Julia perched precariously on the footplate, burns long in the memory; a comet tail of laughter, waves, grins and greetings following on behind them. Julia White, farmhand, has arrived.

CHAPTER FOUR

Farming of Sorts

September 1981–May 1988

My attempts at being a future farmer-horsewoman find opportunity in a new place, with a move, aged eleven, to the outskirts of the nearby market town of Newbury, on Greenham Common in West Berkshire. Our little house is on the outside edge of a housing estate, named after the country's racecourses. From the landing window, through a gap in a narrow belt of woodland that framed it, horses gallop past in a flash on race days. I walk down to the racecourse stables on those weekends and haunt the barriered walkway, where gleaming thoroughbreds on high tensile fetlocks are led past, on their way to the paddock. Their grooms lean in to hold the power of forward movement through a single leather strap and a chifney bit, their elbow points resting on the horse's swinging scapula edge for leverage.

Our neighbours are a young couple of dairy farmers who have bought their first house where they could – not, of course, in the village where their farm is. Occasionally, I get to go with them to their farm to see the cows, bottle-feed calves or get lifts to school in their Land Rover, which smells deliciously of grass and cow muck. Dodds Farm, in the village where I later lived and got married, was bought by a predecessor of our neighbour's family, when the 30-acre farm was parcelled off in the Great Highclere Auction of 1926. During that time, 1,200 acres, including most of the village of Burghclere and several farms, were sold off to pay significant death duties incurred by the Herbert family of Highclere Castle, after the demise of the 5th Earl of Carnarvon three years earlier, in Cairo. It seems extraordinary that the existing 5,000-acre Highclere Estate, which we were once working tenants on ourselves, was big enough then to encompass another whole village. The auction document detailing smallholdings, cottages and farmsteads makes tantalising reading. In an act of feudal benevolence between the family and an arrangement brokered by the retiring land agent and son who succeeded him, the tenants of all the cottages and farms were invited to purchase early at a favourable price. The countryside was depopulated and agriculture still in the grip of a long and deep depression, and a good many of the remote, rural dwellings failed to sell at their asking price. Nevertheless, the auctioneer's programme highlights modern draws: excellent building land, proximity to village railway stations (long since closed), timber rights and good sporting tenure, all within reach of 'no less than three packs of foxhounds'. My local newspaper, the *Newbury Weekly News*, reported sympathetically that 'some of the tenants were old men who had been born on their holdings, which had been in the occupation of their families for generations. When one of these, a grey-haired veteran named Israel Hall secured [his cottage and five acres] against the bidding of an outsider, the audience broke into applause.' Presumably, he couldn't take advantage of the early purchase offer, needing more time to raise a loan. Several of the successful bidders are familiar names. I spot Dodds Farm on the map, out past Windbolts Copse and Featherbed Lane, finding ponds where there are still oozy places. I can feel the collective sense of relief and astonishment released from this place like a marsh gas for those that, having faced the worst, had no more fear of being turned out.

Finding a new riding school is the first thing Mum does to anchor me after Beech Farm, and I am forever grateful for that indulgence. It is a very different and competitive place, run by two brothers, where adults often outnumber pony girls. Alongside the riding school, there are liveries, hunters and a whole upper yard of showjumpers. It isn't smart, but it is well-kept, and, in part, a farm. My riding is tested and improves, and it isn't long until I am working the weekends and being paid a small wage, along with several other girls. Early starts find us catching the horses up in the big fields and bringing them in, sometimes in the dark, sometimes leading three in each hand as the first rays of sun pass through clouds of steam and condensing breath. When we get to the stalls and open loose boxes, we post each horse in, throwing headcollar ropes over necks, trusting they walk into the right box. We groom and groom until we are filthy and they aren't, and tack up for the first rides.

The weather is always uppermost in our minds, affecting tasks and the horses' moods, but the work can't stop. In prolonged spells of deep, iron-hard frost, breaking ice on the troughs takes a mallet and an iron driver, and we tractor hay out to the horses and cows, standing on the back of the trailer, avoiding its rotten floorboards, cutting baler twine with a pocketknife and kicking slices of the same cut and dried summer meadow back onto it at intervals. We breathe in the warm scent of summer in those coldest months, trying not to fall off the trailer as it bounces over frozen ruts and curds of mud. The horses are often fresh, frisky and silly, the farm dogs constant companions, joining in the fun or snuggling with us under horse blankets in the chilly tack room, as we warm up over Cup-a-Soups. In a succession of deep, frozen winters and when snow was expected every year, thick engine grease is smeared on the soles of horses' feet to prevent snow balling up in four-inch stilts. The intricacies of buckles and straps, bolts and a grip on anything mean gloves, even the preferred fingerless variety, are always on and off, or useless.

If there is hunting for a client or a show for someone, an early morning finds us standing on a stool in a stable plaiting and sewing up manes into an odd number of neat little balls, below the neck's arch line (never above). Fumbling with thick black, brown or white thread and a needle, it has to be changed three times for the tricoloured gelding, Jigsaw. They are inspected and pulled out again by our supervisor, a formidable horsewoman, if they are not up to scratch. Terrifying though she is, we become adept. Horses are exercised in heavy rain, high winds and storms, customers or not, hands slipping perilously on wet leather reins, bottoms slick on sodden saddles, going through it all with them.

It seems incredible now, that a just-fourteen-year-old could take responsibility and a hack out, of seven, eight, nine or more riders of differing experience and age onto the roads and common, sometimes to gallop over heather and jump fallen logs in the woods, and return home all in one piece. We don't always. At fifteen, I ride the bigger, stronger, fitter horses, to borrow an air of authority greater than my years.

At the end of the day, the tough, native ponies that live outdoors, Comet, Shady and Dart, Prince and Liquorice, Pearl, Sandstorm, Timber and Kit, are turned out and attention is focused on the big, clipped-out horses for 'evening stables'. Straw beds put up that morning are pulled down from the sides of the loose box and 'set fair'. Horses' legs are hosed, checked for thorns and, when dry, wrapped in thick wadding and felted bandages for comfort and support; plaited manes are teased loose and coats curried and brushed in a rhythm that works up a sweat, else you aren't doing it properly: three strokes of a soft body brush with one hand, and then a cleaning strike across the metal curry comb held like a plate in the other. Every tiny fleck of mud or sweat is groomed out or scraped off with a fingernail and the elaborate origami and tucking of blankets begins. The first red-black-and-yellow-striped Witney blanket, carefully folded that morning, is thrown up over the horse's high withers and unfolded over loins and neck up to the ears. The front corners are pinned like an envelope to make a triangle, with its point between the horse's ears, and then a second blanket or jute rug is thrown over it. The point of the poll triangle is drawn in a snug collar over the jute rug, and a roller or surcingle is done up to secure it like a girth.

Heavy, soaked and drained haynets are slung, dripping, over shoulders and tied up to a ring in the wall (not so high that hayseeds can fall into horses' eyes and ears, not so low that a shoe from a pawing hoof could get caught), and evening feeds are made up to a chorus line of kicking hooves, nickers and heads tossing over the half doors. Once fed, a last round is made to say goodnight and kick the bottom door bolts over, before leaving those loved horses, Demerara, Caster and Limerick, Darcy, Captain and Troy, Cinnabar, Grayling and dear Tanner, my favourite: a chestnut gelding and a strong point-to-pointer, who would rock and plunge and pull your arms out when his feet touched grass, until he was allowed to gallop furiously over it. I push my hands down his neck under his rug to warm them before the homeward journey as he nuzzles and huffs my hair. Then the thought of them all, warm, groomed and comfortable, knee-deep in golden straw, munching hay, sets a warming glow on our different journeys home and sustains us through the week.

For me, home is a two-mile bike ride down dark lanes and bumpy shingle tracks, the intermittent lamp of my pedal-powered dynamo fading with my energy, towards the lights of the estate at dusk. Thin jodhpurs, rubber boots and a worn waxed jacket are poor protection against the elements of an extended day. Wet woollen gloves are near-frozen onto the handlebars of my bike. Sometimes, I get into the warm house and faint, the numbness of the saucer-sized chilblains on my thighs wearing off. I learn not to plunge cold, chapped and filthy hands or poor, swollen chilblained feet into a bath or sink of hot water until I warm up some.

We absorb the knowledge and signals of the season's progressions and its subsequent tasks from the natural world around us: changing birdsong in response to lengthening or shortening daylight being a more reliable indicator than the seesaw of weather or warmth. For each seasonal task, a bird. Grey wagtails with their lemony undersides join their pied cousins around winter mud puddles as we begin bringing in the horses and rugging up for cold weather, and flocks of black-white-and-green lapwings appear in the fields. Stable-yard robins grow their quiet winter subsong with each increment of daylight, with each lowering level of the haystack and each rise of the winter, worm-rich muck heap. And the very day the year turns itself towards the light after the winter solstice, a mistle thrush marks it in strident, rather melancholy tones, from the top of a tall tree, one to another across the wet winter pasture, when we are only thinking of Christmas; his markings similar to the song thrush's but without that bird's apricity. It is all argent, silvery, iron and steel with a mistle thrush. Even the spots on his breast and winter-king pot belly are thorn shaped. His song, like joy capped under a dull, bone-cold ache, has the tang of wet metal gate about it. The pinching, stubborn chill of a bolt that won't go home without effort. A persistent snowdrop cheery weariness in the trudge of January mud, weak February sun, delivered in a minor key, under ice. I love it, but it makes my chilblains ache. It sings a thread that begins in the darkest days of winter, loud into storms, right through to the winter-spring and on, getting inside your head with an edge-of-migraine, tonal monotony until you realise it is the cure. Other birds join in – blackbird, song thrush, the church-bell peal of chaffinch, the bright timpani of the great tit's *Tea*cher, *tea*cher, the greenfinches, nasal *Schneeeew*, revealing the mistle thrush's jazz hook and bass place in the overall chorus, all along. The long, lone intro is over. The song has won through, warmed with a primrose light, and we believe in it at last.

It is time to remove rugs, mix spray for 'sweet itch' among the ponies prone to an eczema-like reaction to midge bites and reduce the grazing of those susceptible to laminitis, an inflammatory disease of the feet from rich grass. Catkins lengthen, loosening golden pollen smudges onto elbows, cheeks and saddle pommels as we duck under leafing trees, and house martins and swallows return to the stables to eat the flies that torture the horses.

Every June, before haymaking can get underway, we pull ragwort. A ritual I've kept and performed every summer since, though with increasing and concerned selectiveness. Ragwort, that tall, sunshine-yellow cluster of daisy-like flowers, is a deeply controversial and divisive plant. Often seen in overgrazed fields or disturbed ground, it's a boon for insects, a lifeline; but it's also cumulatively poisonous and more palatable to grazing animals when wilted, dead or dried in hay. As an 'injurious weed', a term coined by the Weeds Act 1959 when there were a lot more wild flowering plants and insects around, there is an obligation to control it if it poses a risk within fifty metres of grazing or forage land. Most animals ignore it due to its bitter taste, unless there's nothing else to eat or it's present in hay.

We pace the fields, shake off insects and pull it up by the roots, filling wheelbarrows or old feed sacks slung over our shoulders. The spinach-green stain and stink of it on our hands lasts whole weekends and, without handwashing facilities, bitter-taints our lunchtime sandwiches. In big fields at evening, we hug great armfuls of golden-yellow and green, scattering rabbit kits among low-swooping swallows, and pile the trailer high before hotching up beside it all for the ride home under a rising summer moon.

It's a plant I'm inordinately fond of, for its memories and the places it took me in summer – riverside meadows, meadows of gold, downland, little pastures in woodland clearings. Time and a chance to notice everything else going on around it: dainty small copper butterflies, burnet moths, the little waspish socks of cinnabar caterpillars, a daisy carpenter bee. Straightening up, picking a caterpillar out of a bra cup, a gilt-edged barn owl makes early evening patrols below a high-flying noctule bat, big as a jackdaw.

In recent summers, I pull ragwort with my daughters, son and husband in the field we rent for two horses we've inherited. It makes my hands itch now, a cumulative effect perhaps, so we all wear gloves. For the carcinogens in it, but, also, in case of mistakenly pulling a thistle in the gathering dusk. For many years now, we only pull what's directly in reach of the horses, and only when the plant wilts and the caterpillars have pupated into the flamenco drama of cinnabar moths. I never worry about breaking off the roots. It's welcome to come again the following year. Ragwort is especially important in providing nectar and pollen for butterflies, bees, hoverflies – indeed, two hundred invertebrates are known to use it, including thirty species exclusive to it. Even the British Horse Society has recognised its importance in these straitened nectary times and does not advocate blanket removal of 'stagger weed'.

Uprooting fields of gold in shorts and T-shirts is a prelude to the main glory of haymaking – and thoughts of 'getting a tan' in the eighties and nineties are discarded after a first day picking up bales, with bare skin scratched and sore and stuck with thistle thorns. On the hottest days, it is a job that demands full coverage, long sleeves and thick gloves. The tractor work is done by the boys in fields emptied of animals since spring. In a likely spell of dry weather, the long grass is cut, then 'tedded out' by the clever, cheerful, red-and-yellow haybob, behind the tractor. Tedding, 'floofing' or 'whuffling' involves a series of long spinning rake tines flinging, turning and stirring the lying hay about and spreading it out to dry. Then the tines and gates on the machine are adjusted so the tines 'row up' the hay into long, green-blonde windrows for haycocks. Depending on the drying quality of the weather, the tedding out and rowing-up tasks might be performed several times, until the hay is left in soft, romantic, snaking windrows again, ready for baling – and leaping over in people steeplechases we are never too old for. The ancient, red Massey tractor and the temperamental baler often let us down, shortening the weather-window of opportunity. But once the bales are made and lying like bricks about the vast fields, our job begins, fetching and hoisting the bales up onto the high flatbed cart behind the tractor. It is an urgent business, and if the tractor is moving, you have to get the bales on first time, onto your knee and up, the baler twine digging into your hands. Go too slowly and the whole procession leaves you behind. One person is up on the trailer stacking the thrown bales into giant, ever-increasing steps, offsetting them like brickwork, until their position standing on the jolting height becomes too perilous and the tractor is waved back to the yard like a carnival float, with us capering behind, sun struck and victorious.

Lunch on these days – sometimes augmented by the brothers' mother bringing a cool box of ice lollies in the Land Rover – is taken in the field, against the shady side of the tractor and gate-ended hay cart, or under the hedge. Later, there are tins of cool Guinness.

Danger lurks in the purple-blue shadows of the long hedgerows, needing only a slip of tiredness, recklessness, silliness or overconfidence. Of not doing things as you should, in cutting corners. Though we are aware, having grown up terrified by the dreamlike horrors of death on a sunny day through the public information safety films of the seventies and eighties – of lonely water, farmyard games, electrical substations and railway lines – we are working, not playing. Nevertheless, there are near misses, reminders – a foot caught on a loose loop of baler twine sends me crashing off the side of the moving cart onto the ground; someone else puts a foot through the broken boards on the trailer; another doesn't stack the bales properly and they come tumbling down. But the tragedy that dims a golden day and sends us home with shocked tear-streaks down our filthy faces is a nimble and unlikely victim. The dogs are always with us. Two, three, four – sometimes, the couple of fox-hound puppies we're tasked with each year to 'walk' and accustom to people and horses. Schwisby is a favourite, a wheat-coloured Bearded Collie cross with an ever-wagging tail and short legs. He rides on the cart or on the tractor plate (once, on the seat with a block of wood weighting the accelerator, driving it), but, mostly, he rounds us up, leaping on and off the cart with much barking and well-timed agility. Except one day, he misjudges a leap off, lands awkwardly, and goes under the loaded trailer's double back wheels. He appears utterly uninjured, wagging his tail, but doesn't get up. Chris the farmer scoops him up and we follow them back to the Land Rover in silent, horrified procession, convinced by the furious wagging tail that all will be well. They reach the strawy back of the Land Rover and Schwisby dies in Chris's arms before he can lay him down.

Haycart stops then for the rest of the afternoon; the urgency of a gathering weather front that had pressed us all day is ignored. Rain falls on the last bales and ruins them, though someone throws a tarpaulin over the cart. Schwisby was one of us but, in our tearful homegoing, nobody voices the fact that it could have been any of us.

Work continues back at the big barn, where the hay is unloaded and put up. The stack is built again like brickwork, with the next level set at a quarter turn above it, to lessen the suffocating gaps it is possible to fall through. There is an old red hay elevator from the 1950s that rarely works but is a boon when it does, delivering hay to the top via its diplodocus neck. The atmosphere is giddier, dustier and occasionally tense in its closeness and the need to hand or throw bales to each other. Two of the older lads from school face off across the floor over something and it begins to get really heated. We reason, laugh, shout even, until one draws his pocketknife, and feigns lunges and we freeze in horror. The other lad grabs a two-pronged hay fork and roars. At the top of the stack, in a split-second decision, I reason the landing is soft and throw myself off with a scream, taken up by the other girls, and 'fall' out of the haybarn. The lads rush to my aid and the situation diffuses with a handshake.

We emerge sticky with sweat and grime, sneezing black stuff. Later, the boys add weight to our tack-room protest in solidarity, when we realise we girls are paid half what they get. It almost works. We are given a small increase with amusement – though we are all of an age, parity is a way off. We are half as strong as the boys, apparently; we take longer, gossip, our 'boobs get in the way' and we cannot drive the tractors or use the machinery. None of this is true. A camp play is made of our girlishness by the farmer, flicking imaginary hair, and we are told to be grateful. There is a different narrative here. We are the bulk of the workforce, to the point that haymaking often can't begin until exams are over or the school holidays begin. We are fit, strong and energised. We adapt and cooperate swiftly where we need to and work just as hard. We are bright, cheerful and chatty and enjoy our work, and why on earth can't we drive the tractor? We are more careful, certainly. I'm not even going to mention any hindrance of a female physiology.

Over the next month, we are pursued everywhere by the sickly sweet smell of new green hay and the fear of spontaneous combustion in the barn. If the hay is brought in too damp or too green, it can heat up enough to catch fire. Sometimes, one of us is sent to push a bare arm between the bales to check the temperature. It's not an effective gauge. Only once, when the scent took on a caramelised quality, was the stack opened up with a tractor, and found to be smouldering gently in the middle, disaster avoided.

The weekends, school and college holidays stretch into full-time work and the repetition of seasonal variety widens. There are point-to-points, shows, spills and accidents; a cracked bone from a kick riding bareback after cider-drinking at a village fete. I still have the horseshoe-shaped scar above my right ankle. There are carnivals we ride into town for, jumping footpath stiles and clattering through housing estates, stopping at traffic lights dressed as St Trinian's girls, hockey sticks tucked under our thighs and stirrup leathers. And there are pub rides to remote places, where shepherds rib us for the sudden smell of horse entering the bar and we them, for their comforting stink of wet wool and greasy-clean lanolin. But there are other farm jobs, too, that I relish, always volunteering first – pulling wild oats out of cornfields before harvest, milking goats, moving cows and milking the 'house' cow to help clear her mastitis. I love it all. I am strong and free and alive in the open air, close to and part of it all – the domestic animals and the wild, the growing cycle of the year, the weather. *Outside.*

The yard isn't there any more. The yellow painted stables, the stalls. The haybarn, feed and tack room, the fields and thick, ancient hedges. Favourite shady or sheltering trees. House martins, swallows, the barn owl that sat under the granary roof, spreckle-faced and softly lit in a muted auburn-moted spotlight, glamorous and mysterious as a film star. Part of the yard and fields are now a housing estate: Stirrup and Martingale Close, Horseshoe End, The Halters, Haysom's Drive, Equine Way. I wonder, when horseshoes turn up with a clink against a fork in one of the gardens there, if it's one we searched in vain for. The rest is a Tesco superstore, car showrooms, a Hilton hotel and the retail park. It's astonishing it all fits onto that land.

There are no traces left in the buzzing, hyper-lit aisles of two-for-one offers, but, queuing in a snaking trail for food during the first Covid lockdown under a hot sun, there is a ghost of those summers. My mind is tuned in to those times. I see the shine of a clump of ragwort in a yellow bollard, hear the clink of headcollars in the dropping of someone's keys, the rattle of the haybob's tines in a passing train of trollies. There is a pavement between parking spaces where the dividing hedge was, between the mares' field and the geldings' field. A lone song thrush sings from the top of a lamppost there and people notice – look up, smile and comment across the spaces between them. But no other bird picks up and carries the refrain, passes it on. *I remember when all this was fields*, I think, wryly. But I do. I remember it all – the smell of saddle soap and green hay, the little dog Schwisby, lunch under the hay cart. Every horse, each animal. A flock of birds circles and, for a moment, I see a ragged flock of lapwings, not the pigeons from the retail park.

CHAPTER FIVE

A Pig in the Privy and a Good Fug

Winter 1940–February 1941

Almost before anyone knows it, it is Christmas. Festivities are necessarily and respectfully simple, with a kind of shocked burnt-edge just visible around the lens of everything. A little like the singed packet of raisins, sent on to the Hungerford grocer from a bombed London train, that the children pick through for the plum pudding. The sticky-coaly ones are fed to the chickens with glee. Marguerite sets up the nativity scene in a corner of the oldest barn, against a backdrop of straw, as she does each year; only this year, there are more to see it. The figures are beautifully, expressively and richly painted. There are a poor barefoot pilgrim and child, a Black king and a poor Black shepherd boy, sheep, lambs, a cow, a donkey, wealth kneeling beside poverty among the animals in the straw around the crib. The children are allowed to pick them up, but only if they too are kneeling in the straw. They do this with reverence – but the truth is, the packed chalk floor in the barn is unforgiving to falling plaster kings and shepherds.

There are private thoughts and fears for so many elsewhere, and the unthinkable news of thousands of civilians killed, injured or made homeless during the ongoing Blitz hovers in almost everyone's thoughts. The burnt raisins are sobering to those without a personal connection to the big cities, and the threat of mass starvation is real. Up till the start of the war, an astonishing 70 per cent of British food is imported, and occupation by Nazi Germany of most Western European countries as well as attacks on shipping from German submarines cuts off many supplies. Even onions are all but impossible to get hold of, having formerly come largely from the occupied Channel Islands. Nobody knows what might happen next, or to whom. According to the small 'streamline moderne' wireless in Miss White's caravan and the large, elegant, polished one in the manor house library, an invasion is expected before spring and likely to be pre-empted by a large-scale gas attack. Often, on cold, clear nights, the sound of bombs and gunfire is loud. Often, on days where winter seems to wear its own dull tin hat, the guns and bombs from Salisbury Plain seem very close. Someone had it from someone in Hungerford that a year's food stocks had been destroyed by bombing in Southampton. A certain concerned gratitude for work and duty push out the worst hauntings of the imagination and everyone quite literally mucks in: feeding, milking, turning out and cleaning out the animals.

Farm work does not stop for the day, of course, but is minimised and there is a goose and the plum pudding. Joy, and the wearing of it, and the rituals of the season are a vital tool of resistance in this horribly frightening war. The festivities are pleasant, gentle and friendly, and a party is put on for the children. Charlie and John have cut and carted home a Christmas tree, and it has been decorated with coloured glass baubles. Sprigs and boughs of holly, ivy and yew lie along the great Tudor fireplaces and are poked into picture frames linked with paper chains. Pretty cards are strung up in the kitchen. In the evening, Marguerite is a concert party in herself, playing her banjo with Scout-campfire gusto, and Doris leads the singing with a wonderful clear voice. Julia claps along, laughs, grabs hands to encourage dancing and nudges good spirits, trying not to think herself where the children's parents might be. For some of the children, it is the finest Christmas ever, with newspaper hats, paper twists of sweets and a small present each. Later, the tree's little red candles in their clip-on tin holders are lit and there are games of Snap and

Ludo, and after the children have gone to bed, ginger wine around the fire for Marguerite, Doris and Julia.

When Julia heads back to her caravan and lets Jo and Dina out into the night, a little waft of warm, sleepily seductive air hits her. She turns away, hugging herself tight against the cold in her thin party dress and greatcoat, to see the fields below Rivar Down glitter under so much starlight. There is no moon, but the down masquerades as just another of the big black barns, its ancient gently humped roof as protective and vast and friendly somehow, and she thinks of its inner chalk glowing under a blackout of turf, thin as her dress. She has heard there was once a white horse carved into its flank, long grown over, saving anyone the trouble of blanketing it in turves and gorse, as they have done with the strange, elegantly artful white horse at Uffington, a few short miles away. She feels a profound feeling of belonging, a sense of scale and time, and her small, dizzying, ginger-wine-warmed place in it, like a seed of corn planted, to be harvested. Just then, a blue bauble-coloured star falls from the heavens. She silently claps, drops the paper-covered light of her torch from the crook of her arm onto her foot and, feeling suddenly self-conscious and girlish, turns it into a brisk clap to get the dogs in.

Having been master of an independent adult life, Julia finds being told exactly what to do a welcome novelty, having almost never experienced it. Her responsibilities, beyond her dogs and feeding herself, are to report to Shalbourne Manor's kitchen at quarter to nine to receive the order of the day.

The little apple-green Cheltenham caravan is parked out of the way, sheltered behind one of the big barns, in a paddock shared with four Welsh Mountain pony foals. At times, a sweet intelligent face peers in through each window and she is inclined to draw her curtains for privacy. They rub and nibble on the van at night and Julia jokes she's merely exchanged New Forest ponies on the doorstep with Welsh Mountain ones. But she is comfortable in her little van – though little it is. At almost six foot tall, she can just about stand upright in the middle. With her arms outstretched, she can touch both ends, and with her hands on her hips, she says, her elbows brush the sides.

It seems extraordinarily small. I try this out in my little writing hut and our (grown up) son's tiny bedroom and it doesn't seem possible. Jo and Dina's baskets are under the table and the rest of the floor space is taken up with the stove, haybox, water cans and Julia's boots. Fortunately, she says, she has the right sort of temperament for this kind of cramped living. A 'Wiltshire' slowness and patience, a quite reasonable methodicalism. No room to lose your temper in here, she says, the whole place would be wrecked in minutes!

I am stunned to hear she has a housekeeper – Julia, *really?* A cleaner for a home so tiny, you can stand in the middle and touch both sides? I nearly fall off my chair. It seems funny and ludicrous, and I go through the house, telling everyone: a daily *housekeeper*, in a teeny tiny caravan! But Julia writes unashamed: 'A nice woman from the village comes every day to clean up the caravan and do the washing up and sometimes some cooking. The perfect life with almost no domestic duties at all!' I soften, because this did not mean she was idle or didn't 'do' for herself; far from it. Most middle-class households had daily or live-in help of some kind. She grew up with a maid and cook in her large, Victorian childhood home and had live-in domestic help on and off thereafter, who likely doubled as friendship and company. It would have seemed odd to live utterly alone, and the choice would have been between taking in a lodger or a daily help. I check myself against the privileges and conveniences of my age: washing machines, hoovers, fridges and freezers, electric cookers, food bought from supermarkets, radiators. And not forgetting a greater tolerance towards the regularity and thoroughness of housework. Julia is clearly unafraid of hard, dirty, physical work – she'd just prefer to do it outdoors. Who can blame her for that?

In winter, the van walls run with condensation. Clothes and bedding must be wrapped and swaddled, even when sleeping, in ground sheets. The Valor Perfection heater, a tall, robin's-egg-blue portable chimney on three neat, curved little legs, is lit permanently against the cold. Collared with latticework, it has a flat top for cooking on.

The 'dinner' hour is from 12.30–1.30pm and Julia has bread, cheese and tinned sardines, or whatever is available from the village shop. But tea after work, at 5pm, is taken in the house with Doris and Marguerite. She often stays to have a bath, changes into slacks and spends pleasurable evenings alone in the van, reading, listening to the Forces Programme on the wireless with its blend of drama, comedy and quiz shows, when the Home Service gets too much, and cooking supper between the single gas stove and the Valor Perfection heater. On Saturday lunchtimes, the butcher brings her weekly ration: a little bit of steak and two chops. Not much, but she boils them up with some vegetables into a grand stew in the billycan, then places it in the haybox, a wooden lidded crate lined with sweet-smelling hay that acts as a slow cooker. Julia knows the importance of effort, when feeding just herself, and the outdoor work makes her hungry. She makes her breakfast porridge the same way, so that it is hot and lovely in the morning, and the haybox doubles as a heated seat or footstool in the evening. She is warm and content with Jo and Dina for company and enjoys the good fug of the caravan. But blackouts over her windows and ventilator grills stop off fresh air circulation and I am alarmed at the clear carbon monoxide risk. Nodding off on several evenings, her oil lamp flares in protest and goes out with a pop, waking her in the dark. I think of Hardy's Gabriel Oak in *Far from the Madding Crowd* falling asleep in the fumy fug of his sealed shepherd's hut at lambing time, and of him being saved by the wit of a passing Bathsheba Everdene. But no one passes the caravan after dark or thinks of the danger, and I am astonished at how terrible and easy it would be for Julia, Jo and Dina to fall asleep like this and not wake up, when she seems otherwise in a place of such safety. After the lamp goes out for the fourth time, she correlates this with the intolerable headaches she's been waking with, thinks to sleep with the door open a crack, and is saved.

One morning she is woken by the pigs, who have escaped and come rootling around the van, scratching their bristly backs on the underside and rocking it, spooking the pony foals and sending Jo and Dina into paroxysms of excitement. The pigs are soon rounded up, although one of the piglets cannot be found. Early the following morning, an elderly lady knocks and apologises; didn't want to wake the house but have you lost a pig? She has a coat on over her night things. 'I have had to use the neighbour's lavatory, because you see, there is a very nice piglet in my privy. Curled up all cosy and I don't want to disturb it. Could someone come?' Joe Eggleston is sent to retrieve the pig and by midday, the village shop's customers are in on the joke and Julia has made a new friend in Edith, owner of the privy, and starts spending frequent evenings with her in her cottage. But a local policeman sharing the joke is alerted to the presence of a mobile residential van, a luxury not permitted by wartime regulations. Despite protestations of necessity, that Miss White is not 'olidaying', Jack Palmer has the idea that the wheels be removed and the van propped up on big blocks of wood to comply. The plan works, although proves a nuisance when the van must be moved in the heat of summer, to the shade of a big oak tree.

It is a bitterly cold January with penetrating frosts and deep snow, mid-month. It is at this time that the horror of foot-and-mouth disease comes to the village farms. It is confirmed at the Tuckers' small farm first, just a couple of hundred yards from Baverstock Farm at the Manor. By lunchtime, large red notices have gone up at the Tuckers' and no one is allowed to leave. Charlie Tucker and Jack Palmer, married to Charlie's sister, do not go home that night, nor can they for the next two months. The Tuckers are miserably cut off from the rest of the village. Men from the Ministry of Agriculture descend to begin the great purging of the farm, while the family can only watch, helpless. The cows, pigs and sheep are slaughtered on site and buried in deep pits, and the barns are gutted of their careful stores of hay, straw, grain and feedstuff. Small fires deal with these, but are put out early, for fear of attracting the enemy. The carcasses and anything biodegradable is quicklimed in the pits, rather than burnt for the same reason, and this is some blessing. Clothes, and anything left standing, are disinfected. Poor old Harry, utterly overwhelmed, takes to his bed.

At Shalbourne Manor, a scheme of isolation and protection is drawn up. The Jersey milkers are kept to their fields around Baverstock Farm and the hardy black (quite wild) Galloway beef herd live out at the furthest point from the Jerseys, with their bull, Jingo, a tame Aberdeen Angus. With a big cereal crop between the cow herds, the farm is effectively divided in two. Joe, Charlie and John keep with the milking herd and board at the small, thatched Baverstock Farmhouse, and Jack, Doris and Julia look after the Galloways and Jingo, from Shalbourne Manor. Jo and Dina are sent away to kennels. The two small groups wave and holler across the distances, and Jack and his wife conduct a socially distanced relationship, with the cottage garden wall between them, that renders them shy as teenagers. Footbaths of Jeyes disinfectant are deployed in gateways, and vehicle wheels and horses' hooves and legs sprayed down. The weather makes things so much harder. These are very harsh winters. Exactly a month after January's snowstorm, snow falls harder in February and the village is cut off again. Ice loads the telephone wires and there are fears of a repeat of the extraordinary ice storm of the year before that broke off huge branches along the avenue at Ham Spray and elsewhere. In the north of the country, snow falls for fifty-six hours straight, burying six train carriages under fourteen feet of drifting snow north of Newcastle. Over one thousand people have to be dug out. While acknowledging the hardship, I feel a pang of loss of winters like this. The ones we used to get, which I remember so vividly I can taste them, smell their cold, blue-shadowiness; feel the bodily, simple restorative joy of a hot bath and dinner truly earned and needed. The sort of proper winter we rarely get now, where each frost might be our last.

The water freezes of course, but it cannot be carted out to fill the troughs in the usual way: it would be unwise to spray to soaking the carthorses' feathered legs. So, the wheels of the water cart are taken off, and the cart, shafts and all, is mounted upon the trailer like a faintly ridiculous ceremonial bier, to be pulled by the tractor. Twice a day, it is filled with a hose at the farm and, with Jack driving, Doris and Julia sit on a shaft each, on top of the trailer, armed with an ARP stirrup pump and dangling a bucket of Jeyes fluid between their legs. Their carnival float, pulled by buttercup-yellow Racing Lizzie, makes quite a sight through the village and, despite the bitter chill, it is a light-hearted and silly (if entirely practical) part of the day. Once out in the fields, the stirrup pump is put in the buckets of Jeyes and sprayed liberally over wheels and boots and the troughs filled. Bales of hay are cut loose and thrown up into racks to save being trampled, and oat straw is shaken onto the ground to supplement it. The cattle push, bellow and snort, clouds of steam rising up from their solid bodies, their breath condensing and whiskers freezing. They wear a silver rime of frost or even a layer of snow along their backs under a coat so insulating, it does not melt.

In between, when the ground is thawed enough, Jack and Miss White go about ditching, following the 'crust and crumb' method. Jack digs the 'crust', working backwards with his spade, while Miss White works forwards after him, spading the 'crumb' off to one side. Often shin-deep in freezing water, it is a cold, dirty and back-breaking job. Julia misses the warm friendliness of the milking barn, the soft velvet of a Jersey flank against her cheek, the squirt and smell of rich, creamy milk filling the metal pail, but she is happy to be working outdoors. At night in her caravan, she applies cold cream to her ruddy cheeks and cracked, chilblained hands.

There is a scare at Baverstock one morning, when young John is soused in disinfectant and sent running to report to the Manor's kitchen that a Jersey calf is ill. The vet is called but, to everyone's great, shaking relief, diagnoses a chill. But then the Hills' farm, on the other side of Baverstock, comes down with foot-and-mouth, despite every precaution taken. It's a clean and modern farm and just as devastating to the Hills as it is to the Tuckers, but they too must stand by as their whole, fine herd of Ayrshire milkers are destroyed. Again, for fear of visible fires, the village is spared weeks of acrid smoke that jolts a memory for me. In the second year of the new millennium, foot-and-mouth spread horribly across the country, not long after my parents sold their house nearby and moved to a smallholding in Devon. Surrounded by dairy and beef farms, they were almost immediately quarantined. Across the whole country, footpaths and bridleways were closed, signs hand-painted in desperate, dripping red paint went up alongside locked gates, footbaths and trays full of disinfectant. Travel was advised against, especially between rural areas such as ours, and we were prevented for months from visiting.

Newly married, my husband, Martin, is fresh from agricultural college, studying equine management. One of only two males among nineteen female students, it almost completely reversed the gender cohort on the agriculture and gamekeeping courses – except there were no women on those courses at all. For him, not born to farming and with little chance of owning or even renting any land, a career in horse management, particularly breeding them, was a more accessible option. A way in. We took a horse on loan; a big, bright-mahogany bay called Falcon. In those few months when we were both working, pre-parenthood, it was a short-lived luxury; a passion we shared. Confined to the sand school arena and barred from the bridleways, woods and fields, Falcon became a bored then challenging ride, but we'd both relished it. It became a game, me sitting the flying leaps over ever higher fences and the joie-de-vivre bucks, until I didn't, and a last, corkscrewed handstand sent me flying on my own into a crumpled heap in the sand, bloody-nosed but fine. I got back on, but felt bruised enough to take some days off work with a strange kind of disorientated sickness. It took me the week to realise I was pregnant with our first child. Riding horses like Falcon was not sensible any more and, unacknowledged then, something in my confidence shifted slightly. Anyway, he was something we definitely could no longer afford, so he eventually went back to his owner. I missed my parents during that time of what felt like literal confinement; particularly as they'd planned chickens, ducks, a small flock of sheep and a couple of cows in their retirement. But although that happened later, a characterful, long-haired Angora goat named George, which had come with their smallholding as an incumbent, joined the ranks of the slaughtered as farm after farm around them became infected or part of the contiguous cull. Their new neighbours wept as generations-strong pedigrees were destroyed. Many gave up entirely. The pyres of burning cattle and sheep and the acrid pall of smoke around the country were apocalyptic. When we were finally allowed to visit, we were greeted by the army at the entrance to their lane and sprayed down.

During this time, Julia spends more time in the manor than her caravan, missing her dogs, but grateful for the added knowledgeable company of Jack Palmer. There are tremendous discussions between Jack and Doris about farming over the last cups of tea in those evenings. Julia listens intently, head resting on her hands, elbows on knees. After the bitter weather outside, it is warm and comfortable around the great fire and there is still, at this point, plenty to eat and cigarettes to be smoked. The conversations often continue out in the fields. Jack is interesting, skilled, kind and generous with his knowledge. Small, wiry, with keen intelligent eyes and a weathered face, Jack has farmed in Wiltshire but also in Canada. Julia has travelled there and they strike up a genuine friendship, with much to talk about this marvellous country. 'Just like our own A.G. Street,' quips Julia – they have all read several books by that Wiltshire-Manitoba farmer-writer, including *Farmer's Glory*, and they listen to him on the *Brains Trust* programme on the wireless.

Eventually, two months' quarantine is up and, by some miracle, Miss Doris Mason's farm remains clear of the disease. There is a joyful reunion between the two cattle teams, and it is clear Joe Eggleston as head cowman feels the relief deeply. Doris and Julia go to see the Jersey cows, and, with her characteristic fortitude, Doris is upbeat and buoyant, only showing the strain when Joe briefly does.

Julia visits the Hills' farm with Doris to offer condolences and help to begin again. A closer relationship with the Tuckers means it does not need to be said. 'There'll be compensation,' says Fred Hill. He is pragmatic and uncomfortably brusque at first, so they both feel the useless twinge of survivor's guilt, until he says simply, 'It were so quiet. When all the animals were done with. Do you know, not a bird sang? For three days, the birds stopped singing.'

God, the potency of that phrase; its *currency*. The immediate recognition that a situation is so profound and shocking, the world ceased to function normally. Something unnatural occurred and something natural responded. It hits me in the chest like a ball I didn't see coming. I immediately call to mind other times I've heard that phrase *the birds stopped singing* on the television, radio, in books, online, usually by witnesses to wars, terrible explosions or natural disasters, recalled after the event. I can hear my fireman dad saying it, dropping his mutually protective armour of dry humour and scorn in a rare moment: five words to convey the shocking aftermath of a tragic motorway pile-up on the M4 near Hungerford in March 1991. In the space of nineteen seconds, fifty-one vehicles collided sickeningly during patchy fog, killing ten people and injuring twenty-five, in a resultant series of explosions. 'All the birds stopped singing.' And then our chimney sweep, recounting again only last year the terrible, all-too-familiar details of the time a local farmworker (his former classmate) gunned down members of this community on a sunny market day in 1987; the pans burning dry on the stove, a playground of children frozen in terror, radios playing on in stopped cars, and *all the birds stopped singing* for days afterwards.

What is this phenomenon? Do they really? What makes us notice, or, more to the point, imagine it or say it, when most people don't notice the birds singing anyway? Particularly in these times of such depleted birdsong. Is it the high tinnitus of our senses tuning out from the world in an aftershock, a kind of aural faint, so we're not hearing anything that might distract us from what we immediately have to deal with, or shield from?

I ask my husband, Martin, about it. A paramedic for more than twenty years now, he worked for a time next to the office Dad had. It's something he recognises in times of threat or urgent concentration, where life – someone else's – hangs in the balance. He describes it as a useful tuning out, a dialling down of distraction and a switch to life-saving mode. It's curious, though, why we don't say 'I couldn't hear what anyone else was saying' or 'I couldn't hear the traffic'. Why the birds? Is it because they represent the natural world that holds us; and in this moment of acute vulnerability and shock, we realise simultaneously the importance of that life-supporting cradle, and that it is also just a random accident of space, stardust and evolution, and owes us nothing? Is it the fear that our mother earth has deserted us? That we are actually alone?

And isn't it funny, and not funny at all, how we use something so key to the aliveness of the natural world of which we are part, to illustrate how profound, arresting and uncanny it is that the birds fall silent? It's a phrase that drives a point home with such power. But we are in the thick of a long and accelerating process of stopping the birdsong ourselves. It haunts me, this phrase. It means something is terribly, terribly wrong. I am haunted by the variety and abundance of plants, insects and those clever, beautiful, uniquely avian vocal syrinxes we've squeezed out, squeezed to death, one by one, in slow motion.

We are in the midst of the kind of ecological collapse Julia, Doris, Marguerite, the Tuckers, Hills, dear Jack Palmer, Joe and the boy John, the Partridges and their remnant Bloomsberries at Ham Spray House, couldn't begin to imagine, even among the horrors and privations of war. I get inexplicably angry and want to confront them: did you not see this coming? This silencing, these extinctions? But of course they didn't. Who does when they are just doing their best to improve their lot, hold steady – hold *on* to life as they know it, at war and under threat of invasion and starvation? And in the company of such abundance of wild life. They could not, perhaps, imagine it so diminished. They'd think me unhinged. Here they are, assembled at the start of a new phase in the art, innovation and work of farming, of feeding us all, full of hope and action for all that is good, but at the same time about to step on a parallel path to destroy all that they stop for, notice and love, in those back-straightening moments. I see them looking up from the fields, a lark's-eye view, a passing rook's, and I want to shout down, *When did we stop noticing the silencing of the birds?* But it comes out as a musical, slightly hysterical elegy, raining down from on high, of living my own life and witnessing this: a rook's *Crahhh*, knowing I am an unwilling, culpable part of it. Somewhere, there's a link we might forge between us – still can – reaching across decades with the power of our imaginations and community good, that overlap in this time, this place, and that are about to get much closer. What could they have done? What am I to do now?

CHAPTER SIX

Ranching

1988

After some distinctly unimpressive A-level results (except fine art, and a quarter of a disastrous business studies qualification, from which I salvaged touch-typing), I'm at a loss at what to do. University has not been encouraged, and I continue working at the yard until the astonishing opportunity comes to work on a horse ranch, and later a cattle ranch, in Canada.

A family friend, a sort of adopted uncle who'd spent two years living with my dad as a teenager, had emigrated to Canada some decades before and kept in touch. Would I like to work for my flights, board and keep? He and one of his daughters, who was a good dozen years older than me and whom I knew and loved from occasional visits to England, owned and ran a 'Dude Ranch' – a kind of western experience that offered summer camps for kids, rides around the ranch and into the foothills, and trips into the Rocky Mountains of Kananaskis Country, west of Calgary, Alberta.

I'd never been on a plane, but it already felt like destiny. I'd had a dreamy, yearning blueprint of 1920s and 30s Canada since childhood from my grandad, who'd gone out there to work, aged just sixteen, on someone else's ticket. They'd baulked at the last minute and he took his chance as an unemployed farm labourer during the agricultural slump.

I'd grown up on Grandad's wistful, bittersweet stories of Canada, where he'd worked on a farm in Nova Scotia, and then in Ontario.

He'd been accepted as part of a family that sat around a large table at mealtimes with plentiful food. Something he'd never known. He worked with two heavy horses, Queenie and Bess, that he grew to love, and was taken on several occasions to meet the Chief and community of the local Mi'kmaq Nation.* Those interactions left a reverential mark on him, and I wonder at the solidarity he may have instinctively felt then or retrospectively felt in the retelling; he and his mother were largely cast out from the circle of their own locally nomadic, Romany community, when my grandad was born illegitimately. Their family, in turn, were moved off the open land and shut into inclosures or 'rehabilitation compounds' in the New Forest; the 'Nevi Wesh' in Romani, in a similarly sinister model to that imposed on Indigenous people in Canada and the US.† Whenever he spoke of those meetings, there were long pauses where he struggled to find the words, hands open, palms up or curved around those elusive, invisible thoughts, fingers fluttering, shaking his head just the once, before an irreverent joke chased the thoughts away. He talked of those tall, false wooden-fronted, western towns, the Northern Lights, cabin walls, snowshoes, beavers, moose, kindness and a relative sort of plenty. He'd break the spell with a ruffle of my hair and the cry 'ah, *marlish*', a word I heard only him use, and guessed was Romani. I later found it came from his time in Egypt in the Second World War. An adopted Yemini word, *marlish*: 'it doesn't matter, it isn't important, it is of little consequence'.

He'd make my brother and me sweets he'd learnt to cook in Canada – coconut ice and rich fudge as well as thick Canadian

---

* Some sounds in Indigenous languages such as Mi'kmaq or Tsuut'ina do not have comparatives in English (for instance, there are no ejective sounds in the English language), so a phonetic attempt will often only be able to be the closest approximation to the correct pronunciation. However, the pronunciation of Mi'kmaq could be written in English as 'mee g-mahk'.

† Enclosures in the New Forest are historically known and named as 'inclosures'.

pancakes with real maple syrup that he'd send off for. He'd tell us the story again, of how, as stores master in the Egyptian desert during the war, he'd given his own pair of boots away, making thick pancakes to strap to his feet instead. Always the joker. He is delighted when I go.

We exchange illustrated letters, full of questions for each other. When I get home, he tells me he'd wanted to stay; there'd been a job for life for him there. He was given a silver dollar as a gift and pressed to return. But back home in Portsmouth, he met with such poverty again; his mother, stepfather and little sister needing him. He couldn't go back. Was ashamed to have lived such a life. He sold the silver dollar and went to work in the city on trams, then buses, cheerfully enough. I search 'silver dollar, Canada, 1931' on the internet. It may have paid for food for a few days. One side depicts an Indigenous man and a 'coureur des bois', a voyaging European trader, paddling a birch-bark canoe together, the Northern Lights arcing above them. I still have his precious Eaton catalogue, something that would have been thumbed and ordered from in every Canadian home. From the latest fashions to farming implements and even flatpack homes, it brought the prospect of modernity, comfort and ease to hard lives and very rural communities.

Home for me becomes a ranch outside the foothills hamlet of Bragg Creek. There is nothing between us and the Rocky Mountains and our nearest neighbours are a cattle ranch. Weekends are busy and social with people who keep their horses with us, but the weeks, around the camps and excursions, are often just three of us, living together in a one-room log cabin. It had been an improvement, some decades before, on a smaller one that still rested on the sleds that horses had hauled it in on, when the place had been homesteaded. Local legend had it that one of the team of horses pulling it died, and the homestead was decided there and then out of necessity. Both cabins are built of rich-coloured spruce or cedar logs, axe-notched and slotted without nails, though the older one is silvered with age. They are warm, secure-feeling and comfortable, the unlockable doors on both are crowned with the broad, thorny umbrellas of moose antlers. Michelle, my age, from the nearby rural outskirts of Red Deer, and Tom, a cowboy in his early twenties from the prairies outside of Stettler, are my cabin and work fellows. Michelle and I sleep behind a thick curtain pulled across a corner of the cabin and Tom either on the saggy horsehair settee or in the old cabin, under a beautifully made patchwork quilt, deep-grimed and grey with age and likely as old as the cabin itself. We have enough electricity to power lights and an oven. Water comes from a well we have to trek down to, prime and pump weekly, and the toilets are earth closets, a hundred dark and starlit yards from the cabin. A pot and a wooden spoon hang on a cabin corner nail to bang on quiet nights, in case of coming across a bear or mountain lion. The family, and others who keep their horses here, come up from the city in their campervans at weekends.

We are a good team, we three, and quickly inseparable. Michelle and Tom are instinctive, easy horse people; gentle, thoughtful and funny, and they have a reverence for my classical 'English-style riding' on flatter saddles that I find perplexing as I get to grips with heavy western saddles and ropes, and learn a more relaxed western-style of riding. We learn so much from one another, and love the work, people, breathtaking landscape and the horses with a passion.

The horses run free in a big herd. There are around forty, each with their own characteristics and foibles, loyalties and challenges. We keep three back in an overnight corral in case we need to ride anywhere for help, supplies or to go out and bring in the herd in the mornings. Sometimes, on those mornings when we've been up partying or yakking around the fire till late, we bring the herd into the corrals as the customers pull in, in a galloping cloud of coloured bodies, swirling dust, yips and whoops – and all the reckless confidence of youth and slick teamwork. The horses are everything: work, transport, leisure, friends. We think nothing of taking rides out all day, then riding off somewhere in the evening – sometimes to the saloon bar in Bragg Creek, unsaddling and tying the horses outside to the rails or challenging each other to bareback galloping races. We ride the horses into the cabin, sit on their backs as they doze around the campfire, or head off for a night ride in the foothills. The most exhilarating is the last: riding out as coyote voices join together in a building, harmonious chorus from all around that leave you spinning; coming across elk or moose grazing in the fragrant, treacherous muskeg bogs, spread antlers looking like brackets to hold up a small planet; spotting a porcupine and riding around the beaver dam, with the moon melted onto the water and a beaver tail slapping through its motion-rippled ladder. We live in the saddle. We have proper showers perhaps once a fortnight. The thighs of our jeans take on an enviable sheen of waterproofing dirt and grease that all self-respecting cowboys aim for. We are fit, we are tough, we are gloriously filthy. We work hard and we scrub up well for those occasional eye-blinking trips to the stampede and rodeo-themed bars under the lights and warm Chinook winds of Calgary 'Cowtown'. The föhn clouds of the strange and beautiful Chinook weather system that holds sway in this mountain-prairieland form stunning, up-lit arches of cloud, sunrises and sunsets that blush the mountains, our cheeks and hair golden.

For the trips into the mountains proper, we trailer the horses in a short distance to corrals at the trailhead, sleeping the first night top-to-toe under sleeping bags in the back of the pick-up under the most stars I have ever seen. Mike, whose business this is, is a mountain guide, specialising in tracking big-horn sheep. The rams of these incredibly agile, impressive animals grow great, weighty horns that curl like loosened ammonites. Hunters come with licences to shoot them, while others increasingly come with cameras. Hunting is a big, historic and cultural part of Canadian life – and this is big game country. But from subsistence to trade, to tourism, respect and rights, hunting has been complicated and usurped by colonialism; even used as weapon and control against Indigenous Peoples, denying them their own culture and existence. I am barely aware of this but learn, as this new-seeming old, old country seems to be too. And, even in the 1980s and 90s, conservation is presented as key to hunting culture, the restrictions placed on it and, sometimes, the reasons for it. From what I see, respect is paramount and the numbers of licences given each year fluctuate according to species' populations, through draws. The mountain trips are sometimes hunting ones, with guests hoping to bring home a 'trophy' big-horn ram, whitetail or mule deer, moose, elk or even bear. 'Trophy' is the word that rankles most. While the animal is eaten, the hide tanned, the heads of the largest are mounted on walls everywhere. I am deeply uneasy and conflicted about this, but can mostly avoid it, quietly, as I do at home. The season is generally later in the year when I will have to go back to renew my visa, and Michelle volunteers as camp cook for the hunting trips. I help taking supplies in and out of camp instead, aware my dissent would be quite literally a lone voice in the wilderness, with a funny accent to boot, from a country that caused so much harm.

But the rides – oh the rides into the mountains! Usually we go in overnight, taking a whole day to ride to a camp to set up, with a string of pack horses. These are steady and reliable riding horses carrying instead a wooden 'sawbuck' pack saddle. Michelle and I learn the skill of saddling up over thick blankets and saddle pads, buckling up and fitting all the wide string cinches, cruppers, breast and hindquarter straps, evenly weighing and loading the wooden pannier boxes, hefting them up and tying them on. Tom balances on each horse's rump in turn on his knees, lashing a long rope to make a complicated diamond hitch to secure everything on: tents, a hay bale, stove and the boxes of food, with six points of anchorage. The safety of this business and the comfort of the horses is paramount and linked. Any number of cautionary tales of horses bolting with still-attached boxes or gas canisters bouncing behind them are told, and Michelle and I largely remain apprentices of the six-point, double-diamond-hitch in the face of years of experience.

Our roll mat, sleeping bag and personal kit are carried behind our saddles and in saddlebags. The lead pack horse is led from the saddle, with a soft rope wrapped once around the pommel in front of us, and the others follow on loose behind or are tied to a few tail hairs of the horse in front.

We learn to trust the older horses to pick their way along narrow mountain tracks, cross fast and deep, boulder-strewn rivers, or negotiate a muskeg swamp without getting sucked into the molasses-thick, deep-thawed peat. Once or twice, we ride past the skeletons of cattle that have succumbed, perhaps chased in by a predator. We are alert to our horses' body language and reactions and know to stay with (on) them if they sense a bear or mountain lion around. The smell of the sagebrush intensifies then. Tom or Mike ride with a rifle tucked into a scabbard under their stirrup leather.

The landscape is utterly breathtaking and constantly changes under the light, weather, season. There are screes, colourful alpine meadows, sparkling lakes and vistas of lodgepole pine and quivering aspen trees between the snowline of mountain peaks, all the way down to the wide clear rivers. I am constantly astonished and drift between being completely present and feeling awake in the lucidity of a dream of a western paradise. The wildlife, too, is thrilling, from those big grazing animals to bears and wolves, to little pikas and marmots, snowshoe hares and pine martens. There are whiskey jacks and blue jays, great-horned owls, hummingbirds, red-tailed hawks, golden and bald eagles, ospreys and migratory monarch butterflies. It is panoramic, cinematic; at once hard to take in and hard not to constantly gawp at.

Back at the ranch, as a skilled cowboy, Tom is in demand and helps out with his brothers at neighbouring ranches. Michelle and I work at round-ups and brandings, where cattle are brought in from huge open ranges, separated into corrals, checked, wormed and then marked with the ranch's brand on a hot iron. We take the best, most responsive horses. Michelle rides her Appaloosa, Lady, and Tom has his Quarter Horse stallions, Doc and Bow, that I also get to ride.

Bow is a neat, fast little black stallion named after the Bow River at Bragg Creek, but Doc is something else. A striking 'paint' stallion, he is patched brown and white (what we call skewbald in the UK) but has a patch of brown in a cap over his ears and two brown patches around pale blue eyes – in Indigenous lore, this makes him a very special 'Medicine Hat' horse; one that bestows luck, protects his rider from harm, has the potential for supernatural powers. His breed-registered name is Big Medicine Man and I love him with all my heart – I think it is mutual. He is big, sharp of movement and so gentle I can ride him in a 'bosel' – a loop of soft, plaited rawhide on his nose. I am half-convinced he is a childhood library-book favourite come to life, from Marguerite Henry's book, *San Domingo: The Medicine Hat Stallion*. San Domingo becomes my whispered, private name for him.

He comes with us around the fire, before being penned for the night away from the mares. One night, instead of nuzzling my neck or someone's pockets, he steps his front feet up onto one of the big wooden cable reels we use as seats and stands there, before lowering his head in a deep bow. We fall silent; beer bottles to our lips, watching the warmth from the fire ripple his mane, deepen the colour of his chestnut red 'hat' and eye patches, so that the rest of him seems to disappear, his head floating, the flames flickering in his eyes. Something pops on the fire and we snap back, all a little awed by whatever just happened. Doc is spiritual and he is also a party horse. Another night we three all get on his back, Tom, Michelle and I, and ride him through the cabin, in one door out the other, across the verandah. He humours us. Is in on the joke. We ride him bridleless and saddleless down the steep slope to prime the well pump. I slide off once, down his bottom. He stops, swishes his tail, I grab hold and he pulls me up.

There are visits to stampedes, including the big one in Calgary, where a procession of First Nations people ride their horses through the streets ahead of cowboys doing the same. Loose horses come with them, right up through the main city streets. Mares with foals at foot, horses sometimes ridden bareback and without a bridle, some painted with symbols, their riders in full, ancestral headdresses and regalia. At the front is a Medicine Hat horse. We attend rodeos, community cookouts and other round-ups. We ride into the hamlet for pancake breakfasts or to the bar, where there are swinging saloon doors and fights on the pool table. I have long stopped wearing my riding hat, my jodhpurs that seem so silly here, even though they were the new, stretch-denim kind, but I still wear my brown lace-up boots. I don't wear a cowboy hat and get sunstroke. Mike's daughter Carol buys me a pair of lovely leather-tooled cowboy boots and I wear those with bootcut jeans.

I think of Grandad, and write often. I tell him about the cowboys, the horses, the farms; the reservation nearby and some of the Tsuut'ina Nation people I've met, who think I am curious and funny with my English accent, but tell me wonderful things about the wildflowers that grow here and what you can use them for.* I am shy talking to Grandad later about them. There is something I can't quite get a handle on and perhaps it is imagined. But there is a hesitancy. A rueful kinship. I don't make the link between the shared histories of marginalised peoples then. The effects of colonialism. Not, in fact, until after Grandad has died, so I will never know if it was something he acknowledged, knew or felt: those forced reservations for Indigenous Canadians and inclosures for Romany Gypsies in the New Forest; the denial and taking away of traditional ways of life; the persecution, the fear. The ghosts of what might've been his life. As elsewhere, Indigenous or nomadic peoples, living on the land lightly and as part of its rhythms and seasons, obstructed settler access to land ownership and the earth's resources. Reservations and compulsory, Western and often residential schools, where they were frequently abhorrently treated, became a solution of assimilation and cultural eradication. Subjugated, disenfranchised, cut off from resources

---

* A closest-sounding pronunciation of Tsuut'ina in English might be 'tswdina'.

and the agency of their own lives, unemployment, poverty and addictions inevitably follow, seeming to justify the settler policies that caused them in the first place. As Keith Thor Carlson writes in the Canadian independent journal *The Tyee*, 'The circle of colonialism [is] complete.'

When we farm, we push people off the land, as well as wildlife.

Grandad came of his own volition, grasping a last-minute opportunity for a better life. He was lucky. Born to an unmarried Gypsy mother into the poverty of a workhouse, if it were not for his mother's tenacity, he could have been one of the ten thousand Romany children, among more than one hundred thousand other poor or disadvantaged children sent to work in Canada, Australia, New Zealand and South Africa. The British Home Children scheme operated mainly between 1869 and the 1940s, though it continued until the 1970s. Under-resourced, and poorly regulated and understood, the child migration scheme lifted thousands of young children from their families, and trained and placed them as unpaid domestic and farm servants overseas. The intention was to give them the skills to work their way to a better life. Many receiving these children saw them as inherently 'bad' and as cheap labour, and they were treated terribly. Many died. Most never returned home. In fact, 10 per cent of Canada's population, around 4 million people, are estimated to be their descendants.

I stayed in Alberta through the astonishing fall – blue skies and lakes, maple-butter-yellow trees – until the first snows began to fall and my visa had long since run out. Back in England, my friends all scattered to universities, I temp a lonely six months in offices and work my way back to a plane ticket and Canada. By now, the snows have receded to the mountains and the ranch has relocated ten miles south-east from Bragg Creek, sliding like a glacier into the smaller hamlet of Priddis, population just fifty. Tom is here part-time, cowboying for other ranches, and Michelle has returned after a winter back home and we share a small ranch house. There are no near neighbours, and when Michelle and I are alone in the week, our only transport is to pick a horse to ride to Priddis Stores, along the wide verge of the highway. I do it on Bandit one day, ten minutes before closing time, when a craving for chocolate gets the better of me.

We set up a campfire circle of planks on cable reels in a little copse of aspens and pines and often sleep there. Fireflies mingle with campfire sparks, seemingly infinite starlight and shooting stars, across the gaps between the trees. We keep a couple of horses in a makeshift overnight pen, for company, reassurance and a route to safety or help, should we need it. We are all flight animals here.

The rest of the herd roam sections of the ranch freely, accessed by difficult-to-manage barbed wire gates, that I know as 'Hampshire gates'. The name, spoken in exaggeration of my accent, 'ampsheer', is adopted with fond humour. Tom teaches Michelle and me the trick of opening these many, dreaded high-tensile barriers that consist of strands of barbed wire attached to two or three shorter, free-floating posts. The opening end post butts up against the fence through an ankle loop of plain wire, and the top is pulled tight and secured by another wire loop or chain hooked over a nail. The trick, when you don't have the physical strength or height ratio, is leverage. I've not been defeated by such a gate since.

The ranch goes all the way back to the fence of what is then known as the Sarcee Indian Reserve, recognised now as the Indigenously accurate Tsuut'ina Nation reserve – and a country's problematic colonial history is laid out right there: between the reserve and the ranch house is another small, age-silvered cabin on runners; a white European settlers' farmstead on Indigenous land. I try to find the old place online and fail, but the stores, the pretty little wooden church and the Farmers and Ranchers Community Hall built in 1900 by Charles Priddis, gold rush fortune seeker, surveyor and ranchman, is still there. Much I remember seems to have evolved, too. The warmth and wilderness experience, the artistic and rural community surrounding Bragg Creek, glows from my laptop screen. The Visit Bragg Creek website also states:

In the spirit of truth and reconciliation, Bragg Creek and the Bragg Creek Chamber acknowledge that the hamlet and surrounding areas are located on Treaty 7 Territory, sacred ancestral lands of the Blackfoot Nations of Siksika, Kainai, Piikani, Wesley, Stoney-Nakoda & Tsuut'ina Nations & Region 3 of the Métis Nations of Alberta. As current residents and land stewards, we are grateful for the keepers of the land that came before us.

Nearby, Redwood Meadows has developed into a vibrant 'townsite': unique in being a largely independent municipality, it is administered by an elected council within Tsuut'ina stewardship, on Tsuut'ina land. One day, three men come into the ranch in a Chevy truck with a trailer. Michelle has gone to visit family. They say they have come to take one of the horses for training, can name the little black mare and her owner, Crista. They tell me they are Sarcee Nation and live on the neighbouring reserve. They are polite and friendly and not in any way threatening, but they are three men and I am alone and had no idea they were coming. The phone line is down, so I cannot call Crista, but I have no reason not to trust them. I can see the herd, and whistle for them. Their heads spring up and, like a dream, the whole herd comes cantering to my call. I let them into the big corral and tip out some alfalfa cubes for them in a long line, the dust whirling as they settle. I can see I've surprised these men in some way, the youngest of whom perhaps in his late twenties, the older man chewing tobacco, as Tom does. Crista's mare is soon caught and, as we walk her to the trailer, the two younger men quiz me on my 'olde England' accent. They tell me of their family history, of the Crowchilds and Manyhorses, and I tell them about my grandad meeting the Chief of the Mi'kmaq in 1929, '30 or '31 and they seem genuinely interested. I tell them he is a Romany Gypsy. As they load up and say goodbye, the older man smiles for the first time and says, 'Thank you, Miss Calls Horses and They Come.' As the trailer rattles away down the long, rough track, I feel giddy with blessing, relieved three men turning up unexpectedly meant only a pleasant encounter. Crista calls when the phone comes back on to assure me of the arrangement.

There are other actual near misses and scrapes. One evening, a black bear unexpectedly appears at the flimsy screen door. A brief, gauzy impression of immense and languorous strength, luxuriant fur smoothed along the mesh, a paw, revealed by a corner tear in the door, padded down with great long white claws that rattle like sabres. She chooses not to come in. There are sobering thrills riding home in intense lightning storms that echo around the mountains, strikes that roll like a bowling ball along the top of a barbed wire fence and uncountable spills with horses. I am lifted off my feet and almost crushed between two loose horses, galloping down an alley chute at a Black Diamond rodeo, and we have bareback races that get out of control. Once, racing towards the boundary's barbed wire fence, my hands become entangled in Cody's long mane and I can't free them to pull up, so we jump it at breakneck speed, endangering us both. Another time, galloping alongside Highway 22, Cody puts his foot down a gopher hole and turns a complete somersault, miraculously throwing me clear, both of us uninjured and avoiding a truck.

We work hard and play hard, taking on other people's horses to train and break in. I am weathered. I am familiar with the grasses, the trees, the wild 'critters' we live alongside. I get used to reading the Chinook fronts that power the rapid changes in the weather out here, and the legendary winds that blow through Crowsnest Pass.

And then it all comes to an unexpected end somehow, indeterminably, hazily. Promised wages don't materialise, though we're brought groceries in brown paper bags from the city, and we're sent away to help at another horse ranch for the weekend. We return to find many of the horses, tack and camping gear up for sale. The ranch community begins to break up. We grieve the horses that are sold. I am heartbroken over Cody. I don't want this life to end. But I realise how cocooned I've been within it. A job that feels like a wild kind of freedom; providing a rough home, a community, adventure and people that look out for me – and me for them.

Michelle gets work as a rider at the Calgary racetrack. Before we leave and the horses are sold, I ride Cody up the verandah and through the house one last time and Michelle takes pictures. We leave hoofprints in the linoleum, a Polaroid tucked into a mirror frame.

CHAPTER SEVEN

The Possibility of Levers

March–September 1941

Miss White looks forward, as they all do, to a day of rest on Sundays. Milking and feeding are on a rota and the mucking out kept to a minimum; all other jobs suspended. She enjoys being 'idle' and wearing clean clothes, but is often at church for 9am, with the rest of the village. She then takes Jo and Dina for a walk, through gates, rather than hoiking over barbed wire fences in her Sunday skirt. I haven't imagined her in a skirt before. Mid-length, tweed and with kick pleats, apart from the barbed wire, it doesn't restrict her from striding out. She strolls with the dogs along The Lynch, through the fields and back along Cox's Lane, or along the medieval Wansdyke and up to the top of Rivar's Down. Here in fine weather, she sits on a gate by a big oak tree while Jo and Dina explore rabbit holes. They are tremendous sportsmen of the digging variety, but never catch anything. Having been mostly cooped up in the caravan, she guiltily indulges them, smiling at their happy, hairy, mud-plastered eyebrows and moustaches.

From the gate, Miss White enjoys the view, swinging a leg like a girl, as the landscape rolls away beneath her, gloriously; the neatly ploughed fields and plashed hedges and woods greening up, barns and animals arrayed unmoving like a toy farm. The sky is a pale blue with wispy, high clouds from which the songs of skylarks rain down. A wide plume of smoke troubles her periphery towards Reading and, squinting, she can see more beyond that, which is

London, seventy-five miles away. The night, she thinks, had been quiet in her caravan. Certainly, no planes woke her or the dogs. Her sensible brown shoes are rimed with the white chalk paste that passes for soil up here. She slipped a few times coming up, laughing with the dogs at herself, and knows the trip back down might be taken in part on her bottom. She didn't mean to come this far in these shoes. Would have been better off in her hobnails, but knows they'd draw ridicule with her skirt and she wasn't going to wear her comfortable, practical corduroys on a Sunday, so up in her shoes, she came. Hawthorn blossom is beginning to succeed blackthorn, dotting the down with white veils among the yellow cowslips where there are fewer rabbits. It is positively bridal. She feels fit and strong, comfortably tired after the week's work, but not too much.

Corn buntings rattle out their songs, among whitethroats, blackcaps, willow warblers, and the repeated 'little-bit-of-bread and no ch*eese*' refrain sung by yellowhammers every few yards. In the longer grass she can hear corncrake and grey partridge – the children were mimicking their calls yesterday in the meadow, with wax paper played over a comb – and she listens to the bubbling crescendo of several curlew at her back: like the winding up of an air-raid siren, only much, much sweeter, she thinks! Below her, a flock of green plover is agitating. For a moment, from this angle, a whole field is obscured by the tumbling of their black-and-white wings, like a chessboard flipped up in a tantrum. Their looping, warbling song a stomach-flip of a jazzy spring opera drifting up, as if one of the children were messing about with the dial on the library wireless. She wants to conduct it all – applaud! Spring doing its thing, despite what man is doing to man, she rues; though she knows full well nature is as cruel. Cruel, yet indiscriminate perhaps? Well, no, she thinks of the weakest. She is surprised to see two figures walking, when the plover flock clears, a third, a child, zigzagging between them. Ah. It is Frances and Ralph Partridge and their boy, plover egging in the fields behind Ham Spray. She imagines them proffering *oeufs de pluvier* in a spring basket lined with moss to their houseguests, in the garden. She has eaten them like that herself, before this war, after the last. They are a little late, she thinks.

Doris had taken John and the other older evacuee children out plover egging weeks ago, showing them how to tread carefully, watch the birds and find the flint-and-chalk-spotted eggs on the bare scrapes of same-coloured earth. She drummed into them the importance of taking just one from a clutch, doing it quickly – and not to take *any* if the hen bird was sitting, when the eggs were all rolled together, points in, and no good anyway as the embryo would now be growing. They'd had the treat of boiled plover eggs mashed on toast for supper, 'Like they have in Fortnum and Mason or The Ritz!' said John. 'What's good enough for them is good enough for us!' Seeing them out egging, Charlie Tucker had bemoaned the loss of extra income earnt when he was a boy, before the Lapwing Act in 1926, collecting eggs to send up to London where they were a delicacy. 'Folks too greedy,' he said, 'taking too many and spoiling it for everyone.'

'Not least the peewits, eh, Charlie?' says Doris wryly. Charlie chooses to ignore her.

As Julia watches, she thinks about the household down there at Ham Spray. Taps her toe on the chimney pots. A house of pacifists and artists, secluded away, as much as it is possible to be in the country, and in wartime. They are misunderstood, perhaps. Bold, playful, haughty. Fragile, maybe. Stronger as part of their elite company. She'd read about the death by drowning of their friend Virginia Woolf in *The Times* earlier this month and wonders at it; pictures a modern, angular, stylish Ophelia in a river and is sad for her. She has read some of her books, has discussed them enthusiastically with Marguerite and Doris.

Julia looks forward to Sunday afternoons – a traditional 'country nap', then tea and a sociable evening in the library at Shalbourne Manor. Sometimes, to ring the changes, Julia invites Marguerite and Doris over to her caravan, where they get slightly blotto over wine, a game of cards, the sleepy heat of the Valor Perfection heater and a lack of oxygen.

Between them, Doris and Marguerite are demonstrably leaders in their community. Taking initiative and stepping up to any manner of responsibilities that Julia likens to a modern, willing and mutual take on feudalism between the women and their community. The neighbourhood accepts and expects it of them; and they do it so well, so naturally and with a large measure of deference, awareness and respect. She admires their energy and the way that, though the war may have curtailed some activities, it brings scope for others. They are equally determined women. Doris is chief air raid warden and billeting officer for the district, an executive of the National Farmers' Union, Scout commissioner, churchwarden, president of the area's Women's Institute and serves on the Parish and District Council; she also sings in the Bach Choir. Marguerite runs the area's first aid post and is a Girl Guide commissioner, Scout and Cub leader, author and poet. Having some experience leading Girl Guides, Julia is thrilled to become Doris's assistant Cubmaster, complete with warrant and a uniform. Between the three of them, practised as they are from childhood in camping and cooking outdoors, signalling and tracking, navigating and knots, they run Cub meetings, the Shalbourne Scout Troop and a Girl Guides Company in the loft above the garage at the Manor. They even manage a few exuberant wartime camps when farming and foaling allow, roping in Miss de Beaumont's brother and nephew. Around half the children are evacuees and all are quite wild and undisciplined, galloping around like colts, but they and their leaders enjoy it all very much. In the village, the Kingston Room, built in 1843 by a former incumbent of Shalbourne Manor to provide 'a Bible education to the poor', is used as a village hall, and hosts whist drives, dances, plays put on by The Barnstormers drama group and a travelling cine projector for films; an extended, welcoming rural community defiantly socialising and keeping up their spirits behind the blackouts.

I take down my foxed and dog-eared copy of Miss de Beaumont's *The Way of a Horse*, published in 1953 and reprinted in 1972 and bought from a childhood village fete for the '10p' still pencilled inside the cover in a looped hand. Posters of horses she bred, descendants of those pictured inside, adorned my bedroom walls. She wrote several books, including a biography of Baden-Powell and a guide to tracking adventures for the Girl Guides, as well as poetry.

In her introduction to *The Way of a Horse*, Marguerite de Beaumont says:

> *I have had much to do with young people and young horses, both are very similar in many ways ... Anyone who has no love for his fellow men, no understanding of their problems and difficulties, will find it hard to follow the way of a horse, and to give him the understanding and care, which can be the outcome only of a kind heart and an intelligent brain.*

Far from being the headscarved and terrifyingly fierce horsey woman I imagine, it seems she was a great observer and listener. Patrick Crean, an evacuee and Shalbourne Scout who remained a lifelong friend, remembers 'her patience and affection elicited a trust and response from the horses that was remarkable to watch ... but she also had an extraordinary insight into human nature.' In working with her animals, Marguerite is humble and willing to learn from others; older horsemen, small girls, Romany Gypsies. She knows three Romani words that, whispered into a horse's ear, inexplicably calm it, and recalls a childhood incident in a New Forest village shop when a Gypsy woman who had been watching her suddenly clutched and kissed her hand, telling her she would 'have many, many and *fine* horses' before holding open the door for her and bowing.

And she did, this 'far-famed owner of the Shalbourne Stud', according to a Reading newspaper in 1953: among many were prize-winning Honeysuckle and June, Ladybird and Sweetbriar, Zephyr, Ebonita and Raqi Al Hussum, the great, grey Arab stallion. Bred in Baghdad and raced to great acclaim in India, Raqi was brought to England by the Chipperfield's Circus brothers, who had gone to Sri Lanka to purchase elephants. Much beloved,

Raqi retired to stud at Shalbourne, where he never did learn to graze grass, but would nod and prance along to music, and had an inordinate fondness for dates, which were purchased especially for him.

But meanwhile, the farming year rolls slowly on, falling back in its sticky wheel ruts at times, then surging forwards. With her boots and gaitered legs half-submerged in the freezing water of the ditch they had worked on earlier, Miss White is learning hedging. Slashing initially at the excess growth with a long-handled billhook, before Charlie, Joe or Jack follow behind with an axe, or short billhook, they teach her how to cut through most of the growth, to bend, lay the pleached branch down and weave it through to make a secure, thick and living hedge. In the bitter cold of a late spring that seesaws back and forth, they often sing or whistle, sometimes mimicking the early birdsong; the blackbird or song thrush particularly, with his repetitive notes. Miss White joins in, her extremities numbed, her core too warm, her hessian sack apron smeared by mud. '*Sisyphus, Sisyphus*,' she repeats, in time with the song thrush, quietly, then louder, tipping her head side-to-side like a metronome. 'Listen to him sing that! Trying to push spring on, up the bally hill, only for winter to roll all the way back! *Sisyphus, Sisyphus!*' Joe laughs, catches the joke, explains the Greek tyrant King Sisyphus's punishment, of having to roll a boulder uphill for eternity, to a bemused Charlie. 'Ha!' Charlie says. 'Ha! That'll be about roight. I only know it as *Cherry dew, cherry dew* [he adds a falsetto] and we are about as far off from that as we are *straw*berries!' They laugh heartily at that, snort and titter for a while after; replace 'strawberries' with other fruit, all in such short supply now. '*Orr*anges!' says Charlie with feeling, setting them off again.

I wonder how the men feel towards this forty-one-year-old single woman apprenticing herself in their world – and for what aim? Are they suspicious of that? Why has she not just become a Land Girl? I am aware of my time-distanced perception, the assumptions of my time, taught or presented too often through a male agenda-led retrospect, from men who returned from the war, perhaps damaged or disenfranchised themselves, or were the sons of those men. It is not necessarily a feminist lens. I want to lean over a gate and ask them. *Interview* them in my best, smiley, in-confidence, BBC magazine voice, my bicycle leaning against the bosom of a thick and fulsome hedge, vibrating with chirping sparrows: 'So chaps, what do you *rilly* think of these women, these *spinsters*, learning on the job, running the show? Isn't farming a realm of men?' I want to provoke them. But I don't believe they were offended. Irritated, or threatened sometimes, when they got together and spoke about it; imagining a future beyond the war. I imagine them derogatory at times, accusatory. Did they comment, guess and jibe about the women's sexuality and their relationships? I imagine so. Did they know? And do I? I can be certain about Marguerite and Doris's romantic relationship, though I don't know if they were public about it – but not so much about Julia's sexuality. It both doesn't matter and it does. But the war and necessity cracked so much open. Broke further the leather harness and traces of those social restraints already broken, kicked over or weakened by the First World War, a still-fresh and reignited memory; the fields and farms and relationships depleted of men. I imagine some of the community gossiped; perhaps saw these three women, and others like them, as both a breed and class apart, while others speculated privately, or accepted it was possible and necessary to all rub along together. Like the shifting baseline syndrome of what we accept as abundance in nature (from a baseline of what we experienced when we were young, compared to what abundance meant to the baseline our parents or grandparents would recognise), we can be blind to what kind of acceptance or awareness of sexuality and gender relationships existed then on a day-to-day, getting-on-with-it attitude in a rural community. Often, because of the human desire and need to get along together and support one another, in more sparsely populated and remote rural communities, difference is more readily accepted and absorbed. I think those men might regard my proffered confidence and enquiry as rather tabloid, as we might call it today.

As for farming, there have always been women. Milkmaids, work gangs in the fields, women driving carts or animals to market, gleaning and harvesting, growing and cooking, looking after the farmyard animals, menfolk, the elderly, poor or sick in their community, and children. It is interesting to note that in the censuses we set so much store by, of a hundred years earlier in 1841 and 1850, we forget we are looking through a male administrative lens. We assume the women and girls registered as 'maids' or 'domestic servants' were working *indoors*, when many were agricultural workers. In addition, wives and family members not receiving a wage aren't recorded as employed, and women appearing in farm wage books are not allocated an occupation in the census. Reading the rural novels of Thomas Hardy and Mary Webb, or Flora Thompson's *Lark Rise to Candleford* trilogy, there's a different story, though this would have varied from place to place, season and need. Certainly, neither the menfolk nor anyone else in Shalbourne village appear to have any trouble with this farm, run so very well, efficiently and involvedly, by two women. That they are ensconced in a manor at the centre of the village helps, as well as them both clearly being gentry, though, crucially, not men that sent anyone 'over the top' while they sat back at a distance. A class-based feudal acceptance would have still held some sway, but only because (for so much had changed and continued to) they are also active, reliable and respected in their community. They help. They organise things, they lend out employees and farm equipment; they are visible, approachable, know people, take an interest; are positive, kind – and *fun*. They try to live the examples and morals of the yarns they tell to their Cubs and Scouts and Guides in the loft above the garage. All in a way that the neighbouring, more insular, remnant household of Bloomsberries at Ham Spray appeared not to be, so much; for all that they did and are celebrated for.

Miss White's friendship with the affable and generous Jack Palmer grows. They talk of crops and cultivations, hedge and ditches, cattle and pigs, and the hundred and one things that go to make up farming in England as well as Canada. Their enthusiasm, as scholar and teacher, knows no bounds. But Jack also gives Miss White valuable lessons around resourcefulness, working alone and particularly the possibilities of levers. How to handle, wangle and move heavy loads and implements in and out of awkward places when you are not physically strong enough to do it. In time, it proves revolutionary information.

Jack excels at both the knowledge and the passing on of it. In the backwoods of Canada in the 1920s and '30s, self-reliance and safety were paramount. Collecting firewood alone with horses and a wagon in deep and lasting snow often meant an overnight camp. Jack also spent weeks ploughing long prairie miles far from anywhere or anyone, that made the big Wiltshire fields seem like postage stamps. But it is the ingenuity of levers and angles that really sticks with Miss White – how to drag heavy things about with chains, a horse or tractor, how to roll and slide weighty objects up and down planks when it is impossible to lift them. He shows her dodges for unsticking trailers and large implements from mud or snow; how to get things through awkward gateways or around difficult turns, and how to 'tack' up or down steep and slippery hills safely. She learns much she can draw on later. Something Jack has a presentiment of. 'Ingenuity and leverage gal; that and a dose of perseverance. Always have a try, you can probably do it.'

As the spring soil warms by increments, Jack helps Miss White complete her ploughing apprenticeship, just as he is offered a job as bailiff, with his own cottage, in charge of a large farm in Devon. Though they are all as deeply sorry to see him go, as he is to leave, Doris insists she will not stand in anyone's way, even midway through the agricultural year. Julia feels lucky to have known the man and learnt so much from him. She tells him this. They all do.

Their sleep and fears and waking hours are still rattled and disturbed by the sound of aircraft, guns, the news on the wireless and in the papers as well as plumes of smoke off in the relative distance. The Blitz continues horrifically on the cities and towns around them, preparations and alertness for an invasion remain high. Bombs are dropped on nearby Newbury and German bombers fly along the streets, machine-gunning at houses. People are injured, but not killed. In the local park, children put out an incendiary bomb, covering it with earth from the flower beds.

Spring jobs turn to summer jobs and harvest. It is, of course, all hands on deck, with others drafted in from the surrounding area, coming in on foot, on the footplate of Racing Lizzie, and by horse or bicycle, including various members of the Scouts and Guides. Charlie and Joe have gone ahead to 'open the ways' for the machinery to come in. They take the edge of the fields of wheat down with the whetted scythe and bundle and tie the first sheaves. Doris drives the tractor with the newer, wider Massey Harris reaper binder and Charlie drives Doris's pair of dapple-grey Percherons with the older Albion model. Each machine mows, collects and binds the wheat into sheaves, which are collected by the followers, who shock them into stooks like golden tipis to dry. The rhythmic vanes of the big reels of the reaper go round like windmill sails, gathering the corn to the cutting bar. Each bundle is picked up, tamped on the ground to line the stalks up, at an angle. The heads or ears of two sheaves are waggled together to hold them, and they are pitched, three on each side, into a tent shape, allowing the air to flow around and through and fully dry them. There is some friendly competition between tractor and horse team, and the horses finish their day's acre not long after the tractor, whose binder keeps breaking the twine at the knotting.

Old Harry Tucker, helping shock and stook, holds loud and laughing counsel over the tractor–horse rivalry. It is good to see him back on form, after being so incapacitated by foot-and-mouth on his farm. He jeers and waves his pipe, encourages the children to join in, and moves his feet in a hobnailed dance on the stubble, kicking up dust, each time the new, tractor-drawn binder stops. Tea is at five in the field, under the shade of the hedgerow with food, beer and cold tea brought out in leather panniers laid across the broad back of one of Marguerite's prize Highland mares. Her long, silky mane is plaited up with yellow and blue ribbons and eared straw. She is such a picture, the children are awed.

In the evening as the moon comes up from the hedgerow, as if winched there as a theatre backdrop, breathtakingly close and luminous, the children still up are found 'camping' in the tents of the stooks and rounded up. Small animals rustle and make surreptitious, urgent adjustments to their new living arrangements among the stubble and sheaves. A barn owl appears in silent grace; a benediction, rowing through the low rising of harvest dust as it settles and rises again as summer mist; a haze of gold that turns to silver in symbolic alchemy. The moon elongates the shadows of the stooks that seem to import a monumental seriousness on the scene. A job with great meaning and higher purpose well done. 'It looks like a scout camp, a jamboree of tents!' says Miss White, but knows it is something both much greater than that and, also, no less great than that noble intention. A human, human thing. A great pact with nature.

She has been invited, at the expressed wish and clamour of the Shalbourne Scout troop, to become a Scout member herself. Having worked alongside several of them on the farm, she has been declared 'a jolly good Scout'. She accepts with humour, and the inner warmth of the biggest compliment she has ever received.

CHAPTER EIGHT

Not My First Rodeo: A Branding

1989

Determined to bring Grandad new stories back, I manage to stay and work on a farm and a cattle ranch as a cowgirl myself, with a break to travel along the Trans-Canada Highway, through Banff, Golden and Kicking Horse Canyon, past teal and ice-blue lakes and glaciers across the Great Divide of the Rockies, to Vancouver. I have a spell of time on a farm in Hanna, Alberta, on the Great Plains. The farm is out on the prairies that roll on for gold-lit grassy miles and, I am told by almost everyone I meet, 'Out here, you can watch your dog run away for a week.' There are horses and some cattle, but, mostly, the farm is arable. Only barns, houses and grain elevators break the horizontal expanse and the water from the taps is sweet and earthy, and the colour of strong tea. At harvest, one of my jobs is to sit on top of the combine harvester, behind the cab, and collect grain for moisture testing in a paper cup. I sit cross-legged on the roof of the old red Massey, riding into the sunset above the churning header chewing all the pale wheat up, and spewing thick gold braids of straw out behind. After the grain auger has emptied the shush of roaring grain into the tractored trailer, I am allowed to stay up there, sailing through the prairie sea of wheat on my red ship, in a golden cloud of glittering, sunlit chaff.

I visit Tom's homeplace outside the small prairie village of Stettler, with its tall, wooden, burgundy-red Parrish & Heimbecker grain elevator beside the railroad. It's now a museum, I discover, one lost afternoon online. Tom has two older brothers, Davey and Henry, all in their twenties, unmarried and orphans with no other family here. Like Tom, they are kind and funny and look out for me. Their grandparents emigrated from Ireland in the late 1920s, when Grandad was here. For a $10 fee, they'd taken a settler's grant for 160 acres of prairie, in an arrangement that was not available to single women, First Nations or Métis people. To retain and own it, they had to clear and farm at least 40 acres and build a house within the first three years. They hauled two old railroad cabooses in place to live in initially, and began, achieving their dream. But whatever happened after that, the boys had lost both their grandparents and parents by the time they were in their late teens and twenties. They are close, the three of them, and there is a grief they don't speak of, visible in the care they take of each other. The house and land are now Henry's. A large, lonely blue-and-white clapboard prairie house, roofed in green cedar shingles. It has a wide, railed, all-round porch, and no creature comforts inside. No softness. The cupboard doors hang open and opposite the kitchen windows, the railroad carriages are still there. A white lace curtain flows out of a broken window, like someone, a woman, a mother, a wife, shaking out a tablecloth. The ancient windmill pump whirs, turns and creaks in the wind that scours the place.

The house was bought, as most were, from an Eaton catalogue. 'The Other Canadian Bible', the Amazon of its time and something that would have been well-thumbed in every Canadian household for a hundred years. Its pioneering ordering and distribution service meant isolated, rural places could have any mod cons they could afford, from fashionable or practical clothes to pharmaceuticals, curtains, farm machinery, books, toys and flatpack houses. I still have Grandad's much-loved copy. Better than a silver dollar.

I spend my last few precious months at Hays Cattle Ranch, in High River, Alberta, where Tom works. He and his fellow cowboys and farmworkers live in little cabins purpose-built beside the feed lot, with all their meals provided in a cookhouse attached to the family home. Al and Hazel McKinnon run the ranch and have two daughters my age who invite me to stay with them. I am embraced generously, as family. The house is also a large, comfortable ranch house straight from an Eaton catalogue of another time. Though there is no pressure to do so, I have a natural guilt that I should be helping Hazel in the cookhouse, but I am out on the range with Tom. We ride every day, herding cattle, mending or building new snow-proof fences, and Tom teaches me to drive the tractor. I love the cows and the way the horses work with them; there are community round-ups that last whole days and everyone helps out at each neighbour's chapters. Cattle are rounded up into corrals and pens, and calves roped and held with great skill from the backs of responsive horses while they are immunised, branded swiftly with a hot iron, tagged, checked and, if they are steers, have their testicles removed. It is calm, fast, clean and brutally efficient. My job is to dash in with tags and needles and immunise them – and to dodge the testicle 'sweetbreads' thrown at me to make me scream. I refuse to. We lend a hand at other brandings, including a Hutterite ranch; a warm and welcoming self-sufficient Anabaptist colony, who dress conservatively in clothes they make themselves.

One predawn morning before a camping trip into the mountains, I'm woken by a gravel skitter on the window. I open the sloping attic skylight to the most spectacular aurora, so close I could push my hands into it. I climb out of the window in my nightdress, wrapping a borrowed dressing gown around me, and sit on the green cedar shingle tiles of the clapboard house. Though I have seen the Northern Lights many times before by now, every encounter is different, each one awe inspiring. Tonight, they are spectacular. There are pale violet ribbons, green shards that scatter across the sky and plunge down again like organ pipes; there are white searchlights, red theatre-velvet pulsing glows, beams and rippling drapes of fluid, cellophane light in lime and purple. Kaleidoscopic, cinematic and rapidly changing so I can't look away for a second, they are immense and all around. I feel I could step off that roof and walk into them, or that it might sweep me off with the *swosh* of disembodied, deep magenta wing. I think I feel music and there is a high sweet-wrapper crackle that fills the vast sky above, a thrum; strange electrical static, whispers that descend into whooshes with raven-wing taffeta softness and a swooping whine. I try to grasp what it is like, even now. I've heard its echoes in the old, bouncing, dial-up internet tune, once at a rave, in the moments just before a faint, and frequently in starling song, those colours carried suggestively through the spots and glints on the bird's feathers.

I feel like it entered me through my open, amazed mouth and never left; there in the rustle and rub of stiff fabric, a high radio tuning inside my own head. A richly coloured, Quality Street tinnitus. The sound made by the aurora is accepted and known to the three cowboys watching it from below and to other rural Canadians I meet. But since? I have been doubted every time and it's hard even to find anything definitive online. The light show doesn't cease. It fills the sky, retreats, comes back with the flourish of a glass-green silk scarf, a hood, a cloak, a yellow-gold crown of pillars; operatic, purple beams where my mind assigns it a swelling orchestra, rising, wordless choral crescendos. I am overwhelmed and utterly awed.

Time is running out and my visa has expired again. An A-level quote from Thomas Hardy's *Tess of the D'Urbervilles* plays on repeat in my head, when I try to understand how deep this has all gone through me; permanent as a brand burnt into hide through hair and smoking, so that it hurts for a while: 'Experience is as to intensity, and not as to duration.'

Daily, the wild flock of Canada geese build on the lake outside readying themselves for migration with their haunting cries. Fall cedes to winter, and I know I cannot stay. Chinook winds push and pull the weather as if playing about with stage curtains. It snows heavily and I have to borrow snowboots and have a go at snowshoes. I go outside with wet hair one morning and my ringlets freeze to jingling icicles. I am reminded the temperature can drop to -30°C. But when a Chinook mountain wind comes in, the snow is gone in hours and it is fall-warm again. Rancher Al McKinnon tells me how, in Pincher Creek in 1962, a Chinook wind lifted the temperature a steep 41 degrees in an hour, from −19°C to 22°C, and sent everyone dizzy with migraines.

I try different ideas of staying. Work visas, Olds Agricultural University. Information is hard to come by, pre-internet, without an address of your own. I tell anyone I meet, 'I'd like to stay, work on a ranch, learn how to farm.' Most raise their eyebrows or laugh outright. 'It's sure tough out here in winter,' I'm told over and over. 'Not much for a young lady to do.' I hear the words echoed in the campfire favourite 'Four Strong Winds' by Ian Tyson, Alberta's melancholy anthem. Or I get, 'You'd make a grand country girl,' but they are not talking about me working outside, on a ranch, on a farm. They are talking about my marriageability. Tom produces a ring, but I have to tell him no. No, this is not what I want at all, I'm sorry. So sorry if you ever thought it might be. I shut my eyes and suddenly picture myself flapping a lace tablecloth out of a stationary caboose window, crumbs flipped to a prairie wind. I'm nineteen. And I think he knows really. I am too much of a flippertigibbet, I say, and he laughs, squeezes my hand and repeats the word, adopts it.

My plane ticket is bought. 'Four Strong Winds' plays on the radio of every truck I get into in those last weeks, ensuring I am haunted for a lifetime by the lyrics of yearning and the hard, romantic life of an Albertan itinerant cowboy. They all come to see me off at the airport. And I cry and cry and somehow know I'll not return.

Every autumn since, it is the sound of geese that triggers such strong feelings of yearning and wistfulness. Though the origins of the feelings might have faded and been overlaid, the feelings track a familiar path. An emotional muscle memory that floods and washes through me in that season of endings and beginnings. I love the season to come, with its North American echo-play of crisp autumn days, glittering frosts and deep, hushed, blue-shadowed snow. Drifts, almost beyond reach now, though the anticipation of it remains like grief. The seasons unravelling, buffering, blurring.

Autumn-fall change is its own rural *ingraination*: an agrarian calendar marker repeated as generational habit, folk memory, the ghost of recent past-pattern – the new agricultural year of Michaelmas.

It's a whole season that toys with endings and beginnings in the slow back-and-forth between weathers, signs and signifiers, as if a Chinook wind has come to bear. It allows us time to muse, consider, come to terms, come down, to say goodbye and quietly look forward, in the leaf-layering and ultimately enriching practice of change and growth. The rhythmic, longing cries of geese, a comforting kind of melancholy, has me reaching for the small frying pan, a dab of butter, batter, brown sugar and proper maple syrup. I make them slowly, one at a time, with love and a bunch of good country tunes lined up to sing along to. In a tradition it took me many years to connect back to Grandad's, the sound of Canada geese on the move heralds our Pancake Day and a yearly Michaelmas reminder that I'm neither a farmer nor a farmer's wife.

It's been a difficult start and end to the farming year here in 2024. Many crops were washed away by heavy and frequent rains and had to be resown. It's nearly Michaelmas and the late harvest is still underway, postponed repeatedly by unseasonable storms. I'm thinking about Miss White and her threshing 'sheen' as the back garden is almost obscured by the passage of the combine harvester in a halo-smoke of golden-grey chaff. I'm thinking about the prairies, the corrals, the smell of Ponderosa pines, myrtle and muskeg peat bog. How I never got to go back. How I never made it happen.

In the garden at dusk, the air is filled with the cornflake-box smell of harvest and the billion-bee roar of the combines and, so it seems, Canada has come to visit: the moon appears above the treeline, huge and marbled with a harvest-dust filter of deep orange; a spacehopper-moon, joyous, buoyant. When I post my photos of it on social media, it becomes apparent that the #RedMoon trending is coloured not by localised harvest dust, but by unprecedented wildfires raging across Alberta, Canada. By smoke particles from burning pines, sagebrush, wooden houses, community halls painted by communities, and new, hopeful grassland reserves running with reintroduced buffalo. Airmail from Canada. A ghost, a guilting, a reckoning; a terrible, end-times beauty.

Impossible to ignore how another country has advanced climate breakdown while simultaneously experiencing and dealing with it. Alberta has been producing oil since the 1850s, but the extraction of tar-heavy bitumen from its oil or tar sands now ranks as the world's most destructive oil operation, according to *National Geographic* magazine. Nearly two million acres of boreal forest and carbon-storing peat bog have been cleared since 2000; the open-cast mines, depleted riverbeds and toxic lakes of chemical 'tailings', visible from space. The lakes leach a carcinogenic soup of ammonia, lead, creosotes, mercury, benzene, arsenic and naphthenic acid into water sources. Birds die, fish develop strange deformities downstream, and cancer and disease levels among residents – and these are Indigenous lands – are disproportionately high. The bitumen seams in the banks of the Athabaskan River were discovered by First Nations people who mixed it with spruce resin to waterproof the canoes featured on Grandad's silver dollar. But the European, colonial-inspired mining and agricultural industry that grew up since has consistently stripped and denied the right and means to farm to the first farmers of Canada.

Expansion of the tar sands continues and Canada is warming twice as fast as the rest of the world, according to the 2019 *Canada's Changing Climate Report*. Climate breakdown is deeply rooted and driven at scale in a colonialism of patriarchal capitalism, motivated in opposition to community, connection, nature and welfare. I think about the sticky black bitumen 'pitch' that coats and preserves the grain-filled barns in Shalbourne and Inkpen, and the narrow asphalt ribbons of roads that lead everywhere. We are filthy with it. And, as Irish farmer and writer Keith Brennan said on Twitter/X, 'For all the arguments against radically changing farming, for staying, spraying, slurrying, fertilising, there's this: farming is the canary in the climate coalmine. It's farming climate is coming for first.'

At this late, late hour on the climate-breakdown clock, we need radical change and galvanising organisation around land use, nuanced and community-driven, from leaders that include and listen to everybody, differently, but on the scale we managed in the Second World War. It strikes me that those excluded from the very start, Indigenous communities and women, are best placed to lead that, deeply rooted in wisdom, stewardship and the connections between people, land and nature, as they are. I am trying not to sanctify the Shalbourne women, but I can't help but wonder what the women they inspired might have gone on to do, had they had the chance.

Back in the late 1980s to early '90s England, I try and try but cannot get a farming job. I am willing to learn, to train, to work for less, but the UK is in recession. I scour the print ads in the local newspaper and ring up farms. The phone is put down on me once or twice. I quickly stop saying, 'I've worked on a ranch as a cowgirl,' and just say, 'I've worked on a farm.' I am laughed at, treated like an idiot, a wind-up, every time. One farmer a mile from my home tells me, 'It's not a job you can wear your stilettos to, love.' Another asks me, perplexed, 'Well, what does your father do? Does he farm?' I feel embarrassed for trying. I find work at a stable yard that is supposed to include training for British Horse Society exams and entails a fourteen-mile round trip on my brother's racing bike to get there. I love the job, but leave after just months when no training materialises. For the next couple of years, I pinball between office jobs, doing paid and unpaid work with horses at the weekends, until I decide to do that full-time again, working in a yard on a farm by myself.

It's often cold, hard, lonely work, but I love it. On very cold days, I sneak down to the garden centre for a warm up and a hot pasty. It is here, although I don't get to know him just yet, that I first meet my husband, Martin. He has a pet and animal feed business at the garden centre, and we wave as we pass each other on the lanes when he makes deliveries in his old, unreliable truck. I exercise three horses per day, often leading another, and it is in riding repeatedly past a neighbouring farm on the hill that I meet Honor Atkins. Born in 1919, at the age of seventeen Honor started a farm in Surrey with a single Jersey cow. She became a Land Girl during the Second World War and built up a milk herd and delivery service with her pony, Robin. She moved to Hill Farm dairy, Enborne, neighbouring the one I work at, in 1956 with her parents and sister, and farmed it, keeping a Jersey dairy herd, pigs, hens and Dorset Horn sheep. She never industrialised her process and used a Lister cream separator, a hand-turned machine that the founder, Robert Ashton Lister, exhibited and sold via horse and buggy across Alberta as a traveling businessman-inventor. Miss Atkins sells her milk (a treat, thick and lovely on my cornflakes), rich cream and eggs locally and never marries, living with a sister who provides back-up labour. We exchange comments on the weather, the cows, who had seen the little owl that day, on a sometimes twice-daily basis. If I am riding a patient horse, I let them graze the bank and ask her how she got into farming, again and again. She was 'lucky', she says. Her family supported and allowed her dreams. Her sister helps. These are treasured conversations. I want to know her better, to have a tour of her dairy, to meet her butterscotch, silky-flanked cows; to lend a hand. She is in her mid-seventies then, usually headscarved, in a navy quilted jacket or an oversized tweed one with breeches. She farms until she is eighty-one, and dies aged ninety-five, having been that rare, rare thing: a woman farmer in her own right, for sixty-five years. I wonder, now, if her sister really was her sister.

I get myself to university, where I study English literature, media and fine art instead of farming, but bend all my studies to nature and the rural and wonder if it's possible to 'farm' that way: reading and writing about it, interrogating and painting it instead. I take part in and instigate environmental protests, all the while working part-time with horses, which is where I finally meet my husband, through the clearing steam of a neatly stepped muck heap. We share dreams of horses, of fresh wild air, and flirt and bond over cycle rides and feed deliveries around the farms in his tiny Bedford Rascal van. He is wonderful. We find rural work: he sells his small business and trains in horse breeding and management and, afterwards, works on a small farm with horses, where we help with sheep and lambing. He is also a gardener where a flat comes with the job. When his hand is broken at work by a kick from a horse, he loses that job instantly and the other, the one that comes with our flat, becomes precarious. Martin takes a job then as a rights of way officer, and I work for conservation charity, the British Trust for Conservation Volunteers (now TCV,

The Conservation Volunteers), where I mix office work with outdoor work, learning drystone walling, hedgelaying, coppicing and surveying, and become an officer for the groundbreaking Natural Pioneers Millennium Award, enabling people to take action for nature in and with their communities. I find myself in my element.

When our children come along, it is clear our combined wages won't support rent and childcare, so I leave work to care for the children and Martin finds employment on a thoroughbred stud farm that comes with a cottage. After that, we move to Inkpen, living in a rented cottage on one farm, opposite another and passing through more to get anywhere. Still riding borrowed horses, still helping out with the occasional bit of farm work, busy immersing ourselves in the community, family, work. Martin becomes a paramedic, and I work around our three children, as a librarian, cleaner at one of the old farmhouses, a nature columnist, a rural writer. For too many years, our rent takes up most of our income. There is no opportunity to save to buy a house, especially in this most expensive area of rural southern England, among its pretty, thatched old farmworkers' cottages, so attractive to second and even third homers, and no chance to even buy or rent a field or two. In Inkpen, I become fascinated with – no, *attuned to*, though that's not the right phrase either – traces of this old place and the lives, wild, domesticated and human, that went before mine here, however fleetingly. Lives that were deeply invested in its land-body, its fields, its buildings. And I wish, like Honor Atkins, I could talk to them, time travel, and raise their friendly ghosts in a resistance to the loss of so much wildlife, so much community and so much connection. They would care, I know. They would be angry, I am sure. I'd want to give them foresight and responsibility. And I think they would recognise the part they unwittingly played in so much loss, as we all might, and want to put it right. It seems a silly, gauzy thing to try to hold on to – an old net curtain flapping out of a broken window – but it won't let me go. It's a haunting. That. That's the word.

CHAPTER NINE

Manor Farm, Camp Fashion

Michaelmas 1941

Almost twelve months have passed, and Miss White has worked the full cycle of the agricultural year and learnt much. Of herself, she feels competent, fit and hardy but very much the apprentice still. One Sunday afternoon, Doris calls at her caravan for a cup of tea, conspiratorially mysterious, suggesting Julia might want something a little stronger. She has a proposal. She sits, wriggles her buttocks into the upright sofa of the caravan with a restless excitement and clasps her hands together, waiting for Julia's billycan to boil. 'Oh, don't keep me in suspense, Doris!' Julia laughs, anticipating an invitation to a committee or some such… 'Well, you might be grateful I did!' Doris retorts. 'There is a farm for sale in the next village in Inkpen. About three miles away, over the border in Berkshire. I think we should try and buy it, go into partnership. You can live there and do the farming. You want to be a farmer in your own right and here is the perfect opportunity!'

There is, at first, stunned silence from Julia, then a bluster of denial of any qualification or enough earned 'right' to dare to do so. But, when the tea is eventually made, much reassurance follows, much practical talk and no-nonsense encouragement. Doris pats Julia's knee, gives a friendly wink and leaves her to think about it. Julia cannot contemplate her afternoon nap. Paces the caravan, managing just two stooped, small steps in each direction, watched by the dogs – who make her feel self-consciously ridiculous, so that she abandons the pacing. Sits, considers. She is an optimist. Doris will be three short miles away. She has made friends here. 'Well,' she says out loud, to the fug in the caravan, to Jo and Dina, brown eyes blinking under muddy eyebrows, suddenly thinking of Jack and his levers and fixes, 'have a try, you can probably do it.' She sets off towards the house to tell Doris and Marguerite her decision, has a little leap on the way, tapping her heels together. Things are about to get a lot less comfortable, in many ways. But if not now, when? If not her, just someone else and it is wartime. Extraordinary things are happening because they must and, actually, because they can.

She and Doris visit, prior to the auction. The farm is in a lovely spot in the centre of a very spread-out village – more a collection of hamlets, really, separated by woods, fields and common. The farmer, Mr Bertie Lawrence, has had a hard time coping during the bad slump of the thirties, has lost heart and income and is selling up. The two women wonder privately if this has been under pressure from a War Ag visit (the War Agricultural Executive Committee). The grading of the farm is the lowest, C, 'under supervision'. At this time of great need, farms can be confiscated from those farmers deemed not up to scratch. Mr Lawrence's 400 acres wash right up to the foot of the Downs at their highest point of Walbury Hill and include the soaring arc of Gallows Down, also known as Inkpen Beacon, with its ancient long barrow jockeying the leap of its rise, flag-poled in place by the leaning, wooden gallows post of Combe Gibbet.* Julia, Doris and Marguerite are keen on history and regularly discuss the latest revelations and discoveries of the time, swapping theories and following the work of the rising number of prominent, skilled and respected women archaeologists with enthusiasm, such as Tessa Verney Wheeler and Peggy Piggott, as well as men like E. Cecil Curwen, and Alexander Keiller at nearby Avebury. They are excited to find the long barrow on the land, a 6,000-year-old burial chamber of those early agriculturalists – 'Farmers, after all!' says Julia – and are not fazed by the presence of the gibbet, though it draws the eye from anywhere on the farm. For them, it is an artifact, a marker, a

* Inkpen Beacon sometimes refers instead to Walbury Hill, as throughout history beacons have been held on both neighbouring high hill tops.

piece of history and deliciously spooky at times. Julia believes in science utterly, but has a penchant for the supernatural, too; an interest, a curiosity, particularly in numerology – the magic and meaning of numbers. She is a woman of her time, naturally. The neatness of swapping one Manor Farm (Shalbourne) for another (Inkpen) appeals to her, and her childhood home was The Gorse in Manor Park, Kent. Nevertheless, she and Doris are rather taken aback at what they can see of the ruinous state of the farmland, house and buildings, and two ancient farmworkers' cottages. Even so, they attend the auction in Newbury, plant their feet with courage, give each other a surreptitious squeeze of the hand and sensibly expect the place to go for much more than they can manage. The place falls to their bid of £7,000, around £438,000 today, which wouldn't buy a three-bedroomed house in the village currently, let alone a large farm. They are a little stunned, and elated.

That evening they have a small party, with a dusty bottle of very good wine and some jazz tunes on the gramophone. Their plans grow more ambitious as the night goes on – an archaeological dig! Julia watches Doris and Marguerite dance and whirl in the light of the first fire of the season. Both tall and slim, and not stooping as some tall women feel inclined to; Doris's face, pleasant and handsomely angular, a wry twitch of a smile never far from her lips; Marguerite with softer features and an open and merry expression. She thinks, how fortunate to have met them, how wonderful they are. How each has their own separate working life, ambition and goals; how they are independent of each other and equal, yet share and revel in each other's hopes and dreams. It seems to her then that a woman can be anything she wants to be, in a relationship such as theirs; of deep, unquestioning and natural equality and support. She is not dotty or naive enough to think that circumstance, money and class don't come into it, far from it, but thinks these are such bright-burning times for women, and that others respond to that too – she thinks fondly of the men on the farm, the children, other women, unembittered, resolute, making the best of it, and in the rosy glow makes a pledge to herself to honour all that in Inkpen, the very best she can. Doris turns to her, laughing, says, 'The Sapphic life, eh!' Marguerite hoots, Julia raises her glass and, despite herself, blushes.

She spends much of the remaining time at Shalbourne in preparation, poring over maps and plotting with Doris what equipment they will need to borrow, share and buy. She and Doris ride or drive over several times, making plans, meeting with Mr Lawrence and attempting to get a handle on the place, which seems to grow more alarmingly ruinous each time. They are keen to take on those already employed on the farm and reassure the tenants in the tied cottages that this arrangement will continue if it proves satisfactory to all. 'You might have to be strong, Julia,' says Doris. 'Firm and kind. They'll know more than you do, and acknowledging that will get them on side. Whatever you do will be an improvement on their current lot, I'll wager.' Julia is pragmatic; sounds, in agreement, more confident than she feels, but is used to managing on her own. Knows full well that a good, sustained and steady dose of positivity, interest and acknowledgement of experience is often a welcome surprise. Goes a long way. But her first decision must be carried out before she is even in place, and it is a hard, if necessary one. Norman Painting, the Lawrences' revered dairyman of twenty years, and his beautiful herd of Jersey milkers must go. Modern standards of hygiene under War Ag regulations won't tolerate a dairy with such a primitive water supply, so it is no longer tenable. Julia reassures Mr Painting that this is neither slight nor judgement on the excellent condition and care of his animals, milk or management. But it is hard for him to bear.

Miss White and Miss Mason officially take possession of Manor Farm, Inkpen, at Michaelmas, 29 September 1941, and the beginning of the new farming year. Julia must strike out, leave the nearness, comfort and immediate camaraderie of the Tudor fireplace chats, the clean, well-maintained farmyard and its fields of honey-scented, wild white clover, for a cold hearth and a virtually uninhabitable house. She has plenty of misgivings, but, in her forty-first year, feels strong, in good health and equal to any discomforts she may have to endure, not to mention the unforgettable fact of there being a war on.

About ten days before she is due to quit Shalbourne, Miss White is settling in for the night in her caravan when she realises she needs the loo. Jo and Dina barely raise an eyebrow as she pulls on her greatcoat and boots and clomps across to the house, to see if the side door is still unlocked. There is the thinnest fingernail moon over the Downs and a strange greenish-orange hue to the sky. It makes her heart hammer in her chest and she pauses, wondering what it means – the eerie glow from a fire perhaps? A raid? She tries to place it. Bristol direction? No, to the north – Oxford? A chemical light, a factory? Her eyes adjust, the need for a wee forgotten. Higher up, overhead, a wave of green, then pink blush. Suddenly, joyfully, she knows what this is – she has seen them before in Canada – the Northern Lights, the aurora borealis! They intensify as her eyes adjust. Green shards, pink beams, the heavens aflame; it is extraordinary. She goes to the house, calls Doris and Marguerite, on their way to bed, 'you really must come and see!', catches John and two of the older evacuees not yet in bed. The lights come quickly, the night so dark and under a blackout, their eyes don't take long to adjust. The children are at first a little afraid, still not quite trusting of the dark, let alone what these celestial curtains, blowing in a wind they cannot feel, are. Marguerite and Julia try to explain the cause, try to remember the science behind what seems like a portent. Joe Eggleston appears out of the night, extinguishing his lamp, having been up to check a sick cow. 'I saw the green through the barn door,' he says, 'and I thought, I know what that is! In Cumberland, we see it sometimes. But my, this is strong.' After a moment, he goes off down the drive to get his wife and throw bits of stone up at the Tuckers' windows. The little party move down the drive and out through the big, permanently open iron gates into the village square where there are a dozen or so others gathered. The Tuckers come out and stand amazed, turning round on their heels. 'What can it all mean?' Mrs Tucker asks breathlessly. Harry holds an old-fashioned nightcap in both hands. 'Well, I nivver. I wouldna known what it was. I'd a thought it was God and the angels, kids!' He winks at the children.

The magnetic storm of 18 September 1941 remains one of the most intense ever recorded across the northern hemisphere. Shortwave radio transmissions are knocked out, teleprinter machines print nonsense. Telegraphs are lost from Rome, Berlin and Moscow, and England loses contact with parts of Europe. Electricity supplies surge, wobble, dip and flare, and night is turned into day by the phenomenon.

There are moving streamers, rivers and rays of lime, neon pink, lavender. A rare auroral corona of silver light beams down from directly above. In the East End of London, in Southampton, in Plymouth the light awes. There are fears it is a new assault, a German death ray, invaders from Mars, religious omens, a message of victory from on high. Telephone services are disrupted. In the US, during a public radio broadcast, Bing Crosby sings appropriately, 'Where the blue of the night meets the gold of the day,' and is interrupted by the scraps of a telephone conversation between two men. It fades out, before a call between two women gets patched in: 'I fixed it for Eddie to pick up a guy for you and afterwards we'll go to the party,' one girl says. 'I guess it's OK,' her friend replies, 'but how do I know the guy Eddie's bringing for me is all right?' A nation wonders, worries, cheers, is scandalised. Bing resumes his crooning. The war continues regardless, taking advantage where it can. The RAF uses the unforecast light to pound German positions in Norway and France, while the Germans find a Canadian convoy out in the North Atlantic, sink a ship and kill eighteen sailors. The *New York Times* calls the storm 'an ethereal blitz'.

In the square, many are lost in private thoughts or blank wonder. Unbidden teariness, words, questions, sentences spoken out into the night to an indifferent, perhaps, solar system. 'Will it come good and will it be all right?' 'Will he come home?' 'But surely it's a sign from God.' 'Let it all be over.' On several faces, the lights are so bright, if one looks carefully enough, tears of gratitude, fear and sad wonder glint green. Eventually all slip away, and the troop at Shalbourne Manor weave up the short drive, their necks aching. Julia stays outside the caravan a while longer, puts her hand on the door, remembers she still needs a wee and has missed her chance to go to the house. She squats in the dark behind the barn, looking up at the aurora, crystalline above her, trying not to topple over backwards as she does so, grinning, glad. It's a bold move, to take this aurora as a sign that all will be well in her new job as farmer. But she does so, privately, taking it to her heart. A lever to the darkness. A new start, fresh as the night, a graduation of sorts. An irreverent, needs-must wee in the dark.

On 29 September 1941, Miss White hitches her caravan back to her Rover and slow-drives it the three short miles along the rutted, straw-lined lanes. It is perhaps at this point that we begin to meet. Although our habitation of this place is some forty-five years apart, there are already common places, common themes, people in common – something laid down, picked up.

Julia sets to work immediately, recording daily notes of work and progress in her new, smart, black-and-red Day Book and Cultivations Record, with Doris coming over most days to help. Both women are newly shocked at the state of the place, of the task ahead. It is far worse than they had realised: filthy, rat-infested and dilapidated. Years of cow muck has simply been dumped and swept out of the barn doors and left to form a seeping, semi-solid pond in the middle of the yard, which the cows must walk through on repeat, spreading it everywhere. The roofs of all the farm buildings need repairs and, as they run their eyes along them, a stately elm wafts an elegant-sleeved limb over the granary roof when the wind gets up and sweeps a dozen more tiles off, like playing cards off a table. 'Lawkes – what have we done, Julia!' snorts Doris, giving her arm a friendly squeeze. A fine old barn, black tarred in pitch, thickly thatched with a wooden threshing floor at one end and concrete cow stalls at the other, looks secure. Its huge double doors, big enough for loaded wagons to pass through, almost face each other and Julia puzzles at the odd angle, before realising the actual doors are indeed immediately opposite and safely padlocked, and the open 'door' is a hole big enough to drive a cart and horses through.

Miss White and Miss Mason call a meeting with the men, 'all real, skilled countrymen', and find them stiff and reticent, particularly in the light of Mr Painting's dismissal, but keen to clean the place up and get it back on its feet. They are clearly uncomfortable and suspicious of a woman taking over. Miss White knows she'll have to prove herself. She does not expect (or have any desire for) deference to her class, which is somewhere around the lower uppers, as her parents might've done; her generation has experienced a great levelling and humility in that respect. She needs to get these countrymen on side. She must step into her position as owner-farmer, while being compelled to listen to and trust them; to defer to their experience when needed and, indeed, to invite their knowledge, authority and collaboration while remaining in charge. She feels this is utterly reasonable, fair and friendly. It's not what the men expected at all; neither is it what they've ever experienced. This Boss Miss has taken them by surprise with her honesty, cheerfulness, hardiness and warmth, and it is not many months before they begin to settle into a happy affability and loyalty. But not yet.

Here is Arthur Walters, who lives in one of the two tied cottages with his wife and two little girls; Jack Hitchens, cowman, who lives in one half of the other cottage with his wife and 'about ten' children (Jack's brother has the other half-cottage to himself and works elsewhere). Billy Edwards, cheery from the start, is horseman, and Bert Wright, skilled thatcher, rick builder, hedgelayer and King of anything else. Old Bill Knight tells the women he is foreman to Mr Lawrence – though gets some sideways looks from the others. He appears as ancient and dilapidated as the buildings, but has clearly earnt his place here. He becomes 'yard man'. Between them all, a plan is hatched to begin: clearing and cleaning buildings, mending fences and working out what repairs must be done first and what equipment they will need.

Julia and Doris turn their attention then to the house for an hour or so. Manor Farm House is a rather lovely and large eighteenth-century farmhouse, with an additional second pitched roof added at its back in the last century, so that its roof forms an 'M' shape. It is virtually uninhabitable. There is no sanitation, mains water or electricity to the house or farm. A well, its inefficient antique pump that needs priming with two kept-back bucketsful of water each time, and a dirty rainwater tank are the only water supplies for the whole place. They tour the house, grimly noting rat holes and mouse droppings, then Doris stops Julia on the upper floor: 'Can you see what I can see?' Julia scans the room; a window frame is held open and prevented from collapsing alltogether, by a car jack. Up here, too, is a bathroom with a water closet – that cannot be used as there is no water. The whole house is painted throughout in gloomy battleship grey and when they push open the door to the dining room, they find a large elder tree growing up out of the middle of the floor. The whole place is full of absurdities. Doris pinches up the front of her corduroys and begins to skip and sing, 'Here we go round the mulberry bush' as Julia declares it good fortune to have an elder tree at the back of a house, but not necessarily *in* it. 'At least you won't have to bother with a Christmas tree!' Doris bats back. Outside, they find a ghastly stinking privy with a bench and two holes to sit on, over a very full pit that clearly hasn't been emptied or treated in an age. 'Very matey,' says Julia and they begin, uncontrollably, to laugh, until they have to lean on each other, tears running down their faces.

Julia has arranged for some of her furniture, linen, cooking utensils and clothing to be sent up from her house in Burley, which she let out to a family before coming to Shalbourne, but, for the first few days, stays in the relative luxury of her caravan. She has engaged Fred Brazier and his wife from Shalbourne, as tractor driver, housekeeper and live-in help, and when they and the few essentials from Burley arrive, they all three brave the house in rooms they have scrubbed and freshly painted. Julia cannot brave the privy though. She does not enquire as to what the Braziers do. When necessary, she disappears into the little copse nearby, taking a trowel when needed, camp fashion.

The two little cottages that come with the farm are ancient, picturesque and primitive. The Rushes, the Walters' place, has very low-beamed ceilings under a thick, low thatch, a chalk floor, swept and laid over with rush mats and rag rugs, and a pretty, productive garden. Miss White makes sure to visit, taking a small offering of ham wrapped in brown paper, chats easily to the two little girls and is welcomed. To the other, even more primitive cottage, she takes a packet of currants and a little butter. The Hitchens live in one half of the cottage. It has just one small front room and a lean-to back house under a sloping thatch, where there is a washing copper, and two little rooms upstairs. Copper pans gleam over the hearth in the now-October light and children flow in and out, representing every stage of childhood. Something gamey simmers in a pot hanging from a saw-edged ratchet over the open fireplace. Mrs Hitchens is uneasy and Miss White does her best to be chatty, complimenting her on a bonny brood and talking of her plans for the farm that include cows; and how much she'll rely on Jack's expertise. She accepts a half-cup of broth tea then, scooped from the pot, sans the scarce meat and vegetables bobbing in it, tries to quash the feeling she has been swept back one hundred years and focuses on Mrs Hitchens' fashionable pinned curls and print apron. Then, 'Ah!' she says. 'I have one of those growing out of my sitting room too! It must be older than the house!' Mrs Hitchens, initially confused, realises Miss White is referring to the 'stairs' up into the little upstairs bedrooms; a tree trunk, set upright into a hatch, with notches cut in for foot and handholds. 'It's more permanent than a ladder,' says Mrs Hitchens, looking down at her hands. Julia flushes with embarrassment, but quickly rallies. Enquires about the 'next door' occupied by her brother-in-law and leaves with friendly encouragement and the affirmation that she can see improvements need to be made. They shake hands warmly.

Making her way back the short distance to the farm, over the brook, Julia is deep in thought. She is surprised the Walters' cottage has water laid on from a mains on the lane, but is in no doubt that living conditions must be improved for her workers and their families, as well as herself and the farm. She pictures the Hitchens climbing up to bed via the tree-trunk stairs and shakes her head. Thinks of Mrs Hitchens climbing them all the times she has been pregnant; wonders if they hand the littlest ones up – and how all twelve or so of them manage to live in such a tiny place. She thinks how this spread-out village, just three miles along from Shalbourne and a little further up into the Downs, is that bit more remote, that bit poorer, and in parts a lot less modernised. She feels the weight of the harness of responsibility upon her. She wonders where on earth to begin.

They start with the stables and horses. Apart from an old horse hay rake abandoned to the nettles, all the farm machinery has been sold off. With horses, they'll be able to set to work much quicker. With a good eye for a horse, Julia buys a lovely pair of dapple-grey Percherons, Dollie and Silvertail (or Sylvie), and a useful, gentlemanly, big bay gelding with a curled moustache called Boxer, along with two tip carts and some sets of harness at a farm sale. She and Doris have ordered two tractors and several implements, but deliveries and transport are perishingly slow, due to war movements and bombing. They decide to rear heifer calves and build a beef herd instead of a dairy one, and one early evening, just before sunset, Miss White wanders down to the big old barn to see how quickly they can get it ready. Pushing open the big door, there is a whooshing sound that puzzles and startles her. Switching on her torch and sweeping it around, she sees the walls moving, heaving as if furred and alive. Rats, thousands of them, swarming over the floor and up the walls and down uncountable holes in the riddled feed manger and boards. She has never seen so many; suspects few have. A barn owl ghosts through the beam and out of the cart-sized hole in the side of the wall. I'll need an army of you, she says ruefully, backs out, horror-struck, shivers and shuts the door. The rat problem is urgent and of national concern and importance. They are in the house as well as all the buildings, and they simply cannot move forwards until the situation is under control.

It might be hard to imagine rats on this scale, but I can. I am fond of rats. They are intelligent creatures and have their place in the world, but their numbers can quickly get out of control. They do very well, living alongside us. When the field behind our house is put to corn then harvested, we get an influx into the garden – although not on that scale. They are also attracted by pheasant shoots and a ready supply of corn. I have been out with the gamekeeper in the Land Rover at night, driving over Miss White's former land, counting barn owls in the moted beam of a lamp, when whole fields have moved with rats as they break from the maize cover (also grown for pheasants) in their dozens and, sometimes, hundreds. Neighbours here, one in a now-replaced estate-owned wooden cabin unsuited to our climate, and another in a 400-year-old estate cottage made of cob and 'clunch', have an ongoing battle with rats chewing into the house. A supply of wire wool holds them up for a while.

Meanwhile, back at Manor Farm, the professionals are called in with copious amounts of phosphide poison and the farm becomes littered horribly with dead rats. They are collected in sacks as soon as they are spotted and Jack spreads them out in the furrows behind the plough, where they are eventually harrowed in with the seed corn. A grim sowing, but one he is certain makes the corn grow. Miss White writes later that this was not very noticeable.

The barn is made good enough for now, set thickly with straw and twenty-five red, white and roan shorthorn calves just a week old are installed, along with three nurse cows. These are housed separately and their milk rationed out to the calves, so all get an equal measure. The calves are taught to drink from pails, by first suckling the fingers of a hand dipped, then immersed in the milk, until they learn to drink independently.

A new flock of lovely, amenable Light Sussex hens has taken to laying eggs in ingenious places, including high in the thatch of the big old barn. Miss White thinks nothing of climbing the long ladder up there and scooting along the beam to root out the warm eggs, careful not to disturb the barn owl, sitting tall as a sentry at eye level on an opposite beam. Towards the end of October, a terrific storm of wind and rain blows the rick sheet off the roof of one of the barns being retiled for the calves. Tiles begin to fly, slice through the air and shatter. While Arthur and Jack move the calves hurriedly to safety, Miss White, Billy and Bert tackle the tarpaulin, wrestling it up two ladders and back onto the roof in the gale. Miss White climbs up to the ridge and sits on the rearing, flapping sheet while the other two tie it down. But the wind comes straight off the Downs, uninhibited by trees, and at one point she is nearly airborne with the sheet and has to lie flat along the wooden roof structure. Bert and Billy call Arthur and Jack to hurry and grab the other whipping corner ropes, and Miss White half yells, half laughs, 'We are sailing the high seas and about to have a man overboard!' Afterwards, they grin and laugh, drip and shake their heads, over hot tea in the farmhouse kitchen. Apologise for a swear word or two used. But a woman farmer is more than a nine-days' wonder in the village. Often, Miss White finds she is being watched; responds with a defiantly cheery wave and greeting. Days after the storm, she hears Billy address a group of women collecting rosehips for syrup in baskets along the lane – they have stopped to peer through the hedge: 'Ain't you lot ever seen a woman at work before?' Julia smiles. Senses the beginnings of a thaw. Gives herself a quick, little hug.

PART II

INKPEN

CHAPTER TEN

Fiddling and Watering

November 1941

Billy and his new team of horses are piling up rubbish in great bonfires that must be extinguished each night for fear of bombers. Repairs and the whitewashing of walls are continuing apace and Bert Annetts from the village, known for a lost reason as 'Jailer', is taken on as maintenance man. But nature won't wait, and farming must begin immediately. With the tractors and equipment still on order at Oakes in Hungerford, Miss Mason lends Racing Lizzie, a two-furrow plough and her tractor driver, Maurice, to begin ploughing in preparation for autumn sowing. A second tractor and plough are borrowed from a neighbouring farm for Arthur, as well as a tractor-powered hay press to bale the thatched stacks and get the winter fodder under a roof. But then comes a disappointment and setback from Oakes: a cargo ship bearing machinery from America has been sunk by enemy action. Lives have been lost, and their brand-new Allis-Chalmers crawler tractor has gone to the bottom of the Atlantic, to await the plough forever there, in the strangest of dioramas.

Dolly and Sylvie are hitched to a second-hand seed drill to begin sowing, but the broadcaster breaks down irreparably and a new machine or parts must be ordered. 'You'd think old Jethro over there would help us, Billy,' Miss White says, thumbing in the direction of Prosperous Farm, home of Jethro Tull, inventor of the horse-drawn seed drill in 1709. 'What's to be done now?' 'I could try there for parts?' says Billy half seriously. I get the joke. I can still recall the plates reproduced in my O-level history book on the Agrarian Revolution, from Tull's *Horse-Hoeing Husbandry* (1731), and going to see the farmhouse. But this is no laughing matter. There is the very real prospect of losing the farm if they don't do enough. With all their neighbours drilling and unable to help, Bert Wright comes up with the solution. He has a fiddle. After some initial confusion from Miss White, he fetches his old broadcaster. Those Julia has seen consist of a body-worn hopper fed by a sack of seed that pours into a spinner. This is operated by a fiddle bow, long as a driving whip handle, sawn back and forth in marching time, to cast the seed about evenly before the sower. Billy's isn't a fiddle, just a deep, kidney-shaped tray, like those worn by usherettes at picture houses. Bert reassures them that casting soon after the plough, when the furrow slices are still stood up sharp as knives, ensures the seed will hit, then fall down the sides into the furrows in lines as neat and then buried 'as if you'd machine-drilled 'em'. He shoulders the broadcast tray, fills the bag, adjusts the straps and away he goes, flinging measured handfuls of seed corn out to his right then left, in time with the march of his opposite hobnailed boot. Corduroy trousers tied at the knee, waistcoat done up and jacket over the top, he strides as a god over the land, like the engraving in a book Julia has, stored in a tea chest in the house: Clare Leighton's *The Farmer's Year*. 'He who still feels some warmth come up from the earth, flinging his bounties upon the world,' she paraphrases. 'Hear ye the Parable of the Sower,' replies Billy, touching his cap.

Over the next days and weeks, Bert covers 150 acres like this. Setting his tray down at last, his back is clapped like the strong, glossy neck of Boxer by the men in turn. Miss White is profoundly grateful and tells him, 'Bert, it was a pleasure to watch. You have quite saved us.' Bert remains unmoved, though she detects an almost imperceptible dip of an eyebrow. Billy offers to bring him a nosebag. Arthur asks to buy 'two ice creams please, madam'. Dolly and Sylvie finish off the job, harrowing the lot in.

Very early on, there is a visit from the War Ag, whose official task it is to survey, grade, advise and monitor the efficient running of each farm, its production of food, the right sort of food, cleanliness and the keeping down of pests. A wartime farmers' Ofsted. Doris attends the visit for support. She and Julia are acutely aware of the risk and responsibility they have undertaken, of Julia's inexperience and that this is a matter of national importance. Doris is fond of quoting Winston Churchill's speech to the National Farmers' Union last October and does a thumping great impression: 'We rely on the farmers ... The farms of Britain are the front line of freedom!' Julia says how grateful she is that Doris has put this trust in her, letting her get on with it, and doesn't want to let anyone down. 'Now, now,' replies Doris, 'repeat after me: On my honour, I promise that I will do my best...' Julia starts to smile; it is the Guide Promise. '...To do my duty to God, the King, my country and Miss Doris Mason, to help all people at all times except Hitler.' They bump shoulders, laughing. 'Remember, a Girl Guide smiles and sings under all difficulties!' Julia slaps Doris fondly on the arm, 'Oh do stop. I am not going to sing to him!'

State intervention has come unprecedented with the privations of wartime, changing Britain's countryside, physically, politically, imaginatively and proprietorially, at profound and lasting level. The 'National Farm' is born in the popular collective mind as well as governmental psyche. By hauling agriculture compulsorily out of the muck and poverty of the depression into the clinical efficiency of industrialisation at scale, and pulling together, growing, land-working and giving it our all, we do not starve. In fact, the lower third of the population's diet improves.

So much of the sentiment, practice and approach linger on from this time. There is a feeling that farmers are ideologically 'owned' by us and subject to our and our government's demands, needs and blame, becoming both heroes and villains. But the farmers themselves also own or steward land with an agency (within economic and policy restrictions) that we, separated on the other side of fences or confined to footpaths, do not have.

And what was laid down then has presented us with bitter challenges of an existential kind further down the line. The nature and climate crisis worsens and becomes harder to manage. Most people are divorced from the land and how their food is produced, and farmers are often left poorly rewarded for what they produce and unsupported in doing it to benefit nature or access to people. The challenge of our time is not just how we feed the growing population sustainably, justly, securely, amid terrible new wars and finite resources. It's how not to exacerbate the rapidly changing and unstable climate, even as we work in it. And it's how to stop, then reverse the effects of species blinking out, one by one. We seem unable to get a grip on the seriousness, urgency and interconnectedness of the challenges we face and our implication, access and part in them. What a deeply strange and complicated position we have put them, and ourselves, in.

I want to be kind to Miss White when I think about these things. I want to remember that the jigsaw-box romance of the past, of seed fiddles and smocks and close-knit communities, of farmyard geese and knowledge, steam engines in duck ponds and brass-charmed heavy horses was absolutely a functional reality, but it is one often missing the harsh realities. The muck, mire, lack of basic utilities or warmth and short, hard, cramped lives. Miss White is going at this with a firm hand set upon the plough: improvements, electric light, water, better conditions for all, progress and defeating a terrible, terrible enemy. Farmland wildlife in 1941 is just *there*: abundant, sorting itself out, occasionally troublesome, frequently uplifting and a joy. To most, that's all there is to it. And imagining something like climate change, and that this agricultural revolution might have consequences of concern beyond the war, surpasses the reach of most people's scrutiny. What binds all of these female farming and countrywomen together is their thoughtfulness, collaboration, humility, an imaginative literariness, an expressed love for the world and a fresh enthusiasm to take things forward. To change for the better, and not just to do what is asked of them. They have a huge cultural history of what that is like behind them and are quietly, actively rebelling against it, using this opportunity to get on and change things, reacting and adapting to so much more than would ever challenge or cross a male farmer. This is not to blame male farmers at all, or to preclude men from those simply human traits, but it is to ask, what happened to those women, who should have made up 50 per cent of the farming workforce and decision makers? What did we lose when the farm gate was shut on them? A diverse workforce enhances creativity and innovation in problem-solving and drives better, more inclusive decision-making. A diverse agricultural workforce would be in a far better position to respond to what we are dealing with now, and, who knows, if women hadn't been sent back off the land and not allowed to return after the war, would we be in the mess we're in now?

But meanwhile, under siege in wartime, farmers must improve and modernise, grow what they are told, destroy pests and plough up any 'redundant' meadow or pasture for cereals. *This* is Julia's war; *her* war effort and she wants passionately to make a difference in a way she can, improving things for people too. She admires and wants to learn from the old, the existing knowledge, but be at this forefront of progress too, making great strides with the science and technology available. But can she and Doris impress this so early on upon the War Ag chap? Powers of dispossession remain in force until 1958. They both know the system isn't always fair; is open to abuse. They listen to farming author and radio broadcaster Mrs Frances 'Frankie' Donaldson on the wireless; another woman who seized the opportunity to go to agricultural college and bought a farm when her husband went to war, as well as lone parenting their two children. What she does not broadcast on the BBC, but records in letters to her husband, is how, despite earning the full support and high regard of her farming neighbours, 'the pooping little men of the district branch' seek to put her in her place and dispossess her of Gipsy Hall Farm in Wilmcote, Warwickshire. Two or three of them conspire maliciously to spread the impression the farm is going down since she had it, when, in fact, it is doing otherwise. She feels under siege from 'crabbing, sour, second rate gossips' and malign influencers (all men), particularly when she seeks to get rid of her bailiff, who isn't very good and undermines and belittles her at every opportunity. Gipsy Hall Farm is eventually graded 'A' under Frankie Donaldson's own steam, becoming a model farm producing record crop and milk yields and with immaculate accounts books. During the inspection, the War

Ag advisor replies to his chairman that it must've been the show place of the Midlands before, if it has indeed 'come down' since she had it. They agree her critics might've taken a passing look at the farm first, before condemning it merely on account of her being a woman.

But on the other side of their valley, Starlight Farm, run well enough by all accounts by Miss Boston and her former Land Girl Miss Hargreaves, has a different outcome. Initially designated 'B' by the visiting surveyor, it is downgraded to a 'C' by their supervisor, who also happens to own the farm next door. Once the 'C' is given, the two women are evicted without compensation or the chance to buck up, and their War Ag supervisor-neighbour adds Starlight Farm to his own landmass.* He is heard locally expressing strong views about women farming on their own, with implication in his tone. There is no man! No husband, father, brother, uncle, son, running the place; and how strange and *unnatural* that two women should live together, farming it alone. They are often seen walking and idly picnicking together. Thursday Market gossip in Newbury has been rife with speculation and opinion about Miss Boston and her partner, as well as the scruples of the War Ag supervisor and the wretched eviction. Julia, Doris and Marguerite have discussed what they presume at best to be a self-serving injustice, at worst, a vicious and opportune unhousing and land grab from two hard-working women, resented for living as a couple.

I feel an unexpected frisson of familiar dread at this, too. Some trace or whiff of proprietorship, of propriety in the countryside; the garden of our long-tenanted estate-workers' cottage is rather wild. 'No Mow May' has extended into June, July, August and throngs with frogs, toads, newts, grass snakes, butterflies, hoverflies and bees. A few rats. It draws attention from the estate farm manager. I am firmly told not to let nature take over. The house and garden are in poor repair, which we barely mention, lest in return the sparrow boxes and the jasmine that other birds nest in must come off the wall, the

---

* This story is beautifully and most movingly told in Rachel Malik's historical fiction, *Miss Boston and Miss Hargreaves*, loosely based on the life of her grandmother.

starlings' under-tile nest holes be filled in. Or my outspokenness on conservation or support for the Right to Roam (responsible public countryside access reform, as enjoyed in Scotland) crosses a line somewhere and we are graded a 'C' as tenants, and given notice.

The supervising farmer that attends Manor Farm is Mr Frank Moore, a respected, experienced 'yeoman' farmer who survived the slump. He is genuinely interested and encouraging and seems to be in it for no other reason than he wants farms and people to thrive and do their bit. He grades the farm 'B,' ticking the box 'personal failings' and writing the reason 'lack of experience'. But he recognises progress made, the willingness to learn, the positivity and energy. Frank Moore proves to be supportive, visiting often, working out cropping plans and giving good advice around prices and markets, and introducing Julia to other farmers and auctioneers. They end up great friends.

Though she has a run-in with Old Bertie Lawrence, who might have sold the farm, but retains the six ricks of his last harvest, which the team are obligated to thresh and get to market. 'OB' is not well liked and quite disgusted that 'two sisters', which they are not, have bought his farm. He wants the two barley ricks threshed first, to catch the early market, but doesn't say so to Miss White, so 'rascally' Joey Edwards sets his traction engine Nightingale up with the sheen, to do the four wheat ricks first. Work is underway when OB arrives, his shoulders and arms set with tension. A row bubbles. A twinkling Bert tells Miss White to 'look out for OB and his hat'. She remains puzzled until Old Bertie loses his temper, accusing Julia of making him miss the early market deliberately. She attempts to apologise, says that, as yet, she is ignorant of markets.Looking at Joey's face, and the men, who look away, their shoulders beginning to jiggle with amusement, she doesn't suppose they are. Bertie Lawrence wags his finger, shouts about women in their place and ignorance, some furious, incoherent, possibly lewd half-sentences spat about favours and – does she catch 'matey with them friggin' inverts up the road'? Then OB runs out of words, sweeps the cap from his head, throws it down upon the dusty ground like a gauntlet, glares at her, then jumps with both feet up and down upon it. Behind him, the men on the sheen, the rick, at the elevator, are doubled over, slapping thighs, backs, heads thrown back, laughing their heads off. She looks away, presses her lips against the fizz of laughter bubbling up, is stung, in front of her men but also feels compassion for him, nonetheless. Arthur warns her later not to. It takes them ten days to do the ricks and, mostly, they manage without Old Bertie.

About this time, Miss White notices a grand old whiskered gentleman that comes to watch them work, leaning on a blackthorn stick. She is introduced to Joshua Digweed, former carter and ploughman all his life at Manor Farm, working first for Richard Lawrence, OB's father, 'the very best of marsters, and a very good farmer', before working for Bertie Lawrence. One of twelve siblings and in his eighties, he remembers ploughing with oxen here as a boy, and all the heavy horses stabled in Field Barn, now lying ruined at the foot of the Downs, and from which they now salvage tiles and wood for repairs elsewhere. He reels off their names in pairs, Beauty and Bonnie, Justice and Auster, Conquer and Captain, ten altogether, and remembers the beer awarded to best ploughman of the day, including the boys. He knows how the chalk-sticky loam builds up on your boots, making your legs and the horses' hooves heavier just as you both grow more tired. 'We'd be at 'im all winter. Tek a tuthree tractors, what, three weeks now? And no hour to groom and set 'em comfortable for the night.' He likes the new grey breed, the Percherons like Dolly and Sylvie, that came from France after the First World War. 'Good clean legs, so the mud don't cling.' Many of Julia's farm men walk with a rolling gait, limp from accidents, or have plough-bent ankles.

I know those very fields and have beat across them for the keeper in pheasant shoots, as we all did as a family, living on the estate. It's not something I would do now; but back then, it gave me a key. I could make more of a sense of being involved while challenging it; championing and instigating wildlife conservation from the inside, as it were, while earning money working outdoors; a muddy boot in both fields, an outlier fence-sitter as before. Trying to understand and influence, spark conversations and change things in this very male, rural world until working within a commercial pheasant shoot became too much, untenable: unquestionably wrong on many levels. That creamy-marl chalk paste, building up a platform overboot of your wellies, weighting you down. The weariness of just walking across the plough into a head wind, trying to speak softly, thoughtfully among certain voices that carry, that in the end, have just been tolerant. I don't regret it. I learnt a great deal and, I hope, made a few people think differently too. I still have friends in those fields, as it were, though there are topics we avoid.

Julia and 'Jos' Digweed become great friends. He tells her about OB and 'a quarrel too many. He weren't a patch on his feyther, and 'e knew I knew it! Wor the sack fer me and too owd to go working anywhere zelse.' Jos is freshly heartbroken by the severance from land he knows better than his own body. Julia asks him to 'come on for her' as an advisor. He has no problem with this Boss Miss. She is simply Boss.

Winter work commences. Chalk is dug with back-breaking effort from the pit in 'Bumpy' field to fill the hole in the yard where the muck pond was. But for now, the pressing need is water. Replacement parts for the old pump cannot be got and sometimes the water has a sulphurous smell. It is boiled with a kettle on the old black range for human use and the rain tank used for everything else and the animals. An awareness of typhoid is ever present. When they need more, Billy goes almost daily with Boxer to fetch a water cart from neighbour Major Huth and fills it from The Rushes cottage standpipe on Hollow Lane. It is then emptied into a trough in the farmyard and baled with a bucket from there. When working, the carthorses drink four to five buckets each, not to mention the cows. All very trying. Julia barely washes.

Newbury Water Company cannot help, stymied by wartime pressures and the wildly scattered nature of the village. So, Miss White calculates cost, distance and requirements in getting water from the mains, a tantalising half mile away, and into the farmyard. There is some difficulty and delay purchasing pipes, but she works out the best route with Jailer the maintenance man, and, between them all, they hand-dig a half-mile trench through unforgiving chalk, which is so much like concrete. Julia stops to ease her back one bitter, iron-hard day, when the clang of her pick on the chalk sings up her arms, shoulders and through her teeth at such a pitch it makes her want to cry, and says instead to Bert and Arthur: 'Those big ditches up there on the hill? Those thousand-years-old Iron Age bumps and the mound? They were dug with antlers. Pickaxes made from deer antlers! Can you imagine?' Bert looks at her askance, as if she has believed a fairy tale; Arthur pauses, doesn't look up. Says mysteriously: 'The soil is thinner up there, like the air.'

They have begun to make an impression on the farm and buildings, though the farmhouse itself remains draughty, uncomfortable and depressing without electric light or water. Mrs Brazier is stoic and makes the best of it cleverly, but the sitting room fire is dilapidated and the coal-fired range seems to have come out of the ark. Frost ferns etching the windows are not uncommon anywhere, but at Manor Farm they do not thaw. Rats and mice are still a problem throughout and much of the time Julia and the Braziers wear overcoats indoors. She is apologetic, but the focus has to be on the farm first. Being on wartime Double Summer Time, where the clocks are put forward by two hours in the spring, and only moved back one hour in winter, to make the most of the daylight and save on resources, the farm working day begins at the later hour of 8am. Without electric light, it is impossible to begin any earlier, and it's something of a relief to get out and warm up with physical work.

The week before Christmas, there is a surprise present, delivered by lorry in the form of a new Allis-Chalmers crawler tractor and a Ransomes four-furrow plough. The tractor is the bright yellow-orange of a beech tree in autumn and the plough is sky-blue and red. They are left on the road that runs through the farm like gleaming new toys. The team gather round and stare at the machines in awe. Farming is progressing at such a pace now, is needed to do so with such urgency, they feel the future has come to bear. The word 'industry' is on their lips like a strange new metallic taste and mingles with the familiar salt of sweat and a running nose in cold weather. It seems they are on a threshold, there in the road, and it is almost dizzying. It is as if they are on a stage they did not know they were on, and someone in the wings has tweaked the curtain, pulled it aside onto a glimpse of the future. That person, they realise, is Miss White. She swallows, excited, daunted, pleased, clasped hands to her lips in thought, aware she has taken a great step – that must be taken – but nevertheless, she must bring her men along too. She has a strange feeling that the present is more weighted, somehow. That they are leaving the past while still living in it, which seems to imbue everything with an elegiac, filmic light.

On the one hand, there is Bert, broadcasting seed on foot to save the day, the *year*; and on the other, these great, tank-like tracks of the crawler tractor. The versatility and brightness of it and its four-furrow – *four-furrow*! – plough. It seems to glow on this late December day. Billy walks around it, running a hand over the body of it, its flanks, the frame of the plough and down to the frog at the bottom, as if he were feeling for heat in a pulled tendon; as if he were wanting to pick up its foot to see if it is fit for work. He thinks about his horses. His skill, his work. Arthur says, 'It hasn't got a steering wheel.' The future has seemed almost unimaginable until now, a nebulous thing. They may all be doing this for nothing if the invasion comes. Just at a time when the tight restrictions of societal boundaries and expectations are loosening, are kinder, more accepting among many, and more things seem possible. Though there are others trying to hold on to social mores and tradition for dear life, outraged and against the unstoppable force of change.

Julia knows she must show confidence in this huge investment, in order to instil it in the men. 'Well!' she says. 'Let's get it off the road and into the yard. Arthur? Fred?' She indicates the seat. They look at the hedge, the sky, their feet. 'Jailer? Billy then?' Billy refuses. Bert says, 'You do it first, Miss.' Arthur steps forward to turn the crank handle as she settles into the bucket seat. The lane is narrow with a ditch on one side and the lorry driver gave the very simplest of instructions, but it starts and she gets it into gear and it moves forward at quite a pace. The big tracks roll around and the men walk, then trot along beside it, giving encouragement. Though Bert feigns indifference at the back and Billy is frowning, chewing his lip, they both tilt their caps up and jog after it, hobnailed boots clickering on the road. The crawler is moved by pulling a lever back on the side you want to turn, rather, she thinks, like pulling the rein to turn a horse's head. She turns by jerky degrees into the farmyard, misses the old oak gateposts and urges it forwards with a double click of her tongue. After practising stopping and having a turn of the yard one way and the other, imprinting the chalk militarily, watched by Boxer with his moustache quivering, she aligns it with the shed and drives it carefully in. 'Bravo, Miss!' says Arthur. 'Why don't we have a try about with it tomorrow?'

The following day, Julia takes the crawler tractor out and teaches Arthur to drive it. He is unconvinced by its tank-like appearance, so she must convince him of her reasoning and research. It is powerful, versatile and will cope with the hills, and when ploughing, the tracked wheels run alongside and not *in* the furrow, not compacting the soil, which interests her. They find very quickly that this is borne out. The 'Allis' manages the chalk-sticky, flinty land well and is very capable of hauling the four-ton threshing kit up and down the steep hills. It turns on a sixpence. Though Arthur discovers that if you go at a bank too hard, it has the tendency to put a great buck in, sending the driver dangerously sprawling on the bonnet, with his arms around the neck of the great beast.

Christmas Eve, and two little fir trees are cut from the overgrown spinney by Dagg's Gully, one for the farmhouse and one for the church, and on Christmas Day itself Miss White and Miss Mason hold a Christmas Party in the farmhouse for the men, their wives and children. Given the restrictions, a magnificent tea is still produced by Mrs Brazier, with help from Julia and Doris. There is rabbit and roast chicken, Christmas pudding bolstered by grated carrot, and sweets. They listen to the wireless, sing carols and light the candles on the tree. Doris cleverly disappears to come back dressed as an excellent Father Christmas and gives each child a present wrapped in newspaper or pretty cotton scraps. Paper is scarce and wrapping paper banned. The Hitchens children have all come along and, dressed in their Sunday best, are self-conscious and uncertain at first, having never been to a party before. But their shyness soon dissipates and they end the party with games and more hearty singing. Everyone thoroughly enjoys themselves and walks home across the fields and down the lanes, through the evening pinking hour of a hundred blackbirds beneath a scattering of bright early stars.

CHAPTER ELEVEN

Night Ploughing and Utilities

January–March 1942

On New Year's Day, with the smell of imminent snow sharp in their consciousness, Miss White, Mrs Brazier and the men gather round the new standpipe in the yard. Billy is given the honour to try the tap, as he and Boxer had the task of carting most of the water. With a splurt and a cheer from them all, the water runs clear and bright and triumphant. Though on checking the pipes before covering them, a leak is discovered on Hollow Lane and the pipes must all be reset. Nevertheless, for a few glorious days, there is running water to the yard. An official engineer comes to sign it off, congratulating them and adding unnecessarily that he has long suspected contamination of the well. Three days later, the pipes, tap and trough freeze solid, and the gang must revert to the old pump and possibly contaminated water. Bert sets to, instigating a thaw in the troughs, lighting fires beneath them with small bundles of sticks.

The snow they felt in the air falls heavily, accumulates, cuts them off, thaws and falls thickly again. Then there are weeks of deep frost, more heavy snow and bad weather, and wild gales into March. On its slight rise, Manor Farm catches the winds that come in roaring, uninhibited swoops off the Downs. The windows of the farmhouse rattle in their rotten frames and snow falls down the chimneys, leaving small, unthawed drifts in some of the rooms. One morning, out in the yard at a dark and shivering 7am, Miss White has just enough light to see one of the tractor sheds come loose in a gale and sail over the as-yet empty pig sties, raining down tiles and smashing to bits on impact.

When the weather makes it impossible or impractical to plough, harrow or sow, everyone is engaged in repairs or the winter work of ditching, hedging and coppicing. Miss White goes in search of Bert Wright one day and is told he is 'up in The Folly puffin'. The Folly is a spinney where Mum lives now, and was still a kind of unofficial common then. During the pre and between-war decades with farming in long decline, many plots of land are abandoned: overgrown fields becoming scrub, becoming woodland. Poor 'starveacres' on which little can grow, surround tumbled cottages that return their own chalk and flint walls, pots, stoves and thatch back to the land like the crumbling of cake.

On the edge of Manor Farm's land, Grade II listed, seventeenth-century Box Cottage is doing just that even now. It has escaped the Airbnb treatment of others, and I watch it almost daily dissolve like a hairy sugar lump. It haunts me. It is too far gone now, but it could have housed a family desperate for a home in the country, in the community. In 1942, it housed two families in a village beginning to change. Land must be in production, in good and purposeful ownership or tenancy, and the great plough-up of diverse, flower-rich meadow, pasture, down, and even park and common land has begun by order. Bert though, is 'puffin' as he always has. Neither Miss White nor I know what 'puffin' is. Julia hears him first, whistling among the coppicing, collecting up the smallest hazel twigs and brushwood into a hand cradle – two twigs tied together at each end, then pulled together into a tight bundle. Here in the most western edge of West Berkshire, they are called 'puffs'. On the commons, similar-sized bundles of spiky cut gorse are 'fuzzy bavins'. Both are used to fire the bread ovens with a fierce little heat. Other copses and spinneys on the farm have been managed on a coppice cycle, to yield fence and hedging stakes, thatching spars – twisted in the middle and bent like hair grips – hurdle rods, beanpoles and pea sticks, canes, basket whips, puffs – and rabbits. In the spring, with the light let in, they are resplendent with bluebells and primroses, wild garlic and wild daffodils, wood anemones and wood sorrel, violets, honeysuckle, butterflies and skippers, dormice, adders, picnickers. All this will soon stop and hundreds of years of coppicing will fall out of practice, though Bert and the others have no notion of this yet. The coppice woods' sort of flora and fauna is a rarity now, much diminished except on nature reserves. The woods are planted with conifers, or 'warmed up' for pheasants with invasive plants such as cherry laurel, lonicera and snowberry, the growing deer population and hundreds of pheasants taking a toll, the woods dimming, dull. But in 1942, the cut trees revive above the coppice stools in a crop for future years and there are willow warblers and nightingales in every spinney in spring; children collect primroses to send to town and woodcock sit in their cryptic camouflage on nests.

Bert coppices, cutting out fence stakes and sharpening them with his billhook into giant pencils, making inroads into the blackthorn acres that walk a low, black thorny bower from the foot of Gallows Down like a bristling cape onto pasture and plough as soon as your bent back is turned. He plashes and brutalises hedges, trims and slices the stems almost through, leaving a thin veneer of bark and sapwood to lay the hedge down within an inch of its life; he knocks off the heels to give clean slopes that shed rain and infection and sets the hedge uphill in the direction of the rising sap in spring. He stakes it, weaves the hazel rods over the top to lock it all in, and whacks the stakes in with his holly beadle, hoping not to find a flint. It's a work of art, efficiently and deftly done, to provide a permanent living barrier, full of life and leaf and nectar, then berries and nuts, birds and mice. He loves to watch the lithe stoats thread like a ribbon through the hedge bottom, bolting rabbits, in an echo of the weave of his hazel rods on top. Little matchstick tails stuck up, bewitching then killing a squealing rabbit treble their size; he admires them, but winces. Laid again once a decade or two, maybe three, his hedges will outlast them all, he thinks, whoever picks up the billhook next, whoever is victor in this war. Unlike the hated and freely available barbed wire that will falter and rust on dead fence posts that rot in the ground. In 1942, Bert does the hedge all around Champions Field, just down from us, and along Bell Lane, as winding as if it too were weaving in and out of hazel stakes. No one does it again until 2010, when our neighbour and tenant farmer Mr Cordery lays it with Gabriel Cave, who bought the field named Village Hall Piece and kept a few dairy cows as well as a donkey that was led down to the church each Palm Sunday.

In February, Miss White has her chestnut mare, Sheila, sent up on the train by her friend from the New Forest. She misses riding, but, from a practical point of view, it takes too long to walk around the farm on foot. She needs a horse. Sheila steps off the train in her protective bandages and rug, and snorts, head and tail held high. She is bright as a flame. Marguerite has dropped Julia off and holds the horse while she winds off the bandages and tacks up. After a brisk trot up the high street, Julia lets her gallop across Hungerford Common and jump the stile in the corner towards Inkpen Beacon. Eventually, Sheila settles to walk the last mile on a loose rein, is rubbed down and stabled next to an inquisitive Dolly, Sylvie and Boxer.

The following day, enlivened perhaps by their newest acquaintance and a day off work, Boxer finds a weak spot in the old fence of their paddock and pushes through, quickly followed by Sylvie and Dolly. Arthur spots them going down the lane towards the village from the Allis, stops it, stands on the seat and hollers – but they've already clattered past Billy, throwing up sparks from their great shod hooves. Julia gets her car out from the shed and Billy and Arthur, having run down the hill, pile into the car with halters to give chase. Boxer is having a high time of it and trots his ladies, moustache quivering with delight, past the blacksmiths, past the Post Office, dodging several attempts to stop them, and down the track through the woods. They come out opposite the pub and investigate the vegetables in the gardens of the council houses. By now, half the village are out, watching, shooing and helping. The car-full catch up, but the three escapees will not be caught easily. Sylvie spins around and leaves a devastation of craters and cries among carrots and leeks, before clattering back towards the pub, where she is so very nearly caught by a woman on a bicycle and the landlord with his belt. Dolly trots off to the Romany family and their horses on the common and is caught with a word by Ann Maria Black. Boxer, who has an endearing fondness for children, is caught next, with the aid of a girl holding out carrot tops. Sylvie, not wanting to be alone, falls into step behind him. Julia walks back later for her car and brings apologies to all in the form of a basket of eggs.

She rides Sheila out to ask Bert for more fence posts for the carthorse field. Bert is rarely chatty. If she asks what he thinks is a silly question, he simply doesn't answer. But if it is worthy of his consideration, she can come back ten minutes later and he will give her a good answer. If she asks, 'Shall we pick up the hay today?' Or, 'Had we ought to lay this hedge first or that?' He will say, 'That is for you to decide' Or, 'If it pleases yourself, Miss.' He is a proud, skilled and knowledgeable man whose opinion and work she already values greatly, though he refuses to accept praise easily. Julia recognises a need in him to retain dignity and control that the history of his class has rarely given him; she is frequently stung by his exposure of her lack; his ignoring her and making her feel small and silly at times, but she is thoughtful about it. She learns to frame the questions around his agency, putting him in control, to say, 'Bert, if this was your hay, would you bring it in today?' Or, 'Bert, you know your hedges best, which needs doing first?' Then he will answer enthusiastically. Julia finds this technique works well with the other men, once grasped, having enough sense not to pretend she knows when she doesn't, while remaining wryly aware that taking orders from a woman is affronting to them at first. She is not above employing flattery. When she and Bert are miles out of earshot from anyone, and when they know each other better, he is full of information and advice and positively garrulous.

Before she can begin on her own house, Miss White, with Jailer, sets about improving those of her farmworkers in the two tied cottages. She is deeply troubled about conditions there. 'All very picturesque but unhealthy, uncomfortable and about a century behind,' she tells Marguerite after Scouts one evening – she has allowed herself time to get back to helping there once a week, missing it. 'My heifers have more space and comfort than the Hitchens and cleaner water now than the Walters!' Repairs and improvements are made at The Rushes and the whole place freshened up and made more draughtproof and watertight, with Bert rethatching the steeply pitched little roof. Jack Hitchens' brother is persuaded to find accommodation elsewhere and the half-cottage is knocked through, so the family of twelve or so can spread out. Repairs and improvements are made to that too; the tree-trunk stairs are reset and remodelled and the cottage connected to the mains water supply and given a standpipe.

Elsewhere, where farmers are desperate for workers, new cottages are being built. Frankie Donaldson speaks about the importance of this on her broadcast. Decent, provided, 'tied' accommodation makes a farm-working job a possibility. 'The job has to have some attractions and perks!' I imagine her saying, laughing. 'And if you can do it, a modern house is a jolly good one.' Mrs Donaldson reckons on a cottage per 100 acres but only manages to build two herself, with some difficulty and all kinds of barriers, instead of the four and a half needed by her 450 acres; she acknowledges in a letter to her husband overseas that the cottages are 'absolutely square and functional, but spacious and warm and modern'. The one we come to live in in 2004 is built in a similar vein in 1953, along with five others in a fresh mood of post-war optimism and hope for farms and communities, and with all modern conveniences.

In the next decade or two, across the field behind us and at the farm that neighbours Miss White's, other ancient cottages with their outside privies are pulled down. Most of those that remain now are beautifully done up and let to weekenders for large sums and not lived in, despite them having an Agricultural Covenant set upon them, meaning they are expressly for rural workers to live in. Or they are knocked down and rebuilt far larger, their security lights blinking on and off in the otherwise velvet dark, to alert nobody, their heating working on a timer, to keep the empty house warm and free from damp. Cleaners come in from outside the village to dust cobwebs away and clear dead starlings from the fireplaces, so that the houses feel 'lived in' when they come. Meanwhile, no new smaller houses, no council houses are built since the nineties for retirees, those starting out or young families, stopping the 'cycle of life' provision for a diverse and vibrant community. The remnant rural working class and the young are squeezed out. Tenanted cottages for local people are harder and harder to come by, are damp or poorly maintained, while those let for the occasional weekend are freshly decorated and maintained to a high standard. Roofs leak. Windows drop out. Joan, in her nineties, has a crack in her flint and cob cottage through which she can see the Downs undulate. She seals it with scrunched newspaper. Another neighbour's walls are so damp, the stair banister won't stay screwed to the wall. A line of fruiting fungi pops up in its absence. Down Hollow Lane, the same mains water leak that plagued Miss White is never truly fixed, spilling water all the way down the hill, to the place where she joined Manor Farm's pipes, to pool in the snowdrop-filled dip where The Rushes cottage stood for hundreds of years.

Soon, orders come from the War Ag that unite the team further, as a common target for their frustration and disagreement. 'Oh, they allus knows better, them learned suits in government,' says Bert. Doris, and Julia repeat that old adage with a sigh… 'Farmers have two great enemies: the weather and the government; but sometimes, the weather is good!' All know, however, they need both to survive. Agriculture is expanding rapidly to meet the challenge of feeding its nation and the factories struggle to keep up. So much machinery is being quickly invented and got into the fields before it can be fully tested, and with equipment to buy a year before any returns are made, the situation is tight. Miss White's men work a standard fifty-hour week, with a half-hour 'lunch' at 9.30am and an hour off for dinner. 'Gang' working days, during haymaking or threshing, include an extra break at 3pm and they all get Saturday afternoons and Sundays off. She pays them £3 a week, which is a little over the basic agricultural wage as well as a good allowance of perks: as much firewood as they need, plus milk, manure for the gardens, pig meal, straw and tail corn to feed their chickens. She loads the trailer up each Saturday payday and delivers it, calling in at our local, the Crown and Garter afterwards, to treat herself to some bottled beer and an ice cream for the dogs. These days, the pub sells ice cream especially *for* dogs.

The War Ag have ordered Miss White to dig out the pretty over-grass stream that runs between The Rushes and Walk Meadow from a spring in Champions, and whose route the persistent water leak echoes today. It must be dug out to form a drainage ditch and fenced, giving them a drier, more productive field. They haul the largest roof beams up from derelict Field Barn, to build a tractor bridge across it. Along with growing mangolds, or mangelwurzels as the older company call them, for winter fodder, they must grow two acres of potatoes and two of sugar beet. The latter is particularly unsuited to the chalky soil and the work planting, hoeing the rows and getting them up in particular is hard, muddy, cold and miserable work. They must also plough up difficult fields they'd rather leave as pasture and mourn the loss of these lovely meadows. But what can they do when the largest wheat field in the country is now Windsor Great Park?

Ploughing is a challenge on the hills, with their steep slope 'sidelings'. Unlike a team of horses, the tractor 'sidles' and slides downhill, slewing the lines and proving unstable. With the furrow slices falling from left to right, the plough can only work one way across a hill, as the furrows will not fall uphill. Going straight up and down works on some hills, but on the undulations, the fields become an impractical cross-hatched patchwork of odd-shaped pieces. 'Contour' ploughing round and round the piece seems to be the best way. Fred is a nervous tractor driver on the hills, but Miss White finds something profoundly fascinating and satisfying about ploughing with horse or tractor and often takes over from him. They now have a Fordson tractor of their own, as well as the Allis; blue with orange wheels, in the traditional county colours of the Essex farm carts, taken up by the Ford Factory at Dagenham. It has a three-point linkage and a trailed two-furrow plough. Dina loves to ride on the footplate, the wind blowing her ears. She uses it as a platform and foil to hunting rabbits, resting her head and paws on the single foot pedal before leaping into action. All very amusing but equally disorganising as, when her weight shifts to launch off the pedal, she presses the clutch in and the brake comes on, and they stop. She is never fast enough to catch a rabbit. One day, in full flow with the plough on Bumpy, the most undulating field above the chalk pits, Miss White is preparing to turn uphill when the offside front wheel of the Fordson hits a dip, then a flint the size of an upturned mixing bowl. The Fordson drops its shoulder towards the farm and turns over, throwing both Julia and Dina off and thankfully clear. Julia is winded and shaken but, otherwise, they are both fine. She sits for a dizzy minute or two and looks at the tractor, its nose and steering wheel buried in the soil, the ploughshares up in the air like a broken windmill sail. She brushes herself off and goes to find Arthur with the Allis, to pull the Fordson to its feet.

Ploughing Winsley one day, she spots an audience in Hollow Lane and surmises a likely flock of experts among the curious neighbours. Tractors have been on these fields less than a year, and with today's red-and-yellow headscarf on the blue-and-orange tractor, that shoots out a dog every few lengths, a woman driving it is an extra colour-pop of intrigue. She is self-conscious and takes care on the turn to make the new entry quite straight and keep it that way, lowering 'her shining darlings', as Land Girl and writer Enid Barraud describes her ploughshares, to bite and lovingly turn the earth into curling ribbons. She knows her furrows incline to drift and it is at this point she casually mentions in her diary that she only has one eye; that her other is a glass prosthetic. I've no idea what happened – she does not elaborate – and keeps her focus on the raised stick in the hedge to keep her straight. She waves at the congregation and they wave back. They are beginning to accept her warm friendliness and unabashed inventiveness; her willingness to get stuck in and give it a go. She has become theirs already. Julia finds them confronting and curious, but friendly and helpful. They seem surprisingly and independently (often defiantly) keen, to embrace the new with a haughty, *well, why not?* To go boldly out on a limb to accept difference, as if it is nothing; daring others among them to make a fuss. Julia appreciates and admires this about them.

When the weather has been against them in prolonged spells, Miss White takes over at lunchtimes, so the tractor doesn't stop and Doris joins her on Sundays. They are urged by a campaign on the wireless to continue ploughing by night and, choosing the flatter fields, they do. A guiding lantern is placed in the hedge to give them something to aim for and a hooded lamp is hung on a pole that dangles like a carrot in front of the tractor. It is hard, cold, bewitching work. Their eyes soon adjust, but they are used to going about at night anyway. When the moon is up, silvering all before them, they work in a half-light almost like day, though they feel terribly exposed. On several nights, planes pulse or roar over, and there is the sound of gunfire and bomb bursts away towards Reading or London. Fires light up the sky and searchlights sweep cinematically, reminding them of the peril and necessity of their madness. One night, they hear a low-flying bomber jettison its bombs in the direction of Shalbourne Manor. At the following night's Scout meeting, Julia learns one of the bombs hit the corner of a cottage on the Salisbury Road. The family were unhurt, made a cursory check and were not alerted to any damage until one of the Scouts, who had slept through the rogue raid, woke to see the sky through his bedroom ceiling. The hero of the hour, he brings with him a large, jagged shard of bomb casing, found cooled in his bedclothes in the morning.

Night-ploughing is as thrilling as it is exhausting. It feels like licensed subterfuge; it feels like resistance. The smell of the turning soil is richer, the bark of a fox sharper, the glisten of a cut worm behind them in the moonlight a forgiving. They are surprised by how so many of the birds call at night. In early spring, curlew, lapwing, corncrake, stone curlew; the last golden plover before they head off north to breed. Mournful cries that move a person. Demand to be attended, call out the soul. The night is fresh and loud with them. They are aware of a crossover migration of many birds, like messengers of the earth's function, though they miss the comfort of the lighted cottage windows in the blackout. Billy ploughs late in moonlight with Dolly and Sylvie too, the moon dappling their flanks. It is magical to see the great horses pause on the ridge while Billy adjusts his reins, wraps his hands in rags against the cold, surrounded in a steaming halo of lantern light and dragon breath, his horses jingling their bits and tossing their heads in protest at the late hour, but doing anything for him. He sings as he always does when working, his voice richly melodic, his horses flicking their ears back at the sound they have come now to know and love. He and his team disappear into skeining mist, but he knows he can be heard from an open window in the cottage below, with the light pinched out. It makes him feel less lonely.

There is endless trouble with the new Ransomes plough though. It will not go deep enough and merely slices a butter-thin curl off the surface of the earth. Or drives itself into the ground. Then the lifting gear will not work. Arthur and Miss White fiddle with it constantly. There are hold-ups. More night-ploughing. So many of the implements are resurrected and patched from obsolete machinery, parts can't be got and things constantly break down. Kit is invented. The tip cart is adapted to be pulled by a tractor or Boxer. Sheila is proving more of a hindrance than a help. Tied to a hedge, she spins and neighs and paws the ground, lathers herself in sweat, slithers into a ditch and almost gets stuck. More than once she gets away and gallops across a field of newly sown potatoes, puts her foot through her reins and breaks her bridle, heads off over hedges like a point-to-pointer, surprising Bert. Sheila is not suited to farm work and Julia finds her a good, local home with Mr Frank Moore and buys a sweet, sensible bay pony called Tommy from Marguerite. He will happily be ridden or driven in the little trap, and stands patient as a cab horse, pulling leaves or twigs from any hedge he is tied to, rather than trying to jump it.

The horses vanish so quickly from the countryside, in just a few short years, it is astonishing. And with them, so much else – wildflower meadows, clouds of butterflies, blooms of insects, worms from the soil, birds from the sky, and people and their voices from the land. Singing. Mechanisation saves people, it feeds them; it allows ease to those punishing hard jobs and lives and covers the yawing gaps in labour. But it goes off at such a roaring pace and continues on its path, without stopping to look around itself, to pause and reflect, to look at what it might be damaging or destroying or losing in its wake. To notice and heed the gradual silencing of the countryside for the warning it is, rather than ignoring this literal, collective, canary in the coalmine. There are no checks, no balances, no adjustments. No looking out over the side, only observations, stories and laments, too easily dismissed.

It hurts to look back and pinpoint the start of the slow poisoning and starving of the birds and insects with the new chemicals to this time. The ploughing-up of all those insect-filled meadows, the uncountable, bouncing flocks of linnets, yellowhammers, goldfinches, thick as gauze across the vision. The birds that came with the horses – the swallows in the stables, the house martins in the eves, the yellow wagtails and meadow pipits that all feed on the insects around grazing animals and their dung in meadows, the sparrows around the granary, the barn owl in the hayloft and across the fields.

The horses are still relied upon for now. Petrol is rationed further and the breaking down of such new machinery in a spell of good weather may mean the loss of an entire crop. But if all is going well, the Allis, or the blue-and-orange Fordson, can sow and harrow two acres an hour, which it would take a two-horse team more than a day to do.

Three miles away, a German bomber aiming his bombs at the London to Bristol railway line and a local single road bridge misses. Most of his bombs land in the water meadows either side of the canal and the River Kennet, creating new pools, but one flies in through a carthorse stable door. The ploughman and his wife there are woken by an almighty roar, a detonation, and he goes out with a flashlight. The yard appears unscathed, the building all up, just some splintering around the loosebox door frame and silence. He calls to reassure his horses, his team, but there is no sound. He approaches the double loose box with building dread and, his senses heightened, smells then the familiar iron tang of blood, notes a terrible black shadow approaching him from under the door. No, he says, no. Not my team. But there is no saving them. They are both gone, the bay Clydesdale and the black Shire, killed instantly.

He sits on an upturned pail in the yard, lit softly by the dropped flashlight in the low mist coming off the river, and weeps. His wife comes down then, crosses the yard in her clogs and takes in the scene. Swallows. Nothing but service, he says, nothing but serve. He remembers others in the First World War. Has treated every animal, every child since like he owes them the world and would give it if he could. 'What has any of it got to do with them?' he asks.

CHAPTER TWELVE

Harvest, Home, Hurrahing

April–August 1942

Farming and rural work is hard on clothes at the best of times. Mud, muck and animals, thorns, flints and barbed wire, oil and bits of machinery all take their toll, tearing and smearing, abrading and catching, fraying and staining – and the weather, particularly the harsh wartime winters, makes matters far worse. By Miss White's own admission, they all look like scarecrows. Arthur laments several remembered garments he dressed a scarecrow with, before the war. Sacking is employed liberally. Tied around waists, around thighs and in place of gaiters, and worn as capes or even hoods tucked under caps and hats. For lack of baler twine, strips are often peeled from the twining stems of traveller's joy, or bedwine, as they call it. Sometimes used to tie stooks or puffs of hazel sticks, it is readily available. 'We'll all become hedges ourselves,' says Miss White, in her tattered greatcoat. Clothes soaked through before lunch or dinner don't dry out, so the men take to coming out in their Home Guard uniforms. Very smart.

Inkpen Home Guard is a flourishing and enthusiastic affair, and Miss White is keen to support it. She accepts a request from the Civil Defence to step up as ARP Warden for the parish. There hasn't been one and, quite shockingly, no gas masks have been issued at all. Five hundred of the terrifying but necessary things arrive, as soon as she is in post, for the scattered parishioners. They are issued at the village hall, built in 1924 on the edge of Manor Farm's land in an active, hopeful, galvanising memorial of community cohesion, after the First World War. Several of Miss White's men or their wives' families suffered personal losses in that war and its role in bringing the community together in practical, social, healthy or fun endeavour is greatly valued. The Women's Institute set up an industry of fruit canning and bottling there, and there are wedding receptions, dental clinics and Nursing Society meetings; war weapons work and a labour exchange, meetings of the Boys Club, Choral Society and Labour Party, plays and fundraising whist drives, harvest suppers, parties and defiant dances under blackout to a great and exciting variety of bands. Inkpen has two itself in some opposition – The Temperance Band and The Guzzeleers, both remarkably accomplished. Eventually, they merge. Few of them can read music, but they play beautifully, with musical instinct, by ear. They have a smashing uniform and include two girls among the dozen or more 'Bandsmen'. Julia's Bert plays the euphonium and Jailer the trombone, and the band regularly 'blow the roof off' the little village hall. The renowned pianist Solomon Cutner comes to perform, on a treasured piano carried around the corner from Beacon House, the Inkpen home of his friend and tutee, Victor Bonham-Carter; himself a farmer as well as an author and subeditor of *The Countryman* magazine and a champion, campaigner and planner of vibrant village life.

In 2024, we celebrate our village hall's centenary, giving the 'old girl' a party and singing happy birthday, blur-eyed at so many memories of being in the place. On the fuzzy green baize of the borrowed display board among many photos, there is one of Miss White and Manor Farm; another of the men of the Home Guard.

Our reminisces inevitably turn to things we can't sustain any more – a band, a choir, a youth club, falling numbers at Scouts, and at the primary school as no new houses are built, as smaller ones are rebuilt bigger or extended, as rented homes become second or holiday homes, as wealthier parents move in and send their children out of the village to private schools. But, we've been here before, I say, and our old girl and her community has survived. We do different things. As we leave, linking arms, we pass one of the village's oldest thatched cottages that Mum's friends, Lin and Brenny, were born in and who have done – and do – so much in the community. With Mum, they provide tea, coffee, bacon rolls and laughter at the village market once a month and still live here, in housing built just after the war ended. Their childhood thatched cottage is chocolate-box pretty and sits on the Airbnb website, next to a village hall it can no longer support.

Miss White has co-opted three Assistant Wardens: a neighbouring farmer, a local builder, Frank Carter, and Lady Clarke Jervoise of Kirby House, our 'Big House'. She receives a wooden box containing twelve triangular bandages, six tourniquets and a pair of scissors in case of casualties. She wonders where the rest of the kit is; it hardly seems sufficient. There is also a gas rattle (temptingly handy for crow and pigeon scaring) an armband and a tin plate for the roadside farm gate with ARP Warden on it – she is disappointed not to get a nice tin hat with 'W' on it, or a uniform, but then, when would she wear that?

At the village hall mask fitting, the parish is jolly and sociable and there are plenty of jokes about the masks being better (years) late than never, and them being no longer abandoned to their own fate. All but one of the villagers is fitted up with a mask – a man with a very big beard who refuses his – and Miss White manages to get two extra infant masks for her dogs. Not that she thinks she'd get them into one.

She is also issued with three tons of emergency food to be stored at the farm, in case the village should be cut off by enemy action or find itself under siege. Tins of biscuits, tea, sugar, dried milk and margarine, corned beef and ham are tucked away out of sight in the granary and changed regularly by a visiting wholesaler. It is beautifully packed and secure and must, she imagines, be always fresh and wholesome. I am first surprised and then heartened that the government would go to the lengths and expense to support its scattered outer parishes and resist occupation to the bitter end. Manor Farm's employees and residents are told by Civil Defence that they must not tell anyone about this secret bountiful larder, and they don't. Two stirrup pumps for potential fires, however, are utilised for whitewashing the cow sheds and stables.

In the 1940s, Inkpen's Home Guard becomes a legend in its own right. All Miss White's men belong to it except Bert Wright, who says he is in the fire brigade. To her secret amusement, that sometimes rises unbidden to her lips, Julia later finds out by chance there is no local fire brigade. When Bert is eventually conscripted into the Home Guard, he grumbles that he 'doesn't agree with all that left right stuff'. She is quite sure he doesn't. A brother four years older than he, and one of twins, was killed in Flanders in the First World War.

The Home Guard meet most Sunday mornings at Manor Farm or occasionally at the village hall, and Julia readily accepts a request for help with exercises. The small town of Hungerford challenges Inkpen Home Guard to capture a roadblock on Strongrove Hill, past Undy's Cottage on the road to Marlborough. The Inkpen contingent devise a plan to go by train from the village of Kintbury, four miles away, and avoid detection. Miss White and a neighbour, masquerading as innocent housewives, meet the men, who cram into the two cars and speed towards the roadblock, making a surprise 'attack' from the rear, firing deafening blanks from their rifles out the car windows. Julia holds her nerve and 'Hungerford' is captured without much resistance, but a 'bang off' thrown at the car means she has to swerve violently to miss it. Or was it a hit? After an hour of deliberation from the judges, when much fraternisation between the parish Guards takes place, Inkpen is deemed to have dodged the 'grenade' and is victorious. She is given three cheers from the Inkpenners, who are raucous on the return journey.

On another occasion, Inkpen comes up against the tiny neighbouring village of West Woodhay. Sergeant Goodhart, a rather imaginative civil engineer, suggests employing a Trojan Horse tactic in the form of Miss White's big trailer, loaded up with straw bales around the sides. The Home Guard soldiers cram into the dusty innards with neckerchiefs tied over their mouths and noses to ameliorate against audible coughs and sneezes. It is cave-like and somewhat comforting, this wall of protection and concealment they have sown, grown, cut down, threshed and baled, all in a year where the world is on fire and the future uncertain. They feel close and docile as cattle, as if for a moment they have given themselves over to whatever will come. Julia pulls her load into the hamlet with the blue-and-orange Fordson, smoothly, unchallenged and with suppressed glee. 'Who would suspect a woman?' Sergeant Goodhart says, twinkling. 'How terribly naive,' she says, with an arched eyebrow. She stops and bangs the Fordson's wheel arch with a hoof pick from her pocket, so the sound rings out and reaches them. The soldiers push off the top bales, jump out with a roar and take West Woodhay by surprise. Woodhay quickly concede before they all repair, ribbing each other mercilessly, to the Crown and Garter for refreshments. Fun, like passion, like dancing behind blackouts, like recklessly and suddenly falling in love or lust, or like stopping to take in the land and its people in a certain cinematic light, appreciating afresh what you have and forgiving the most entrenched grudges, is a form of resistance too.

But when the village of Ham's Home Guard come to capture Manor Farm, the invaders are thwarted almost before they begin and take unkindly to the mocking banter. They elect to approach through the woods at Dagg's Gully, putting up cawing rooks and woodpigeons clattering off in alarm. A rookie error at the rookery. A sign any gamekeeper, trespasser, naturalist or lone female wildlife watcher knows is as good as an alarm bell. The Inkpen men all turn and face the spinney, fold their arms or point their rifles and wait, clapping and jeering when the Ham men come through. Frustrated and embarrassed perhaps, some members of Ham's Home Guard do not see the funny side. There is pushing and shoving. Someone goes down and someone else steps forward, hats are whipped off heads and thrown, collars grabbed and a fist hits a bristly chin. Sergeant Goodhart and Miss White come running, blowing whistles, employing the gas rattle. Inkpen remains unbeaten and in roaring form.

Late spring, the death of a rat precipitates work starting on the farmhouse. The old dwelling is divided into two parts; the oldest north-facing half is eighteenth-century and is where the Braziers live, until Fred hands his notice in, mistrusting the tractor and deciding the work isn't for him. They remain friends and Julia is grateful for their winter of sacrifice in this cold and dilapidated house. Mrs Walters offers to come on for Julia as general help in the house and she, Arthur and their two little girls, Rosie and Dorrie, move in. Julia enjoys having the two little girls around very much; and with two, and sometimes three, small evacuee boys, the house is busy and full. The Walters have the north wing, which gives them a lot of space, as well as the large kitchen, dairy and a bathroom (sans water and plumbing, of course) with beautiful wide, elm floorboards. Julia has the wing facing Gallows Down and Walbury Hill, with views of Rivars Down, above Shalbourne.

In the drawing room, one day, an occasional bad smell intensifies into a familiar reality: a dead rat. She clambers down the breakneck stairs to the water level below the old house – the cellar is a veritable indoor pool, two feet deep in winter – but no dead rat is spotted. Jack and Billy find it, pulling the lath and plaster of the cellar ceiling down. Miss White knows this, because they have placed the rat on her doorstep as proof, for when she comes in to dinner. While they are down there, they discover one of the huge oak beams supporting the upper floors of the house has been dangerously compromised by previous improvements, leaving the great supporting beam sitting on barely an inch of brickwork. If not for the rat, the sitting-room floor, furniture, Julia, Dina, Jo and perhaps the children would have found themselves disappeared into the water-filled cellar beneath, this year perhaps, or next.

Ever-versatile Jailer builds a supporting pillar, and Julia is forced to think about the farmhouse and the winter to come – it is a miserable prospect. If not for condemning the Braziers to suffer alone on her behalf, she would have decamped to the caravan last winter. She doesn't want to lose the Walters and has a duty towards keeping the girls and the evacuees warm and comfortable, so she concedes to Jailer's sensible suggestions with relief. The house is renovated as best as they can manage over the summer. Julia is glad to see the back of the last grubby, depressing grey walls patched with ghostly blanks where another life once hung. A continuous-burning stove is installed in the shared dining room and downstairs at least is much warmer. By the end of the summer, mains water has been got into the house, with a coke boiler for hot water. WCs are installed at last; although, when she pays and thanks the painter, he tells her the lavatory seat is freshly varnished and she can't use it for another three days. Vexing, to say the least.

The seasons roll on, marked by activity in the fields: rolling to consolidate, tiller and root the growing corn, and to push the flints down after the 'winter heave' brings them to the surface. There is harrowing and weeding of root crops with the horse-hoe, and singling mangolds, turnips, potatoes and beets. The farm is slowly filling with animals. Four geese have become fifteen and are a joy to see around the place, their eggs and the occasional bird, a treat. The calves are turned out onto the grass pasture, bucking and skittering, and everyone pauses, smiling wordlessly to watch the joyous spectacle, and there is a field of ponies from Shalbourne to bring and sell on.

The tricksy, time-consuming process of haycart (haymaking or *aycrut*, as the men call it) is got going in fine spells, with all hands involved. Much time and discussion are spent on decoding the weather reports given on the BBC, and reading the weather coming to them over the hill. For haycart, they have a mowing machine, an angled side rake to make the lines or windrows, a swath turner and an old American car, missing most of its floorboards. Jailer has adapted a hay sweep, like a giant fork, to attach to the front of it. Miss White drives, sweeping mounds of golden-green hay before her, delivering it to Jack and Billy, who fork it onto the elevator. When it breaks down, as it inevitably does, one man must stand halfway up the stack in the 'pitch hole', receiving a forkful of hay and passing it on up to the stack builders. Bert then thatches the stack with 'yelms' (bundles) of long wheat straw, so it has some protection from wind and rain. The sweet-smelling and soft hay that comes out of traditional haystack building is, Miss White assures me in her diary, much better quality than the new way of baling windrows straight off the field, which, admittedly, needs much less manpower.

She makes the two types: 'hard' seed hay, mostly ryegrass sown in a one-year ley for the purpose, or soft meadow hay, which contains a rich variety of wild-growing grasses, fragrant clovers and bedstraws, and falls before the mower in a puff of purple and gold pollen smoke in the June sunshine, that thousands of butterflies rise up through. *That* is one of my favourite scents – and it seems I'm not alone. It is replicated as 'coumarin' in expensive perfumes, or simply by lying in a sun-baked field in June or July.

There are, of course, Land Girls to help. Billeted and shared between the farms in the village, these women are 'awfully nice girls', hard-working and a breath of fresh air. Julia and Doris are delighted to welcome more women on the land and are amused at the effect they have on some of the shocked and unprepared men. Arthur comes into the yard flustered and perspiring one already-hot summer morning, having failed to deliver a message to the girls to come to the hayfield. While the dew evaporates, they do the morning job of hoeing roots in Village Hall Piece. Miss White goes to see what the matter is, which Arthur is relaying, flush-cheeked, to the others. 'Miss, they have taken their cloeds off. I can't speak to them in that state! You must sort it!' Julia rides Tommy up to the field to find the women hoeing hard in a singing and merry line. In the blistering heat, they have indeed discarded shirts, dungarees and corduroy trousers, and are hoeing in their bras and knickers. Very fetching, she snorts, waves, tells them they are getting on very well but will burn! 'We want a nice suntan!' they say. 'And there's no one about to see us!' One merry girl with a headscarf as bright as her lipstick asks provocatively, 'Do we shock you, Miss White?' Miss White smiles. 'Goodness, no. There was a mould before you, and people who broke it!' The women look delightedly shocked at this. 'Miss *White!*' they chorus. She chuckles to herself riding back, calling, 'Come on to the hayfield, but you might get dressed or the men will not recover!' She leans down to pat the pony on the neck, and says, 'I *have* lived, Tommy, I have indeed lived!' The following day, she asks the girls if they are sunburnt. 'Yes, terribly,' they reply. 'We won't be doing that again, the men are perfectly safe.'

With the government and War Ag Committee urging all farms to double their output, labour is a constant need and lack. The Land Girls, when they can come on for Manor Farm, are a real boon. Other soldiers come and go, as well as Italian and German prisoners of war from the camp in Newbury, who can be ordered by telephone and come with a British soldier as guard. John Dymond often joins in as casual labour at these times and fits in well with the team. He is a big, tall man and could be construed as intimidating, until one gets to know him. Having rolled all around the world, he has settled down in Inkpen, to an extent. Coming and going with the weather or the seasons, he is a sort of professional poacher and hugely knowledgeable. Miss White values knowing him and they become friends. She lets John shoot game on the farm as long as some is shared with her and the farm men, as food is short. They are glad of the rabbits. He keeps an eye on the place, letting her know if a fence is broken or some thatch has blown off a rick. This big, rather upright, soldierly man is often to be seen around the farm foraging with a little basket of flowers or berries. He makes wonderful concoctions and wines from dandelions, elderberries or blackberries and mangolds, and makes presents of them to Julia, at Christmas. On one occasion, when she is short of food and has a friend coming to dinner, she asks if he'd mind getting her two young rabbits. He comes later with two beautiful, fat, cock pheasants that must have been released by Major Huth for his shoot next door, saying very drolly that he was sorry, he'd aimed at a rabbit and missed. A surprising thing to have happened.

That first harvest is never forgotten by Julia. Billy and his brothers, Dick and Charlie, come on to open up the ways around the edge of the oats first, for the reaper binder, with great long scythes. And it is a pleasure to see them work. All in their forties, they used to do all the fields like this, with followers behind, collecting and binding the sheaves, not so long ago. The reaper binder is a Canadian model and left-handed, so that it cuts around a field anticlockwise and throws out the tied sheaves to the right. After that, the followers pull in two sheaves at a time by the waist, rubbing their shockheads together slightly to 'catch' and stand four or six up against each other in tent-like stooks. In her Day Book and Cultivations Record, Julia writes: 'Uncertain stormy weather, all hands shocking up after tea. Geese are blissful. Oats a terrible mess.' In later years, opening up the ways with scythes is too time-consuming, so they go straight in with the reaper binder, despite it damaging the first cut edge a little so the followers must catch or rescue the first delivered sheaves from off or over the hedge or the barbed wire. They make a sport of it.

For a time, the excitement of harvest attracts a gang of wild boys, intent on mischief; Sally Colquhoun, our farming neighbour and a little girl at the time, remembers Miss White as 'quite the harridan' then. There was a lot to keep order on. As the cutting gets close to the middle of the field, sundry villagers arrive with sticks and dogs to catch the rabbits caught in the middle, then fleeing. It is 'fair game' and the rabbits are taken home for tea. It gets dangerous at times and Miss White takes her turn riding the binder, shouting fierce warnings to move out of the way. Six boys from a school harvest camp come to help and, every year, the Scouts. More often than not, they are divided up. Jos Digweed comes to watch and supervise, occasionally repeating an old adage I've often heard while helping the gamekeeper with something and the teenage 'boys' are lobbing corn cobs at each other across the maize: 'One boy's a boy, two boys is 'alf a boy, and three boys is no boy at all!'

One 'whole boy' drives the tractor while another loads with the other pitchers, jabbing the long-handled, two-grained pitch fork into the sheaves with the curved tines upwards, so, with a swing and a half-turn of the wrist, they slip easily off into the trailer or cart. Miss White teaches the boys and some of the soldiers this, but the Land Girls are proficient, it being their second or third harvest. Bert is a renowned and beautiful rick builder and all work to his instructions. Once the rick is built – Manor Farm's are pitch-roofed and round, going in at the bottom with a wide middle girth – Bert goes 'yelming' to thatch and keep them watertight and windproof. Jack is his assistant. Handfuls of straw are pulled evenly from the bottom of the rick, or a loose pile, and lined up and layered into a straight bundle, or 'yelm'. This is carried in a big, forked hazel stick up a long thatching ladder, wider at the base than it is at the top, and laid and pegged with hazel spars. The fields have turned into little golden hamlets of what look very like medieval round houses, though most tower above cottage height. Solid straw houses. Bert frequently wins first prize in rick building at Newbury Agricultural Show and Miss White is inordinately proud of him and the ricks. In fact, he seems to take it in turns to win with Jos Digweed's son, who works for Frank Moore.

Tea comes into the field at 5pm on an old carriage pram pushed by Mrs Walters. It has 'Manor Farm Tea Car' painted in white on one side and 'A rick a day keeps Hitler away' on the other. She and everyone else flop down in the scented, prickly-shorn field in the shade of the rick before they carry on into the evening. It is a hard-worked but jovial affair; their numbers swelled by friends and neighbours and whoever else is on hand. When they are all working in the field together, there is a profound and intense feeling of communal endeavour and cooperation that washes over them all. When the last sheaf in a field is picked up, that person has the honour of calling theatrically, 'This is the one we were looking for!' A cheer goes up and the gleaners, some of the women and all the children, come on to the field to pick up any stray ears of corn to take for themselves, in pillow cases, cans and baskets. The machines are more efficient than the scything gang, but a little corn is always left behind by the men – the husbands of the gleaners and the beneficiaries.

It is a memorable harvest, though not the best. August was wet and windy in part, flattening and lowering some of the waiting corn so it got lodged and was difficult and slow to cut. Some of the oats from Champions have been ricked damp, that field being so full of green weeds and charlock it took too long to dry and Miss White got impatient. The rick begins to heat and has to be pulled down before it catches fire and spoils the oats. There are a few home truths from her men about patience, but she is able to sell the discarded weed seeds from the thresher on as wild birdseed. With harvest safely gathered in, Julia, Mrs Walters and Bert's niece put on a Harvest Supper for the farm people and all who helped. With more than thirty invited, she borrows trestle tables and benches from the village hall as well as plates, cutlery and glasses from neighbours. She and Mrs Walters set a long table down the middle of the newly retiled granary and, using bedsheets as tablecloths, even find a few flowers and ears of corn to decorate the table with. They muster as many hurricane lamps as they can find to hang around the walls and they give off a beautiful friendly glow.

All invited come, and Miss White makes a short welcome speech before sitting at the head of the table with Miss Mason and Miss de Beaumont either side, and Jos Digweed and the Rector at the other end. Rosie and Dorrie act as excellent and very sweet waitresses and they all sit down to eat their own produce – roast goose and potatoes, vegetables and apple pie made beautifully by Mrs Walters. With a barrel of beer set up on the sawing horse, the party goes with a swing. Someone has an accordion, Bert his euphonium, Doris and Marguerite a ukulele and guitar between them, and Jack Tucker comes over from Shalbourne with his fine old hurdy gurdy. Led by Marguerite, they spend the evening singing old country folk songs, with a few new ones they know, and spark up the floor with their hobnail boots. It is wet and windy outside but snug within, and they are warmed by a friendly, joyous feeling between them, of living in the present and making the best of it. Not sure if they dare to imagine what the future might hold. Miss White has learnt so much from them. When she apologises for the decision to rick the damp oats at Champions again, they bang their glasses on the table, drum their feet and roar, 'Ah, there's always next year! We shall do better next year!'

CHAPTER THIRTEEN

The Old Chalk Track to the Sky and a Pocket of Bells

August–June 1943

During the wet spell in August, Miss White finds herself with a lot of hired help and volunteers – her farm men, Land Girls, a handful of soldiers, harvest camp boys, a few girls and Scouts – willing to get stuck into something, but unable to get on with the harvest. She has an idea and puts it to the men. They decide to build a new road from the old beech tree on the Combe Road, down Parson's Hill to the old track, which is rough, deeply rutted and far too steep for comfort, especially as the War Ag insists the hill must now be ploughed. Getting all the required kit up and down will be difficult at the very least. So, in the unseasonal wind and rain, in this exposed spot, they set to, wrapped in sacks, to make a new mark on the land.

Arthur sets off with the Fordson to plough up and down the plotted route so the earth curves away in narrow ribbons. The soil is so thin up here on the high chalk that occasionally the ploughshare gouges the chalk. They wonder if they can grow a crop up here at all. Then the collected gang of men, women, girls and boys begin with whatever implement they have found – spades, shovels, rakes and hoes – to remove the soil. It comes away like the pelt then skin of an animal and carefully, laboriously, they pare it back to white bone. The Scouts decide the road has always been there, a covered up Roman road that gladiators last trod. They work, digging, tamping and levelling in a week of relentless rain that is ruining the rest of the harvest. It's a good distraction if nothing else. They stop for dinner in Wergs Barn and go back out again in the same wet clothes. I'm reminded of conservation holiday weekends doing the same thing. At least it is warm. It thunders. Low cloud like smoke wreathes along the down above them, and before the week is up, the rough chalk road is finished and is such a success, the old perilous one begins to grow over. They are rather proud of their endeavours. Particularly Miss White. The road is marked on the next Ordnance Survey map.

After harvest, the race is on to prepare the ground again for the following year, and deal with the root crops. Sid, another member of the Walters family, is taken on as tractor man and a second Fordson tractor is purchased. This later model is easier to start and painted the same dark green of the now-camouflaged Dagenham factory it came out of, but it has iron tyres with gripping spuds as rubber tyres are increasingly scarce. All the old grass leys must now be put down to wheat, so the meadows and downland of Picket Piece, Pebbles, Black Butts, Hayes, Bumpy and Parson's Hill, using the new road, are all ploughed for the first time, perhaps ever. It's a formidable programme and some of the hills dangerously steep.

Reading Mrs Frankie Donaldson's farming books, Miss White tries filling the blue-and-orange Fordson's tyres with water as ballast instead of air, and this improves its grip enormously. Soon, others are doing this on neighbouring farms and what started off as a Manor Farm eccentricity becomes good practice. Billy is busy carting potatoes, mangolds, turnips and beets to the train station, and carting and scaling dung from the two-wheeled Scotch tip cart, often with prisoners of war or Land Girls to help. Miss White has to tackle the Ministry of Agriculture's form-filling to apply for oak posts and slabbing from Inkpen sawmills to repair Wergs Barn, its yard and skillings (the open-fronted in-yard shelters). After forty questions relating to iron girders, size of site and number of blitzed houses, her modest request is refused, twice. Mr Edwards at the sawmills recommends she apply for 'wood to repair farm gates and implements' instead, and in this she is successful, although, she says as she laughs with him, 'Most of the gates I have are Hosier gates!' Named after the pioneering neighbouring farmer, Arthur Hosier, who invented the mobile milking parlour bail in 1922, I realise these are my barbed wire-and-stake 'Hampshire gates' and smile at how Hosier has become Hampshire between Miss White's time and mine, and the local accent: *ampsheer*, *ohzure*. Wergs Barn is beautifully repaired and thatched, the cows are housed and the mangolds earthed up and clamped under straw thatch for fodder in the skillings. What's left of Field Barn, having been stripped of much of its resources, is rebuilt smaller, and thatched.

I wish I'd seen it like that, instead of the blown-apart state I knew it in, before it fell down. By the time I know Wergs Barn, a few years into the new millennium, it is in a ruinous state, with part of the roof gone and black beams jutting out as if after a fire. Bits of sixty-three-year-old thatch stick out from a corner of its corrugated iron roof. It is a sudden and arresting sight. Neglected and unused, it has become a gothic relic. Had it been upkept, it may well have been a luxurious house by now, and I'm not sure how I feel about that. I look up the name 'Wergs'. It is also the name of the lane it is on – or one of them. Wergs Lane is also Hollow Lane and the latter part of Rooksnest Lane. If there ever were any road name signs here, they weren't put back after the war. Wergs, from the Old English *withegas*: willows; a wet, rushy place. Or *wyrcan*, *weorc*: to do; something done. Work.

Sometimes I take a longer route to school to pass it and go through Manor Farm, with the dog and the baby in the pram. Sometimes, I hurry past. Today, on a still, bright afternoon, I park the pram and the dog under some hazel trees and creep in through a gap where a big door once was, pushing through tall nettles and brambles. Light pours into one half, and in the other enters in laser shafts and beams in all thicknesses – needle, pencil, plank – and I let them play on my hands. There is a powerful feeling of something just settled. Of something that has just left the place. In a pool of honey light on the floor are the rounded cylinders of barn owl pellets. Still a working barn then, I think, and smile. I pocket some to dissect with my son later and squint up at the high roof beams, but the apex of this cathedral roof is in darkness. I imagine the barn owl opening one eye up there on her beam, shifting a foot. I must not disturb her. I cross the old threshing floor and spot a collection of feed bags folded in a corner, some metal sheep hurdles, an elder tree growing up out of the floor that exudes its distinct bacon smell as I brush past. Then in the furthest corner somebody moves, says something cheery in a woman's voice, as if speaking to an animal, clanks a metal pail, rattles some feed nuts into what looks, in the monk-brown light, like a manger. I can smell the sweet, grassy smell of cows then; sugar beet; am shocked the building is still in use. Ashamed of my intrusion, I back out quietly.

I peer in cautiously the following day. The building creaks, shifts a hip. As I'd previously thought, there is no sign that any cows have been housed here for years and I am puzzled. A little spooked, but surely mistaken. I must have imagined the cows. The woman could have been talking to a dog, a cat. Herself, even. I don't know it then, but I think she is there for the first time: Miss White.

About two weeks later, the great old barn comes down in a storm. Branches have been wrenched from trees, there are beaches of flint, gravel and chalk cobbles washed up along the lane. Beside the barn, I find a small collection of spilled echinoid fossils, the smooth, round, track-indented pebbles of shepherd's crowns or thunderstones. The barn's enormous, ancient timbers lie exposed and crossed, like a bonfire, the tin roof lifting like a lifeless pheasant's wing in the wind. Weather-bent planks lie like a flotsam tide, knot holes peering like so many eyes. I picture the barn's sway and collapse. The barn owl fleeing. We are close enough to have heard it falling, but didn't. I am inexplicably sad. All that air, that golden light, mote and storage, that shelter, that place of safety, warmth, animals and work. What's left doesn't seem enough to have contained all those centuries of life it held, the harvests, the threshing, the tides of depleting and building up again, the tithing; repairs and repurposing. The chatter. All gone back to air, seed, dust, nothing. The light let go.

Being listed, a new, smaller, traditionally built barn replaces it nearer to the farm and the old site is planted up as a small copse.

The barn owl moves to a new metal cowshed. But the name remains. Even in council road closure notifications (when we get them), it is: 'the unnamed road from Wergs Barn to Weavers Lane'. In certain lights, especially at night, I can still see its outline. A resistance to the penetration of my headlights or torch, or an afterimage imprinted on the eye, a lasting palinopsia. A barn-shaped space of darker sky. A barn-shaped piece of lightness.

Meanwhile, Bill Knight is given the task of supervising ten schoolboys to lift the potatoes. But the boys play him up and potatoes are thrown. Bill threatens to 'take a stick' to them. Julia has a stern word with Bill and the boys, relieving Bill and, as the oldest boy has set himself up as foreman, challenges him to act like one. Her tactic works, and the boys prove useful. During the early part of the war, schoolboys are allowed to work six hours a day and girls four, and they are often given such tasks as hoeing and do very well; they are missed when new regulations send them all back to school.

Six German POWs arrive to help tackle the hard and hateful job of lifting beets. Julia is always out of pocket with the sugar beet and it does so poorly on the chalk. Half of Inkpen's earth (which she has to pay for in weight) seems to cling to them all the way to the extraction plant by train in Kidderminster. The vegetable pulp left over from the sugar-extraction process is sent back to farmers to feed cattle with and Julia mixes hers with chaff, root tops and chopped mangolds in a sweet-smelling fodder. When I wander into Wergs Barn that day and think someone is there, it's what I can smell; familiar, comforting and evocative, the sugar-beety scent of barn floor and autumnal tar-spotted sycamore leaves; the winter feed-room smell of sugar-beet pulp soaking and swelling in buckets. But what a bitter, super-charged political thing sugar is, from cane to beet: a nation-shaping industry, profiting from the shame of historical slavery and indentured labour of others, through to the modern decimation of wildlife. I look at my Golden Syrup tin pen pots and the familiar nostalgia of their green-and-gold vintage image, the oldest logo in the world. I'm still warmed by childhood memories of Sunday tea's 'treacle on toast', and remember the shock of realising what the image depicted – the biblical, Victorian illustration of bees leaving the honeyed body cavity of a dead lion. Samson's Old Testament riddle 'Out of the strong came forth sweetness' accompanies the image, and while it is hard to decipher its baffling and contradictory meaning (Samson killed the lion), its message on a tin of sugar and that industry's historical association with slavery is suddenly cloying. I think also of the four lorryloads of bees just one teaspoon of the Cruiser SB neonicotinoid seed coating kills, according to Professor Dave Goulson, while it prevents aphids spreading virus yellows disease on sugar beet. The 2018 ban on neonicotinoids has been overridden for the last few years under pressure from British Sugar, though it looks to hold this year. I think of the sugar-loaf sculptures in grand houses and the sugar tax on soft drinks. And I think of all the variations of sugar in my kitchen cupboard; the silver sugar spoon with the little wren on the handle that I use to sweeten my porridge oats in the morning.

In the late afternoon of 10 February 1943, two German Dornier bombers follow the Great Western Railway line running west from London on a 'nuisance tip-and-run raid' upon Reading and Newbury; the latter just seven miles away. Arthur, Jack and Billy, ploughing on the higher ground, see one of the planes bank, and most of them hear the bombs. It is awful not knowing what has happened until Miss White enquires from Peggy Cruse, the journalist at the local paper, calling in at her cottage later. In Newbury, there is no time for an air raid warning. As children walk home from the senior council school, they hear a roar and look up to see a German plane dropping sticks at tree-top height. Eight high-explosive bombs drop on the school, St John's Church, St Bartholomew's Almshouses and Southampton Terrace, destroying them and damaging another 265 buildings. Just the altar of the church remains standing. Fifteen people are killed, including three schoolchildren and two of their teachers. Forty-one are injured, twenty-five seriously. The police and Home Guard have to keep the crowds back to make a safe, organised search for survivors. The forward and dorsal gunners strafe the high street but, as it is half-day closing on a Wednesday afternoon, the streets are all but empty.

Eight minutes earlier, the other bomber flew in over Reading, dropping four 1,000-pound bombs over the centre of town. It is half-day closing there too, but forty-one people are killed; twenty-nine of them dining, serving or queuing for tea in the People's Pantry. The only place open, it is one of the government-sponsored British Restaurants set up to provide cheap, hot, off-ration meals, and give people cheer and somewhere to go. It is run by the Women's Voluntary Service. Michael Bond, creator of Paddington Bear, was working for the BBC on a transmitter in the attic rooms above the restaurant. He was able to make his way unhurt down the partially destroyed stairs. The Dornier guns the streets of Reading too, sending people running for their lives, but again, at teatime on a half-day Wednesday, the streets are quieter than they might be. All the same, the attack also leaves 150 injured.

It's funny how we try to rationalise or make sense of events such as these, using such quintessentially British markers: early closing, teatimes, market day; distance in miles. Because it was a Wednesday teatime in Newbury, the school was all but empty and the streets quiet. Because it was a Wednesday early closing teatime in Reading, the People's Pantry was the only place to be. Because it was a Wednesday, summer school-holiday market day in Hungerford in 1987, the unemployed farmworker, familiar to us all by sight, was able to kill, injure and affect so many people. The night before, I stop on the common with a lad from sixth form on the way home from a village hall party. We walk in the velvet dark lapping the edge of the little town, the Downs silhouetted behind us like the hangars full of grain he works in. Just as I am about to step off the high bank onto the thin black ribbon of asphalt that runs through the common, a barn owl screeches from a hollow oak beside us; momentarily frightened, I feel bodily that I've made a terrible misstep, my brain mistaking the road for the canal, and I shriek at the prospect of falling into the black water, laughing when I don't. The following day, as Hungerford's tragedy unfolds, I am seven miles away, at home. In Reading, you can still see shrapnel marks in the walls of St Laurence's Church, next to where the People's Pantry stood, and on a faded, tractor-flail-battered road sign on the way back to Inkpen from Hungerford, you can count the bullet holes from that market day, or the days before it, when he was practising.

Frances Partridge describes a British Restaurant in nearby Swindon as 'a huge elephant-house, where thousands and thousands ... were eating an all-beige meal'. There are, of course, no British Restaurants in the villages, though there is one in nearby Hungerford. Inkpen is still outside of the reach of takeaways or such things as Uber Eats or Deliveroo, but I'm delighted to discover wartime rural workers weren't forgotten. The Ministry of Food devises the charmingly named Rural Pie Scheme, whereby pies are made locally and distributed via the Women's Voluntary Service or the Women's Institute. I like to think of the farm-workers and Land Girls trailing up to the village hall or the pub to buy theirs, eating them on their way back to the fields. In just one week in 1944, 1.3 million Rural Pies were sold in the scheme that continued with rationing until 1953, keeping the farmworkers producing food.

On a lovely May morning, many of the villagers meet at the little, thirteenth-century church of St Michael and All Angels, for Rogation Sunday. Neighbouring farmer Tom Ward wears a surplice and carries the processional cross in an outdoor service to bless the crops and animals. He walks ahead of The Inkpen Band (an amalgamation of the Temperance Band and The Guzzeleers), who are followed by a procession of villagers and animals. Doris, Marguerite, Jos Digweed and all of Manor Farm go. Julia brings along Jo and Dina, groomed and beribboned, and Billy brings Dolly and Sylvie, their manes plaited and crested with ribbons, wildflowers and may, and the straggling procession winds musically along the lanes to the old beech tree at the top of Parson's Hill, which I will always think of now as the Rogation Beech tree. With a glorious view of Gallows Down and much of Manor Farm, they sing heartily and the rector blesses the crops and animals in an ancient custom. Later in the year, on Plough Sunday, Julia takes her single-furrow horse plough, cleaned especially by Billy, its steel mouldboard polished by recent use in the field, and she and Doris drag it up the aisle to be blessed. The congregation is always swelled at these special services. I am not religious, but there is deep value and comfort to be found in these quiet village churches. Time to be together in an ancient place and honour a rural, village, farming life. A community. The church is so much like a barn, a village hall, a woods, with its rafters made from local oak trees, flint from the hill and blocks of chalk. At Christmastime, I've loved coming out into the frosty churchyard lit by dozens of candles, so that those that lie there with names both familiar and strange can be part of the magic. And so many of them from Manor Farm *are* here. Annetts and Hitchins, Mays and Wrights, Carters, Paintings, perhaps they are all here. I've loved the harvest festivals, where we have shared food and conversation, packing boxes and drinking tea from those ubiquitous Berylware blue or green cups and saucers from the 1940s, still going; that Miss White will have sipped from, balancing a biscuit on the saucer, in this same church hall at one meeting or another. I love the history and rurality of it all; the six bells that ring out in age ranging from 435 years to 25, and named, in age order, John, William Purdue, Thomas, and Hilary Bell (for Mr Bell, who appropriately got the old bells ringing again in 1988) with the last two, Barbara and Michael, added in 2000.

I meet Miss White up by the Rogation Beech one evening. She is looking in the distance at the rabbit damage on Long Sorrel, at the foot of Gallows Down. There are thousands all along here, eating a large area of crop and leaving the ground sour and thistly. The Downs itself looks much barer than it does now. But eighty years on, you are far more likely to see a hare than a rabbit. Myxomatosis cycles round and viral haemorrhagic disease and a loss of habitat means that rabbits, astonishingly, have become rare. I hear Julia grumping to some walkers about the bright-yellow flowers swamping the barley yet to be cut in Upper and Lower Grains. 'How beautiful!' say the walkers. 'Well, I don't like it at all; it's killing the barley!' There is a saying I still hear sometimes, about certainty: 'As sure as charlock grows on chalk.' It has plagued a corner of Home Field, behind our house, recently, where our lovely new neighbour Sally had her paddock ploughed and reseeded with grass by an old grey Ferguson tractor. As if it was just waiting, up came the bright-yellow, choking charlock like a riotous feud, like the 'gutturals of dialect' Ted Hughes writes about of thistles. 'Sharlock,' Miss White writes relatedly in her Day Book and Cultivations Record, in the dialect, and underlined, twice. *Shar lock*. But it is a blissful and favourite spot up here, nonetheless, for us both.

As the sun goes down over Wiltshire, Gallows Down is bathed in a last golden light that picks out every meadow anthill tump, every rabbit's ear, and she softens. Spider silk forms from billions of tiny money spiders ballooning off to join others in invisible aerial plankton but, just now in the slanted, late light, the freshly harvested field in front of us ripples and flows and gleams with a silk sheet, before it lifts and is let loose in strands on the gentle breeze. No chemicals, I think out loud. But sharlock. From the old Rogation Beech, I can see Manor Farm House now, and Mum's house, just beyond it. I am thinking of that Rogation Procession, of the singing and the band, of Dolly and Sylvie plaited up with flowers, and I hear the church bells start up. Quite inexplicably, they seem to come up in the air from the church and barrel over me, ringing their familiar peal in an isolated pocket of sound, like a swarm of bees, and are gone. Here they are and there they go: John, William Purdue and Thomas, Hilary Bell, Barbara and Michael. An air pocket of bells. I feel like Alison Smith in Powell and Pressburger's strange, beloved and beautiful wartime film *A Canterbury Tale*, when she hears Chaucer's pilgrims and their horses briefly, on the wind over the Downs, laughing, gossiping and playing music. I lose an hour in the afternoon on the internet trying to fathom what this strange phenomenon was. Nothing. An aural picture of the wind.

One winter's evening, I go at sunset to find Miss White's road. It's still there on my OS map. I meander along winding Bell Lane, which my children used to call beep-beep lane, for the very same reason that vehicles – a cart with a bell, a car with a horn – would alert anything oncoming around its many single, narrow bends. By the Rogation Beech tree, there is a metal gate, grassy and overgrown, between two thick hedges separating our estate's field with Parson's Hill. Then, this is the place, surely? I climb the gate, making as sure as I can that no one is out lamping or stalking deer, as I'm trespassing. The sunset aligns and illuminates the track between hedges, arched with briars and bedwine, and I sweep down through the long grass. Halfway, my foot slips on chalk and the road is there. Once chalk has been defleeced of its pelt, it takes a very long time to grow back. Hence the prevalence of white horses here. I bend down and touch the chilly chalk surface. I walk on past hares that squat, thinking I haven't seen them, in their forms, and a herd of seven fallow deer watch me from the middle of old Milking Parlour field.

I walk the track like a ghost myself. Like we ordinary rural women do, sometimes. Unheard, unseen, still in those traditional, domestic, caring female roles; country women of a certain age. And there's a great strength, pride and importance in that, holding so much together, that goes mostly unrecognised. But I am also an outlier, unobserved, until I am also not those things. Until I'm heard to counter, seen to question or challenge the accepted, mostly male, approach to country life. The seasonal round of subjects I've learnt to keep quiet about in front of them: hunting, shooting, mowing and tidying, hedge-cutting, tree-felling, spraying, predator control, badgers, when to take sheep off the hill so the chalk flowers can bloom; when to put them back on. Climate change. Access – the Right to Roam. Pheasants. None of this is any of my business, apparently.

And yet time is running out; the hour is late for all of these things and their cumulative and blindly traditional impact on the planet. Though so much has changed since Miss White's time, so little has too, and I'm furious and tired of swallowing it all, trying to fit that patriarchal 'proper country girl' role (it's never country woman, even when you're fifty-something). I'm usually *corrected*; met with impatience, scorn, or outright anger sometimes, that quickly escalates, no matter how genuinely and gently I try to reach out to support, offer ideas and a bridge, compromises or just a slightly different way of doing things that might make all the difference to a species facing extinction.

I am a female farmer of the imagination and there have been successes, positive encounters and outcomes, but it is hard to make them last. I'm known by one farmer half fondly (it's been years) as 'Trouble'. Another pulls up in his tractor beside me, too fast, too close on the pavement-less lane, demanding that I 'smile'. When I do, he says, 'Ah, that's much better, don't make me stop to tell you again.' Another traps me in my field-edge car park one day, blocking my exit with his tractor and making me late for a meeting, to berate me about the length of the bird-nesting season, which I'd 'got wrong' the year before, when I'd simply mimed that birds were still nesting in a hedge he was cutting in early July. 'What do you know? Are you sat in a tractor all day?' he shouted without irony.

But the successes, when they come, however small, with people who are lovely, make my heart sing and give me hope. Like the farmer who let me mark the last three lapwing nests in the village, delaying getting a grass crop in until the parents got the chicks into a nearby paddock. Or the farmer who, when I'd run, flagging him down in his enormous tractor, like Jenny Agutter in *The Railway Children*, to tell him I'd just found a stone curlew nest on the ground, listened, right until I'd finished. Would he please avoid it? I asked. Not only did he, he also offered to enter the what3words position into his tractor-cab computer and populate it across the fleet. The birds could be avoided, even if he wasn't behind the wheel. Right there, industrial agriculture used to save birds.

The golden hour sun is right in my eyes now as I walk down Miss White's track from the skyline. Near a tarpaulin-covered stack of straw bales, I am sure I see her. Walking out from behind them, tall and slim, with her funny, short-legged dogs running ahead. But it is hard to tell; a projection of shadow-play and light, perhaps. The stubble glows golden-grey with long shadows, and I am glad it has been left and not ploughed straight back in; but it is almost lifeless, having been given a final desiccant chemical spray before harvest and another dose afterwards. There are no green weeds; very few birds. No ballooning spiders, no flowing, rippling spider-silk sheet across the corn stalks. Not even the ghost of them. Just a picture of the wind, a projection of the light.

CHAPTER FOURTEEN

Harvest Under Fire

September 1943–September 1944

In the autumn of 1943, the US Army arrive in an astonishing and spectacular procession through the village, and the farm have a whole new complication to deal with. A friend of mine's father peers through his garden hedge at the convoy coming down the narrow lanes, while his big sister and her friend throw apples from their orchard for the soldiers in return for sweets, gum and balloons (that turn out to be condoms). Black Butts is the field at the western foot of Gallows Down, where the steep hill meets it in a narrow, dark seam of blackthorn: a fierce, thorny basket of blackbirds, finches, buntings and woodcock, that plummets into a surf of leafless white blossom in February. A wilderness gap. It is also the forgotten end of the great Wansdyke, the West Country's early medieval linear defensive earthworks. It is named for the god of strange mixture – war, wisdom, poetry and the midweek – Woden, and seems an appropriate setting for battle practice. The wind is often troublesome at Black Butts. It has long been used as a rifle range and this field, as well as Parson's Hill and the land around Field Barn, is partially requisitioned – meaning the farm must also continue to farm it. It all proves to be a great and disorganising trial, not to mention a dangerous one.

The Army, the 101st Airborne Division known as the Screaming Eagles or Band of Brothers among them, build a concrete bunker under the hill and practise capturing it. They arrive in coaches in the mornings, without warning, and block up the Combe Road entirely, rambling off down the field. 'American soldiers do not march,' says Miss White pointedly. She has found the Americans unfriendly and uncooperative. They have marvellous and plentiful rations, which the farm and village know because they are left the empty cartons. But it is the live firing and mock battles that begin without warning or announcement, in a hail of bullets, forcing a hasty retreat. Some soldiers fire over the heads of their fellow troops from Parson's Hill, with lit tracer bullets. They shoot at anything – rabbits, cans thrown into the air, walkers on the top of the hill, farm machinery, Miss White and the men. It is a miracle no one is hit, though Julia hears there are casualties among their own. Bullets zip past with distant laughter sometimes, as she goes about her work. The team proceed with their hearts in their mouths. Trenches are dug all over the field and Julia has to walk back and forth before fieldwork, marking them with long sticks. The horses and cattle are kept to other parts of the farm.

Newly repaired and thatched Field Barn is co-opted as a base, with fires lit inside to cook on, and the men sit smoking recklessly against the ricks. The worst weapon Julia sees used is a flamethrower. One afternoon, it burns down the entire spinney in the corner of the field. This prompts Miss White to speak to the slick and smartly dressed commanding officer – she draws herself up to her full height and explains she is fearful of losing her ricks, the barn and, more importantly, one of her men. The officer looks her up and down a long time before answering. Looks amused, narrowing his eyes deliberately on her fraying hem, a ragged sleeve, her face. Doesn't she know that the American Army has taken over the whole of southern England? They can do what they like in it! She is so incensed, she could shoot him herself. At least they haven't got tanks here. She has seen the fearful damage they do to crops and pasture, driving right over fences and through hedges, even ricks, for fun. Harvesting or threshing continues and is regularly, hastily abandoned under fire. The fields become strewn with live ammunition and bazooka shells. She often has to call the Bomb Disposal Unit in Oxford.

Sometimes, the tail fins of possibly spent shells stick up out of the ground, and the army tie a long piece of string to them, retreat and take cover before pulling them out.

At intervals, a helpful British colonel comes to see what's happening and to consider complaints or claims for damage and disturbance. She feels stuck between the necessity of the Army and the pressures of the War Ag. Crops are flattened or shelled, hedges, ditches and tracks damaged, work is interrupted and good weather windows lost. She is frustrated that, with a little cooperation and perhaps a daily or weekly briefing, this needn't be the case, but there is monetary compensation. She knows, she impresses on the colonel, the importance of training and the sacrifices being made, if they are going to win this war. Once, after an abandonment of haycart in perfect haymaking weather, they watch an intense battle from the Combe Road. Arthur says, 'Well, I do hope they will know how to do it on the day, poor buggers.' Everyone is in sober agreement.

There are some gleeful, stolen-away compensations. The soldiers have plentiful and wonderful clothes and are careless with them. Beautiful pullovers, scarves and gloves; once a greatcoat, left three summer nights on a hedge, before the gang claimed it. Handy ammunition boxes, too. An officer approaches Miss White one day to say their men have lost a lot of clothing – did they ever see any of it? 'Oh no,' says Miss White, wearing one of the pullovers and busying herself with the tractor crank. 'Not at all.'

The Army do pause when Miss White shows up with her collection of Land Girls, prisoners of war and excited schoolboys. Some of the Land Army women have met some of the soldiers at local dances and, needless to say, it takes a while for everyone to settle down. They must dodge the trenches and shell holes as it is, and the boys are distracted, collecting cartridges and shell cases. There are shouts (and sulks) as they pick up and pocket hand grenades, which Miss White gingerly takes from them and leaves in a careful pile. All very hard on the nerves.

Work and life on the farm continue as if things were completely normal; machinery breaks down and is repaired, is borrowed and lent between neighbours. The calves, now older 'stirks', get ringworm and it passes around the team, including Miss White. *All* are cured, human and animal, very efficiently by the vet. The new Marshall threshing 'sheen' is lent to Shalbourne, pulled slowly along the lanes by the blue-and-orange Fordson, with Miss White driving her old Morris car in front to give warning. The Allis crawler has to go by hired lorry. It is quite a procession. Bert and Arthur are away two weeks, helping with the Shalbourne threshing. This tackle is often hired out to neighbours with some of the men, and Julia at times, to operate it. Bert always steps forward to ask the Master for the customary 'Beer Money' when the work is done, and doles it out. Miss White, who on one occasion has worked the baler all day, is presented solemnly with hers – 'Your Beer Money, Miss,' – and is delighted.

Later, she buys an ex-Army four-wheel-drive lorry. It is extremely useful around the farm, in demand locally, and for taking sacks of corn direct from field to mill in Hungerford, where she becomes a well-known figure and earns the nickname 'Heavy Goods'. Years later, she travels to Venice, and on reaching Milan, a porter steps forward to help with her case. He offers a hand and says in English, 'Miss White, excuse me, Heavy Goods. A pleasure.' He is a former prisoner of war, who operated the hoist that hauled the sacks of grain up to the top floor of the mill at Hungerford. He takes her to a café while she waits, comes to collect her and see her onto the train. They wave each other off like old friends.

One day, Miss White is telling Bert something about the Iron Age hill fort, in a pause to drink tea, talking of her ambitions to investigate the long barrow up there. 'They were all farmers, Bert, much like ourselves, I imagine.' Bert looks askance. 'That mound, a thatched clamp of old farmers? I suppose you read that in a book!' To which scathing remark Julia determines to show Bert something that will impress him. A few days later, she has the chance. Taking a neighbour's pigs to Calne, she needs another hand in case of trouble en route with the pigs and invites Bert along, suggesting a stop on the way home at Avebury, the village in the stones, contemporary with Stonehenge. Bert is astonished at the great stone circle and avenue there, the way some of the stones form the walls of cottages, that there is clearly great meaning and engineering involved in their placing, as well as the great man-made mound of Silbury Hill, but it is the museum that really affects him. Julia goes to meet a friend and asks the curator if he will take Bert round. Afterwards, she has a job to get him away. Bert's mind is blown. 'Well. I've never seen anything like that before,' he says. 'Never.' He is quiet much of the way home, repeating this several times over. He is a deeply thoughtful, intelligent and clever man, but has that stubborn, proud, rural working-class suspicion and derision of books and academic learning that is all too familiar to me. I've been in the sights of such coruscating, lasered assessment, time and time again, as a child, as an adult and as a school librarian. Books. It's something Flora Thompson, of *Lark Rise to Candleford*, knew all too well. Bookworm. Idler. Candle-waster. Geek, nerd, *neek*. It has a sting. But Bert never accuses Julia of 'reading it in a book' again and often mentions his visit to others. He sometimes joins Julia in her moments of wonder and speculation about the people on the high hill above them. Sometimes even prompts them. A different sort of curiosity and wonder at the world has caught. I want to give Julia a smile of acknowledgement. I'd like to give Bert a gentle pat on the arm, a wordless opening-up of my hands. God, he'd hate that.

The threshing tackle often gets stuck, being so heavy and awkward, and the ground around the ricks often soft. One day it gets hopelessly bogged down. 'Right. Blocks, tackle, levers!' says Miss White. She takes the tractor and trailer to the sawmills to borrow two big pulleys and a long piece of strong wire rope. With Bert and Arthur's sceptical help and under her construction, they rig it up 'handy billy' fashion, onto a tree as anchor. Arthur repeats variations on 'I can't see as how this'll work'. Bert says, and repeats, 'We never did it like this at timber cart.' Eventually Julia says, irritated, 'Never mind about timber cart, we're going to do it this way now.' The men raise their eyebrows at each other behind her back. They get it fixed and hitched onto the tractor and Arthur is instructed to drive slowly forwards, which he does shaking his head in an unbelieving way – and the machine comes away like a gumboot from mud. She doesn't say anything at first, but stands, hand on hips, smiling triumphantly. 'Leverage,' she says. 'The endless possibility of levers. And boats. It works all the time with boats.' Bert looks askance at this. Arthur says, 'Well I'll be damned.' After this, the team use the method frequently under her supervision, using a tree or the heavy baler as an anchor. Only once does Julia get it wrong and pull a tree over. About a year after the first instance, Bert says out of the blue, 'You were quite right, Miss.' 'What about Bert?' 'The levers and pulleys. I've sin it in a book.' He describes, funnily enough, *Scouting for Boys*. 'A book, Bert?' She cannot resist. 'Something you read about in a book?' She presses her lips together, trying not to smile at the fact that though her system works, and continues to get them out of scrapes, it is not sufficient proof for Bert. But a book now is. He doesn't rise to her teasing, the twitch of her lips.

Ploughing, harrowing, drilling and rolling of the fields continues, with everyone determined 'not to be put off by they Yanks!' Arthur is drilling barley in Hayes Piece near Black Butts, with Billy sat on the drill and Miss White fetching seed back and forth along the headland in the old Morris, when the hitch on the drill sheers off. The Army is using live rounds on the firing range and the tractor, drill and hands are stuck perilously close. Miss White waves, making up semaphores to indicate a problem, but bullets continue to zip through the air alarmingly. She strides across to the Morris and rags it up the hill on the field edge, waving a handkerchief out of the window, and speaks to the officer in charge. Would they please stop firing while they effect the necessary repairs? 'No,' comes the blunt answer, and they don't. She races back to the men and asks what they want to do. 'Fix the drill,' Bert says with Arthur calmly nodding. They begin to dismantle it, and Miss White, screaming through the gears, races back to the farmyard for a replacement hitch. She stays with the men while they calmly fix the new hitch on, holding this or that, as the bullets continue to fly wide of the target at the foot of the hill. Eventually, the drill is got away to a safer part of the field. They do not think the soldiers are actually aiming at them or the machines – damn poor shots if they are – but intend only to frighten them and make a sport of making them jump or run (though the latter might indeed prove fatal). Either way, the soldiers remain disappointed in this show of courage and defiance under fire. Miss White decides to send her men home and do the job of harrowing on the tractor herself, but they are reluctant to leave her, until she insists. The soldiers continue their firing and Julia whistles all the songs she can muster and focusses on that, and the harrows behind her.

In May, the practice assaults intensify, day and night. In Ham, Frances Partridge reports bangs of such sudden, shattering loudness, it turns the household into bags of nerves, jumping like babies and spilling tea. In Inkpen, Audrey Bonham Carter reports the noise so loud, it rattles their teeth in their heads. At Manor Farm, the bangs are loudest of all, cracking window panes, juddering photo frames across side tables, shaking loose bits of plaster off the walls and frightening dogs. In the mornings, it is as if a flock of vengeful ghosts has been abroad, shaking the village houses from within.

Then, the noise, gunfire and shelling stops, and the troops are gone. The fields and lanes are eerily empty and quiet. No birds sing. The weight of something about to happen is dreadful; heavy and light and giddying all at once. As if no one is quite sure of the ground beneath their feet. Days later, the air thrums and the sky fills with one hundred low-flying Dakota C-47s towing enormous Horsa gliders to France. Everyone stops in the fields and comes out of their homes to watch in awe. One of the gliders seems to baulk at the prospect before it has even got over Inkpen. It breaks free from its tether and comes sailing down to land safely in Hayes Piece, ploughing a new furrow.

The relief at working in the fields without being shot at barely has time to register, when the 6th Airborne Division of the British Army arrive. Though they are friendly and cooperative, fresh trenches are dug and more live exercises ensue. This time, however, Miss White must request permission to go on the fields from the requisitioned Big House on the neighbouring estate of West Woodhay, where her own Trojan Horse soldiers were victorious. They must be escorted at all times and not even look at what she has no business in. One night, much damage is done in a night exercise around the farm. Fences are cut and torn up, hedges smashed, whole fields of oats trodden down, and all gates left open. Miss White follows the trail of small arms ammunition and packets of gelignite, picking it up gingerly. Another intense week of night training, shooting and explosions keeps them all wakeful, before they too are gone. This time to Arnhem.

Arthur turns up a live, six-inch mortar shell while cultivating near Black Butts. He fetches Miss White but, reasoning it hadn't gone off and not *just* he, but Miss herself and Sid had already been over it with the tractor, he says he's going to 'chuck it in the hedge'. Julia is forceful: 'No! No! No, you don't!' The Bomb Disposal Unit set it off with a terrific bang, hurling flints and sending the cattle galloping, four fields away. It leaves a great hole in the field that is still there. Though it has a perfectly round-shaped, innocent-looking woods planted around it now.

A fresh wave of evacuees arrives in the countryside as bombing intensifies with the horror of Wellsian 'robot-planes', 'doodlebugs' or 'chaps'. Julia Strachey, seeking refuge again at Ham Spray, hears a terrible noise in the night, and feels sure she recognises it, exclaiming, 'The bally chaps have followed me here!' It is heard and felt in Inkpen too, with a violent, sucking swoosh of wind. But Ralph Partridge, who heard nothing and is unfamiliar with 'the chaps', scoffs and says, 'Probably a carthorse stamping.' But it *is* a doodlebug, a V1. Granny Hezel from Craven Lodge sees it fly along the common, parallel to the road, before crashing into Inkpen Beacon, less than a mile short of Manor Farm and Ham Spray. It blows a thirty-foot crater in the field, and all the glass in at Combe Manor, half a mile in the other direction. Destined for London, one of the new Supermarine Spitfires likely knocked it 180 degrees off course, flying alongside, and tapping it with a wing tip. The next morning, Bob comes to Miss White with a 'Please Miss, may I speak to you?' Bob shuffles, 'Please Miss, m'lavatory has blown down.' The blast has blown the big willow tree down by The Rushes and taken the ancient earth closet with it. Jailer installs a sanitary Elsan toilet in Bob's woodshed, with which he is very pleased. For a while, the doodlebug chap is known as 'the friendly bomb' for its shortness of landing and forced replacement of Bob's lavatory.

From the Rogation Beech, its smooth bark laddered halfway up with age-swollen lettering that could be sixty or eighty years old, the name 'Valerie' and a drawing of a soldier smoking, looking down Bell Lane with binoculars to his eyes – I see Miss White. She is going in to get equipment or 'upset' a fallen shock of oats done hastily. I see her dust off the wide-hipped breeches that she has tucked into her knee-high, button-down, soft brown leather 'spatterdashes' worn over her ankle boots. She tugs the hem of her finders-keepers US pullover over her tall, slender, rather androgynous frame and takes a square of pale sacking to wave. She looks like a wilder, more practical Virginia Woolf or Vita Sackville-West. Her boots and spats scratched, and supple with saddle soap, her face, like theirs, quite long and angular; her eyes, heavy-lidded and a little haunted with the sadness of her age. She strides out, very slightly stooped, waving her sacking flag, not caring a jot how mad she might look. Not one of her men laughs or says a word until she is safely back.

I am conjuring ghosts, later in my writing hut; putting them in place and writing them into being, when I hear the guns: a *dut-dut-dut* of rapid fire and a rolling, booming growl. My pen pot and the thin bow window vibrate lightly. It is a deeply familiar sound, but one that, after a break of weeks, I still mistake at first for something peaceful and ordinary: a neighbour rolling their wheelie bin out, thunder, or the deep, rumbling whicker of one of the horses over the field. I think of the soldiers then, and what they made of Miss White. Not a young, poster-pretty Land Girl, and not like their mothers or older sisters either. A complete anomaly as a farmer. She didn't fit their vision; they failed to see her. They made her, and ergo her workforce in these fields, invisible; dismissed. And yet, she kept on, led her men, the women, boys and girls under her care, safely through. Bringing home the harvest, to boot. I think of the Army not very many fields away now among the winter skylarks, sheep and hares; and I think of the horrors endured and delivered in ongoing and new warfare, and visited on civilians, on children. Mostly, women and children, for God's sakes. I recall the images of the poem 'Channel Firing' by Thomas Hardy. Of 'gunnery practice out at sea' that wakes the dead in questioning; that though they are reassured 'That is not the judgment-hour … Again the guns disturbed the hour', reminding me that though it might be peaceful here, it is but an accident of birth in time and place.

CHAPTER FIFTEEN

Rooksnest Lane and a Pig Club

Winter 1944 and 2024

Julia is wallowing in a scalding hot bath after a bitterly cold day outdoors, looking forward to building up the fire downstairs and an evening listening to the radio. Snow has fallen, snow on ice on snow, and it has all been very difficult. A cold drip lands on her collar bone; then another quite quickly after. She looks up with a sense of foreboding, just in time to see the ceiling bulging directly overhead, ominously. She leaps out of the bath like a gazelle, just before a cart load of snow, tiles and bits of rafter falls in on her, crashing into the bathtub. She shrieks as a spider runs across the floor, quite ridiculously, given what's just happened, and her oil lamp goes out. There are footsteps and shouts of concern and she's no idea whether the rest of the roof is coming in, a bomb has landed (though she's sure it hasn't) or whether they'll all fall through the upper floor. She yells, 'Come no further! I'm quite safe, but go downstairs and I'll meet you there!' She manages to grab a towel and her quilted dressing gown, and tiptoes, dripping in the dark, to her bedroom to hurriedly get dressed.

Downstairs, with a hot tea and the reassuring, pleasant company of the household, she feels much less shaken. Fred has gone back up with her and it is clear, from the lovely, bright and starlit patch of night sky, that the valley between the two roofs of the 'M' of the house has caved in under the weight of snow. When she relates the drama the next morning to the men in the kitchen, warming themselves by the old range, Jack and Bert look horrified, then sheepish. 'Ah,' says Jack after a beat or two. 'Old Bertie would have us sweeping snow out of the valley between the roofs. I guess we forgot all about it.' Julia can't be cross. She enjoys these cosy mornings when they all come stamping into the kitchen in their stockinged feet to plan the day's work and talk of their evenings. Dear Jailer sets to, even in the bitter cold and snow, with Bert and Jack helping and makes the repairs into a kind of sloping attic, between the valley of the roofs. Not to be outdone, Bert comes up with a plan for a different problematic roof. The old Morris car, which is extremely handy about the farm, and quicker than grooming and tacking up Tommy, has a perished and torn soft roof. Bert offers to thatch it. He comes up with a sketch that includes a decorative rick-gable crown of plaited straw on a hazel stick. They are uproarious and Bert dares her to let him do it. By this time, tears are rolling down her cheeks. 'I cannot go about in a mobile rick, Bert!' But they all acknowledge with due pride that 'they' will just think it 'another original but slightly dotty idea of ours'. I love that casual togetherness 'of ours'. For all the years after, if ever an awkward moment, a lull in talk or a chance for a reminisce arises, the design for Bert's mobile rick comes up and grows in legendary status – a foil to the Germans, or 'they Yanks!' Something to spy on the War Ag from, or whoever broke into the village hall and stole jars from the WI's jam-making session. It never fails to produce a friendly-feeling warmth and seems to encompass the national farming situation entirely.

One morning, Frances Partridge telephones, 'Do you have any milk to make deliveries – we have a problem and can't get any in Ham.' Miss White puts her in touch with a dairy farmer in the village and doesn't ask what the problem might be, knowing what she does about Ham Spray. There is plenty to ruffle feathers there if you were of the ruffled sort. She quietly applauds the Ham Spray contingent on the whole; though they hold themselves aloof from much of the community, intellectually and in their class. Such a striking difference from Doris and Marguerite, who are utterly accepted and loved and, well, *dynamic*. The Ham dairy farmer could be against homosexuals, she imagines, *or* pacifists and Conscientious Objectors. But there has always been something of a frost between Ham village and the Spray House that has nothing to do with either of those things. Rural communities often readily accept, absorb and negotiate difference, out of need and reliance upon each other; neighbours that are stuck together and stick together, finding a common unity in the kindness of community. Julia finds out in the end from Mrs Hitchens, who gets it from Mrs Partridge's loose-lipped housekeeper, who has been reading letters. The Partridges share their water tank above the garage for a small rent with the dairy next door, owned by Major Huth, an uncompromising and deeply religious man who owns land up to and including Inkpen. Major Huth's son-in-law, Colonel Boord, arrives affably at the door one morning to ask if the Partridges would go easy on the water – two-*thousand* gallons has disappeared overnight! Perhaps there are intimations of the parties and pools of the recent past, but Ralph Partridge is baffled, 'Good gracious! We only use that water on our tomatoes.' The following day, there is a violent explosion of the human kind. Colonel Boord is shouting, 'You really are a *bloody* man!' and has cut the water pipe. Boord is shaking his fist in Ralph Partridge's face, 'I'd like to bash your face in, and if I did, the whole country would be pleased. I know all about your history. I know you wouldn't join the Home Guard.' Ah, Ralph's trial as a Conscientious Objector has been reported in the papers, so it is that – no matter that he is also a distinguished, decorated and traumatised soldier of the First World War himself. Major Huth is also present and his reply is to cancel the milk delivery for the Partridges, which means no butter to churn, no puddings or milk for the children or mother and baby currently sheltering in the house. That all the cottages subsequently run dry of water and must bucket from old wells means a leak somewhere on Major Huth's part, but he is unrepentant.

Miss White finds the whole thing rather amusing, though keeps that to herself. She has form with Major Huth, a 'somewhat fiery gentleman with a beard'. Without asking, Major Huth had continued to have a pheasant shoot across Manor Farm land. She had not liked seeing his syndicate of 'rich friends with their keepers and smart plus fours shooting my pheasants when we were working so hard to produce food, and hungry'. She subsequently refuses to renew the agreement the following year and her decision annoys him very much.

On Miss White's suggestion, the farm men and families elect to start a Pig Club. She has a workforce of fifteen now, including casual workers, and each subscribed member buys half a piglet and makes a small contribution to pig meal. This is supplemented with a clanking pail of food scraps that they boil up in an old copper boiler Miss White finds in an abandoned ruin of a cottage. Jailer Annetts has made some beautiful pig sties and Julia and Bob Edwards take the little box trailer to buy eight 8-week-old piglets from Newbury Market on a Thursday 'Pig and Paper day'. All very exciting. The men, their families and Julia all take a rota-turn at looking after the pigs, who are petted, named and scritched. Despite this, pig-killing day doesn't feel like the worst of betrayals, only an unquestioned natural and necessary conclusion; though along the road, Frances Partridge lies awake the night before her own pig at The Spray is due to be killed. At Manor Farm the day has a holiday air, of mixed excitement, preparation and a shared cooperative of gratitude, for there will soon be a wonderful feast of much-needed, home-produced protein for all. That the pigs are loved and treated like royalty up to this point is a commonality I read about in Thomas Hardy and Flora Thompson, even though then, the pigs' deaths are sometimes still cruel. Thankfully, by now, the pigs are properly, quickly and humanely killed at home by the travelling butcher, Reuben Annetts, Jailer's father. Though it is illegal to slaughter pigs in the road, they do so on the council lane that runs through the farm, pinking its chalky edges. Afterwards, the hair and bristles are burnt off in a straw pile and the carcasses washed and scrubbed with brooms, before being hung in Wergs Barn. Reuben Annetts comes again, two days later, to divide up the carcasses evenly. Half must go to the Ministry of Food and the rest is made expertly by each family into brawn, sausages, chittlins and faggots, with the cured, smoked ham and well-salted bacon placed in racks under the low kitchen ceilings, to last much of the winter. All very tender. For days, everyone rather overeats and much comment is made in the fields over feasting, contentment and not a few bellyaches. Without fridges, much of the meat must be eaten quickly, and is also given to any neighbours in need. The memories of roast pork last much longer.

One frosty, wintry night, I walk the familiar mile home from Mum's house on the other side of Dagg's Gully, along the same lane that passes through Manor Farm (though it has a slight detour now), clutching a packet of bacon she has given us from the Farmers' Market. It is chill and squishy in my hands. The night is beautiful, cold and clear, with a near-full moon that out-brightens most of the stars. Past the barns at Manor Farm, some of Mr Cordery's little black angus cattle shift and huff in the straw, and a barn owl calls *Ssshhhhht* over Walk Meadow. As I reach the corner where Wergs Barn stood and Hollow Lane rises to Rooksnest Lane, I remember the road is closed and switch off my phone torch, only using it to alert any cars that might come by.

The water supply is being patched in the usual place, just above where Miss White's pipes, still working perfectly well, join the mains. The banks either side of Hollow Lane rise steeply to the trees towering blackly against the glittering sky and the lane darkens beneath their night shade. I consciously do not look at the place where the barn stood, in case there is that barn-shaped lightening against the hill; a ghostly picture-blank, where other lives once hung. Otherwise, I am comfortable, at an enquiring ease, open to the stories of the night. I know where I am for the sugar beet smell of fallen, decaying, sycamore leaves. The road is very definitely closed, with a stagger of deep holes in the ground, and great heaps of chalk rubble and knuckle-bone flints railed off with what look like plastic showjumps. The barn owl calls again.

My moonshadow is sharp as a black paper cut-out, but I am wary of stepping in other shadows, in case they are holes in the ground, and walk the wavering moonlit path between the shadow branches. I shy past the sleeping digger, its arched neck, bucket and teeth too much like a dragon, and irrational as it is, its caterpillar tracks might jerk into action if I look at it. The rooks and jackdaws in their winter roost are conversational, up late with the moon so bright on them I can see their open bills, their throat ruffles, their feathers reflecting a milky-purple sheen. Some watch me walk below. There is a voice then. Someone is speaking. I turn round, but the road is empty. They must be behind the hedge of Wergs Meadow, out in the field? Or Bumpy, on my right? It's a woman's voice asking questions in a clipped and refined vintage of another era, 'And you went to school here, didn't you?' 'Oh yes, madam,' comes the reply in that slow, expressive and measured dialect I still hear sometimes, though the accent is much deeper – Berkshire, yes, but very much *West* Berkshire, so it is almost West Country with a distinctive cadence; I hold my breath and listen – is it a conversation I am hearing? 'When my *far*thur came he didn't have no higgler work so he went rabbit catching for Major *Hoo* ... then his trade wor a *Black*smith... he were the wonderful *h*age of nine-ty-two. When her wor *eighty-nine* he wor hedgelaying and the Dr came by and said, *hey*, it's time you left that alone!' I am convinced now I am hearing Miss White and, who? Bert Wright? I can't make sense of this. My skin prickles. The voices again, 'And then I went fer Miss *White*, building ricks and all *sarts* of jobs what she want'd doin'. Drove tractors. She wor a *good* woman. A *kind* woman and she worked longside us, like any man. They were good days all, through the war and on after ... I worked for Edward's like my farther did.' They stop abruptly and I try to quietly breathe. What is this? Do they know I'm here – are they really there? Should I speak? The rooks and jackdaws have fallen silent. The voice cannot then belong to Miss White and the voice must be Bert *Annetts*, not Wright: Jailer.

Then comes another voice, older, less clear with a deeper accent, talking about hedging and pig killing: 'I travelled on foot between all the codages and farms of Inkpen, Kintbury, Woody, Inglewood, Combe and Ham. There aren't many of the old 'ouses but where I've killed a pig – though they can't make bacon now like the old codagers did. I did the pigs at Manor Farm for Miss White, on the road right here!' I look down at the moon-sheeny tarmac, gripping the bacon too hard. This can only be Reuben Annetts, Jailer's father. My phone pings in my pocket and this strange spell is broken. And then something falls into place. My phone. I pull it out, rooted to the spot, my heart hammering in my chest. I find, in switching my phone torch off, I must've somehow played old recordings I'd searched for from the village website – some research I hadn't quite yet got to. I am relieved and heartbroken all at once and a sort of sobbing and laughing escape me. Some of the rooks scatter with a clamour of caws. It is all very eerie and startling, but also strange to hear Jailer and his father in this spot, talking about hedgelaying, rick building, even pig killing. I'm a bit overcome. I release my grip on the packet of bacon a little, a poor substitute for what they both would remember, and am suddenly very cold and teary. I wanted so powerfully to speak to these friendly ghosts, that I almost did, stepping into the shadows to say a tentative, 'Hello…? Bert? Julia?'

When I get home, things don't add up. I hadn't quite got to this point in my research, in discovering these recordings of Bert Annette's – Jailer's – voice or that of his father's, Reuben Annetts. They are nearly cued up on my laptop in a list of fascinating recorded memories made in the village in 1975 and 1964. I hadn't actually 'found' them yet and I hadn't looked at the website on my phone at all. I listen to the short, eight-minute recording of Jailer and there are certainly some similarities with what I heard, but some differences too. Then when I click on the recording of Reuben Annetts, born 1876, it isn't there. I try again – the link is with the British Library Survey of English Accents and Dialects, which is broken. The message reads: 'Sorry we can't find that page. We're continuing to experience a major technology outage as a result of an October 2023 cyber-attack.' And yet, I seem to have heard it in 2024.

I lose myself in stories and recordings remembered by villagers today that were largely concurrent with Miss White's time. How Norman Painting was asked to bring a heifer calf back from Newbury Market, after finding it tied to his already full horse and cart. It was too young to walk far, so he carried it the eight miles home to the other side of the village. And here's Joyce Uprichard, village hall caretaker for more than fifty years, and who I collected the key from, and had tea with on several occasions when the children were little. Joyce describes old Inkpen as a 'poor little village' really, but one rich in people and character.

There is also a wonderful recording of Lilian Watts, naturalist, wildlife campaigner and a key member in saving the common from being built on. She recalls cycling from the other side of Newbury to listen to nightingales on the edge of the settled Gypsy encampment on the common in 1907. Returning, married in 1935, she rents twelve acres of the common land, the 'Poors Allotment', alongside the Wright family's pigs and the Romany family's horses, clearing some of the gorse and pioneer trees, and studying the plants, lichens and birds there. She discovers a rare pale dog violet, *Viola lactea*, there, and records three species of heather, two of gorse, petty whin, gipsywort, bog asphodel, lousewort, milkwort and dodder, all of which can still be found, thanks to the further efforts and management of the local Wildlife Trust and volunteers.

But the birds she recorded in this small remnant heathy woodland – nightjar, corncrake, snipe, lesser spotted woodpecker, nightingale – are now gone. In the last twenty years of my recording, I've seen and heard the last nesting woodcock there, the last spotted flycatcher, the last willow warbler, the last willow tit. At the end of the tape she recorded, Lilian takes us out on the common and plays us a nightingale; loud and beautiful and heartbreaking and gone. What is particularly shocking, what really gets to me, is the volume, variety and numbers of all the other birds singing in the background too. I remember, even fifteen years ago, the overwhelm of a dawn chorus; the aural blur of rich, loud, solid sound where it was nearly impossible to pick out individual birds. Now, it is full of holes, of absence. The beauty and devastation is that you could fall utterly in love with the awe and joy of what remains, and not know, or be able to imagine what this tiny, torn scrap of a once incredible aural tapestry sounded like.

How did we get to this point where the ecosystem is so depleted? We talk about losing species as if we've lost our keys, a treasured photograph, mislaid something carelessly or by accident – and in part, yes, we absolutely have. But why haven't we stopped doing it, when we know we are? With all the evidence to support how important, how vital to life, nature and the climate is (and just for its own sake, too) so many more of us are falling in love with nature. But we are also making the links between the joint nature-climate crises and climate justice; that those who have benefited most from industrialisation bear an overwhelming responsibility for the crises, just as those least responsible bear the brunt of the consequences. It's taken a very long time, but we are prepared to fight for it, and we are galvanising.

I think of where it began for me, my love of farming and wildlife, the countryside, and I'm taken back to my beautifully illustrated pocket (car glovebox) Shell Guides to the Countryside – Shell, as in the oil company. How utterly and powerfully hoodwinked we've been by those heavyweight companies, in oil, forestry, agriculture and more, which have got so big and so influential that they can blinker, mollify and outmanoeuvre us? But still, we march, we petition, we join forces; we make our language more reasonable, less reactive, more inclusive and diverse. There is much work to do here, but this is how we do it. We activate and more of us are doing so, our voices rising in collaboration and strength even as the birdsong fades. It's a strong female thing, isn't it? I listen to Lillian Watts's recording on repeat. A glorious, riotous cacophony of sweet English birdsong in spring, right on my doorstep. Gone now. A ghosting.

CHAPTER SIXTEEN

Talking with the Farrier About Climate Change

January 1945–December 1946 and May 2008–October 2020

The rookery is loud and thick with birds, and there is a fellow-feeling in them heading to the fields at daybreak, and back again to the woods beside the farm and cottages in the blue light of evening. The men lead them out, or the rooks lead the men. Both companies come home together. Winter thrushes strip the hedges of berries and fill in the gaps the winter leaves have left. Starlings gather in great clouds. Miss White and the men even feel sympathy for the crowds of grain-eating sparrows around the granary and the ricks. Snipe and woodcock are seen about the thawed ground around the muck heaps. Hundreds of plover shift from field to field, looking so much, from a distance, like they've been flung out in great arcs from a fiddle broadcaster and seeded onto the ground. Julia finds a barn owl caught by the foot in some frayed sacking in the granary. She loves to see these bewitching birds and they do a great service on the farm, catching mice and rats. She catches it carefully, clamping her hands lightly around its body, pinning its wings and thinking how light it feels, how insubstantial, compared to its large-seeming presence. It hisses at her and sinks its bill into her finger, drawing blood, before she manages to release it back into the cosy thatch of the granary roof.

The last summer of the war proves to be an interminably wet one and petrol rations are such that the petrol-start tractors, although running on vaporising oil, have to be left running over the dinner hour. And then suddenly, at last, at last, the war is finally over. There are celebrations and such relief, with people hanging makeshift bunting out of cottage windows and, even in the countryside, a sense of giddiness with handshakes, back slaps and kisses, when anyone meets in the lanes. Anyone that can goes into Hungerford or Newbury to celebrate and Miss White gives everyone the day off. As Conscientious Objectors, Frances and Ralph Partridge are cautious at the response they'll get but are welcomed into arms and homes. After all, isn't it logical that pacifists of all people should rejoice in the return of peace? Peace returns, as Mrs Partridge puts it, 'like the pins and needles with which blood rushes back into a crushed limb'.

The end of the war precipitates a bit of a turnaround of staff. Sid Walters and then Jailer decide to leave off from farm work, but they part on good and friendly terms and Miss White is able to take on Bill Watts, who lives in Champions Cottage beside the field of the same name and keeps a wonderful market garden. She also takes on Bert's brother Dick permanently, and then later another brother, Charlie, too. Bert's niece Marjorie comes to help in the house and garden and altogether, says Julia, the Wrights were a splendid family – and part of her own. Julia feels a glow of pride and gratitude for her farm men and their families. No one could beat them for their versatility, practical skill, hard work and willingness to give anything a try. They have got the farm and Julia through the war and are second to none. They have doubted her decisions sometimes, yet always openly, respecting her wishes and carrying them out, and they have never judged her, she realises, for anything at all, other than perhaps her lack of patience on the timing of ricking corn. Bit hasty. Truly, they are quite remarkable.

She sympathises with Frankie Donaldson, this brilliant female farmer-writer-broadcaster, when she states that 'people who know everything are always a hopeless proposition'. Frankie adds to this statement in a letter to her husband that 'the new cowman is an argumentative bugger'. Julia admires this woman farmer, who often had to take her small children out on the tractor and into the fields with her. In her biography, her daughter Carol writes, 'Frankie fought a woman's war, not just bringing up children and doing her bit on the home front, but fighting a battle to become a proficient farmer providing food for the nation, and taking on the hostility and obstruction of farmworkers towards a woman entering a traditionally male sphere of work.'

The industry as a whole has been perishingly slow in addressing the balance of women in farming. Worldwide, today, 43 per cent of agricultural workers are women, but only 15 per cent of them own land. In the UK, although women make up 55 per cent of the farming workforce (including unpaid, contributing family labour) just 16 per cent are 'farm holders' (owners or managers), dropping to 7 per cent in Scotland. Young women are still being advised that the only way to get into farming is to marry a farmer. In 2024, *Farmer's Weekly* magazine launched a campaign called Level The Field, to make agriculture fairer, more equitable and more inviting for everyone, particularly women. The barriers it cites for women are wearyingly familiar, but identified and acknowledged: being overlooked for succession, low land ownership rates, difficulty accessing finance or government support, lack of access to flexible childcare and family needs. Equipment, work clothing and on-site facilities are designed by men for men, and women are still being subject to prejudice. Despite Minette Batters being the National Farmers' Union's first woman president from 2018 to 2024, there is very low representation in farming organisations, particularly at the top levels.

Perhaps it is no surprise that, back in 1945, the farm gate is shut again on the progress women who want to farm have made, and have proved themselves perfectly capable of, equally as well as the men. A kind of fierce and sexist, often misogynistic gatekeeping of agriculture seems to redouble after the war; a patriarchal patting of the heads of the Land Girls and sending them home, to feminine jobs if they didn't immediately marry. To apply some serious moisturiser and nail cream to those calloused hands. Women that have held the fort on their husband's, brother's or son's farms, give back the reins and are waved cheerily away to the farmhouse and the sidelines (where they are likely to continue as unacknowledged backbone and enginehouse of the farm from there). And this defensive gatekeeping of farming from women lasts and lasts, one might argue, through all the decades since. Born, I think, of fear. That women might be able to do the job just as well. That they might, in fact, be able to do it better.

The war is over, but the farm must plough on as usual. The need to keep up food production and standards and embrace new innovation is more pressing than ever, now the men are back to drive this 'properly', and with rationing and the War Ag in place for several years yet. Enid Barraud's joyful, contemporary, lyrical account *Set My Hand upon the Plough* of farming as a Land Girl (reprinted in a beautiful new edition by Little Toller in 2024) describes the heartbreak of this time. Enid, who went by the name of John and lived with their 'close companion' Bunty in a farm cottage, is handed their wage packet with a note and one week's notice, after three and a half years of hard work on one beloved farm. Despite working as well and hard as all the others, Enid/John is to be replaced by Italian POWs and is utterly heartbroken: 'They say just before you die your memory does a flashback over your past life...' They remember calves born and suckling, bitter weather, the hurricane-lamp glow on the straw in the cowshed, corn falling before the scythe. It's a devastating personal loss, but other women, as landowners, manage to continue.

For Miss White, for Miss Honor Atkins at Hill Farm dairy five miles away and for Miss Mason and Miss de Beaumont, and doubtless other women farmers of those years whose endeavour has been erased, farming continues in their more than capable hands. The Museum of English Rural Life in Reading, a beloved haunt of mine, says that:

> *One in ten farms was either managed or run by a woman [between 1900 and 1945]. The majority of female farmers were widows, carrying on their late husbands' tenancy until a son took over. But women also farmed in their own right. Many college-trained middle class women wanted to farm, as did many who had worked on the land during the First World War. In this way each could be 'head of a world of her own'.*

Smallholdings of around ten acres were particularly suited to women farming on their own or in partnership with a friend. However, there were also women who farmed on a much larger scale. In the mid-1930s Farmer and Stockbreeder *ran a series on 'successful women farmers', highlighting the 'valuable work' they were doing 'for the advancement of agriculture'. This was a timely reminder to readers that not all farmers were men.*

Frankie Donaldson's husband comes home to Gipsy Hall Farm from the war and they farm successfully together there, then at another farm. Before her husband returns, Frankie reads Lady Eve Balfour's *The Living Soil* (1943) and is quite changed. Lady Balfour, two years older than Julia White, was one of the first women to study agriculture at the University of Reading, deciding at around the age I did (twelve) that she wanted to be a farmer. It can't have been easy for Lady Eve, but she had class, money and an influential family behind her, instilling the confidence and perhaps a certain superiority that gave her access and a dose of respect. In the countryside it seems, class trumps sex. Having none of the above and not coming from a farming family, no one was going to let me onto an all-male agricultural course in the 1980s and '90s, and they didn't. Farming was in a good place after the war, in no small part down to a female workforce. There had been an agricultural revolution during wartime that continued in the decades afterwards and the investment had to be protected and grown on, so that farms could continue to weather economic storms and be passed on down the male line. Women supported, but they didn't run farms and rarely worked on them.

Lady Balfour was, by all accounts, a phenomenally talented, formidable and dedicated woman farmer and innovator. Aged twenty (masquerading as twenty-five) she was appointed bailiff of a farm in Wales with the support of the Monmouthshire Women's War Agricultural Committee, managing a team of Land Girls. The following year, she bought New Bells Farm in Haughley Green, Suffolk, with her sister and a trust fund, where they lived for a long time without running water or electricity. With Alice Debenham, a neighbouring farmer at Walnut Tree Farm, thirty-one years her senior and something of a benefactor, she began the Haughley Experiment, the first long-term, side-by-side scientific comparison of organic and industrial, chemical-based farming. She had means and a seemingly supportive as well as political background: her father was the 2nd Earl of Balfour; an aunt, Lady Wentworth, a renowned horse breeder; two other aunts – a suffragist and a four-times-imprisoned, hunger-striking suffragette – and an uncle who had been Prime Minister. Lady Balfour co-founded The Soil Association in 1946 in a revolutionary movement that understood the soil as a complex living thing, and was a lifelong pioneer of organic farming.

Frankie Donaldson writes enthusiastically to her husband in Cairo about *The Living Soil* and organic farming, admitting, like every other famer, she uses 'artificials with great liberality and feels a bit shaken'. I think of Miss White and her charlock and couch grass. How relieved she is when miracle chemicals are invented to kill them, leaving the wheat 'untouched', as well as artificial nitro fertilisers that double a grass sward – yet suffocate out the flowers. Miss White was sparing with her use of the latter. Yet still, how easily we believe the precise miracle of these chemicals. Even this year, on Facebook, a move was supported to use Roundup on the village pond, to rid it of the irises taking over, in the belief there existed a chemical treatment that would leave everything else – plant life and pondlife, aquatic insects, frogs, newts and toads – not dead. I intervened, carefully, suggesting the alternative of a work party instead. I can see myself quite clearly, knocking on Manor Farm House door one late afternoon, with *The Living Soil* clutched in my hands, and an armful of books from my own bookshelves now. 'Miss White, may I?' We sit at her kitchen table in our socks, the dogs fussing around our feet. Drink tea from a big brown teapot with a green crocheted tea cosy. This book, and these books, *Silent Spring* by Rachel Carson, *The Killing of the Countryside* by Graham Harvey, *Silent Earth* by Dave Goulson, *The Moth Snowstorm* by Michael McCarthy; Kate Bradbury's *One Garden Against the World*: Miss White, Julia, will you read them? Because something unimaginable will come of this, I say. We are on a wave of massive change now. We are losing, no, *have lost*, no again, have *destroyed* species and habitats. What you see, out here, in abundance – the flocks of birds, the variety, the flowers, insects, bees, butterflies; what you cannot imagine not being there – is going, is gone. And not only that, the soil is dying, rinsing away; weather patterns are changing wildly, becoming unpredictable in ways you can't imagine. We are at a tipping point and sliding.

But the dream of her kitchen table stays in my head, an obsessive argument with ghosts, not unlike the ones I continually have in my head with policy makers, leaders and landowners, some farmers. I am being haunted by these incredible, hidden, spirited and funny women, these imperfect, incorruptible saints and I don't know what to do with it. I feel that with them, I'd have a chance to influence and change the way they farm. To become a kind of voluntary advisor-without-agency, as I have occasionally been in the intervening decades since my Canadian adventure on the farm we live on, keeping wild bird records, surveying and feeding them en masse, asking for concessions for wildlife on the farm and sometimes getting them, inviting tours and talks and engagement with schools, heck, even twice, being runners up in a prestigious conservation award. But it's been a difficult and fraught relationship too, that ultimately ended when the management changed. But it has left me empowered and able to diversify and build on actions for wildlife and community in other ways.

Sometimes, ghosts don't want to talk. Sometimes, the distance is too great. There are things we passionately disagree with, that I cannot relate to or don't think they can. Perhaps I underestimate them. Sometimes, they've too much to say. And, do you know what? So have I! I know that Julia, Doris and Marguerite would welcome me in; would listen, be interested, be horrified in turns, would consider and, I think, do things differently. I walk home, still clutching the books – or perhaps I'm empty handed, the books left on the kitchen table at Manor Farm, my arms still light and rising with a sudden weightlessness, past modern-day Trenchfields and Black Butts, Hayes Piece and Grains, the chemically dressed corn in the ground and sprayed twice before the shoots are even up, and the field blue with slug pellets. It's a bloody war. And it's a war with a mindset, a war with belief. A war with trust and change. And it's a war we are going to have to win with hearts and minds and science.

After the war, the Agriculture Act 1947 established its commitment to continuing to develop a highly mechanised, intensive, industrial farming system. Artificial nitrogen and an increasing array of poorly understood chemicals were considered part of a responsible, well-run farm. The War Ag still had powers to foreclose, or evict without compensation, anyone that didn't run a productive and well-managed farm until 1958, by which time industrial farming was well established and accepted as 'the norm'. Frankie Donaldson is put off pursuing what had been a revelation to her, by the male farmers around her, by the male War Ag and her husband, though they did trial some organic plots. To Lady Balfour's intense disappointment, the government refused to offer support or funding towards organic production. She was seen as a crank. Which she rather revelled in, nonetheless.

Lady Balfour lived with her 'close friend and lifelong companion' Kathleen Carnley, a skilful dairy farmer, for fifty years and was also close to Beryl 'Beb' Hearnden, with whom she collaborated on several successful crime novels. She played jazz saxophonist in a band, trained horses, rode a motorcycle, gained a pilot's licence and flew Tiger Moths like Miss White's brother, and sailed. She and Julia would surely have got on famously. She also had a weak eye and wore a patch over it, and enjoyed touring the country and even overseas, towing a caravan behind a Rolls-Royce car. Photographs of her are mesmerising. She looks every bit the spirited, challenging, serious and thoughtful revolutionary.

Meanwhile, back at Manor Farm, Arthur Walters, Miss White's reliable, dependable, chief tractor driver becomes ill and it becomes obvious by Christmas that he must give up the work. This is, of course, a huge blow to the Walters family in many ways; not least a concern of health, finance and housing security, 'living in' as they do. Forty years on, writing up her diary, Julia laments the loss of this lovely family from the house and her life, including the two girls, Dorrie and Rosie, who have grown up on the farm. I come across Dorrie much later, around 2008. She is married to John, the horseman, and lives in one of the estate cottages identical to ours. Capable and bright, she has worked in the Big House for very many years, as Nanny then housekeeper to our aristocratic neighbour and her siblings. On 'Beaters' Days' after Christmas, when we are all invited up to the Big House, she serves us tea, cake and finger sandwiches and it is always a fun, warm and lively occasion. We come then to ride the horse belonging to the daughter of the Big House. Living in the lovely old estate farmhouse behind us, she is in her late fifties and had fallen off and sustained a broken neck. When we are introduced to her horse, Honey Bee, Elizabeth is in a metal halo device, secured to her skull with pins to immobilise her head and neck until it heals. Dorrie's husband, Horseman John, has suggested we keep Honey Bee ridden, while Elizabeth recovers.

We become great friends with Elizabeth. Delightfully eccentric and full of tales of her younger life and drolly funny, she lives alone, but happily, seeing friends and popping up to her club in London. Between my dearest friend, Sarah, and I, then two of our daughters and my husband too, we share the ride of this wonderful horse. My Sheila, my imaginary 'Emma', she is a part thoroughbred chestnut mare and a former event horse. With Sarah and I not that long post-pregnancy, and the mare having been put out to grass, the three of us get fit together and enjoy many years riding around the estate and over the Downs. We enjoy a lasting friendship with Elizabeth too, sitting in the tack room or in her warm and rather shabby farmhouse kitchen around the Aga. We loan a chestnut New Forest pony called Storm from the goddaughter of our neighbour, for my daughter to ride and to keep Honey Bee company. Horses on a shoestring.

John looks after Bee until he no longer can, and we take over. He is deeply knowledgeable, having been in racing and stud work all his life. I hang on his every word. He tells me stories of galloping hatless over the Downs on frosty mornings at Barbary Castle – the old hill fort on The Ridgeway – crouched low over the withers and necks of some of the finest and fastest thoroughbreds; of strings of racehorses trotting up through Wiltshire villages, striped blankets warming the loins and powerful quarters of their mounts, just north of here, at Wroughton and Wichelstowe, at Hackpen Hill; names and places that resonate with the ringing of hooves over turf for centuries. John is a proud man, reluctant to acknowledge that his aging body won't allow him to do what he loves and lives for. To ride and serve the animals he loves and has built a life around. He can be hard sometimes. When the horse goes lame, due to an abscess in her foot caused by a flint bruise, the farrier comes to cut it out and relieve the pressure. John says we must get the vet to pack and poultice and dress the foot daily – but I've done this dozens of times. No need, I say; I can do this. We order poultices and bandages and put down a thick straw bed and bed down the old cart shed next door for the pony. John watches each day without a word, as I cut the pad into a hoof-shape, heat and soak the slippery lintex in a bowl of hot water, squeeze it out and press it, warm, onto the sole of Bee's foot, resting between my knees as she nuzzles my back pockets. My scissors, thick cotton wadding and bandages all to hand, I pack the foot and wrap the wadding round her leg to hold and support it all, and setting the foot down, wrap and secure the bandage round her leg, tying it all in a neat bow, making sure the knot lies between and not on her tendons on the side, and tuck the ends in. I wrap the other leg for support. John walks away before I'm done, every time. Sometimes tuts. Mostly glowers. For all his experience, this isn't something he's ever had to do before. Five days later, the foot is good enough for Bee to go out into the field. I wrap it all again, with an extra layer of electrical insulating tape for waterproofing. When she comes sound, John looks at me for the first time in days. Says, 'Well, I s'pose that's good work, vetinry.' It's the closest I ever get to a compliment, an acknowledgement. John brings me the most wonderful photos of him riding as a young lad, and older. A lifetime in service.

Over the years, we help Elizabeth out more as an early-onset dementia takes hold of her, and John becomes less able. Eventually, Elizabeth has a series of carers whom we get to know too, who enjoy bringing Elizabeth out to 'do' the horses, and open the kitchen window to let them poke their heads in, when we walk past. John and Dorrie die months apart in 2020, and I wish I'd asked them both more about their lives here. Though I wonder how much they'd have told.

Bee throws a shoe one day and we have to hunt for it. Not only was it fairly new, and can be put back on, there is a danger of her stepping on the nails and injuring herself. I walk the paddock back and forth, then the edge of the stubble we had just cantered over, and find a shoe. But it's not Bee's. It's twice the size. I knock the mud off a carthorse's shoe. It is rusty, but not much. I picture Dolly or Sylvie, for it must be one of theirs, stepping on the shoe's heel in the field, and pulling it off, the plough folding it straight in under the furrow. I can hear Billy cursing. The shoe hasn't got much wear on it. I can see him alongside me, searching for it. Perhaps he would have asked Sid or Bill Watts to join in looking. We all walk forwards together, the horses waiting patiently in a corner of the field, swishing tails, using the opportunity to rest each hind leg in turn as we sweep the ground before us, metal detecting with our eyes, heads bent to the earth in the timeless search for a lost horseshoe.

The farrier comes to trim and shoe our horses a couple of days later, Honey Bee's shoe lost to another decade, for someone else to find. Only three of her four-time walking hoofbeats ring out into the dusty farmyard, and one of those clinks rather than clops – the distinctive sound of a loose shoe, the risen clenches of the nail ends rattling loose in their holes: clip-clop clink-…, clip-clop clink-…. It is a percussion that attracts attention: 'Lost one, gonna lose another?' says my neighbour Betty as we pass the garden gate. The pony taps along lightly behind, unshod.

Steve, the farrier, trims the pony first, carving new white keratin moons from his hooves with an oak-handled paring knife, rounding Storm's toes to help ease his ailments of old age and laminitis, a cumulative condition of too much rich grass for an equine evolved for gorse and coarse grasses on the New Forest. Bee is 'cold shod', whereby the correct-sized shoe is hammered into individual shape, rather than being heated and shaped from a bar of iron in the portable furnace. I miss the hot roar of the burner, the exacting fit, the smell of painlessly burnt horn to imprint and check for size and the hiss of a red-hot shoe cooled in a bucket of water, fetched from the yard.

I lean against the warm yard wall, holding each horse in turn. The action of the nippers and paring knife, the rasping, filing down and levelling, the testing and checking of the sole is a familiar, mesmerising craft. The jazz tap-and-clink of hammer on nail, and shoe over anvil, attracts Hobie, Mr Cordery's terrier, who drops in from Manor Farm for a chew on the pale curved moons of discarded hoof. Every dog loves a blacksmith. He manages to fit three crescents in his mouth and trots off, tail wagging. A horse is said to have five hearts; the rubbery, triangular frog in each hoof is both shock absorber and circulatory pump. A digital pulse powered by contact with the ground that pumps blood back up to the big heart in the near centre of the horse's chest. The frog is the key to the relationship between the ground and a horse's beating heart.

With a hoof held between his knees, resting on his worked leather apron, the farrier talks to me through a mouth full of nails in short, thoughtful sentences. I tell him about finding the wrong lost shoe, and my farming women. There's some local gossip, but before long, we fall to talking about grass and the ground. A record of weather, warmth, moisture or the lack of it, and the response of grass to it, can be read in the growth rings on horses' hooves, like ridges on a bracket fungus, or rings on a felled tree. The farrier talks of the new hoof patterns he sees now, the cracks and contractions of extreme weather, his back bent to the low angle of a coffee table. Each horse has their eyes closed, while he is bent to the language of diagnosing, dousing, responding, correcting, adjusting. It's an old alchemy of mythic proportions and instinct that Reuben Annetts, Jailer's father, was well-versed in. Both our farrier and Reuben, and their forebears, all members of The Worshipful Company of Farriers, their hands on the pulse of the earth, feeling through the feet of horses: earth, grass, horn, weather; a kind of electricity. Steve says he doesn't like these new patterns he's seeing. Says, 'That old shoe of your women's horses wouldn't have known these changes.'

Neither of us names it, but we are talking, all the same, about climate breakdown. The mare shifts her weight and he bears it. The clincher presses the nail heads down with a click to secure the shoe.

CHAPTER SEVENTEEN

Parish Work

January 1947–April 1950

The winter of 1947 proves to be one of the harshest of the century. Miss White is by herself in that rather big farmhouse, without anyone to keep it warm and functioning, or cook for her. Let's not judge her for that last, from the comfort and ease of having heated homes with electricity, appliances and convenient food. She has none of these things and a substantial farm to run to exacting government standards as well as support the men she employs, and their families. Late January, it begins to snow and doesn't really stop until the middle of March. Arctic conditions and severe blizzards deliver almost continuous snow cover, deep frost and ice across the country. In the southern English lowlands, there are level accumulations of three feet or more and drifts in excess of fifteen feet in places, especially on the high Downland. Bulldozers are diverted from bomb to snow clearance and ice floes jostle up the Thames. Post-war shortages and difficulties bite harder, are further exacerbated and bitterly exposed, and there are severe hardships. Many businesses close down for the period, unable to operate or receive stock, and there are coal shortages and power blackouts. Neither Miss White nor the farm cottagers notice any power blackouts, not having it in the first place, but she runs out of fuel for her coal-fired range, which makes cooking rather difficult, and must eke out coke for the hot water boiler to thaw the troughs.

At first, Julia drives into Hungerford for her midday dinner and a bit of cheer at a nice little café, until the snow becomes too deep. Then she wraps herself up in thick layers and, with a scarf over her head and ears, goes on the Fordson tractor for a few days until it gets stuck in enormous drifts on Hungerford Common. She has to walk, first to the café and to recharge the wireless battery, then trudge the five miles home in deep, exhausting snow. Bert and Dick manage to retrieve the tractor, which she feels foolish about, but she hugs herself for managing to recharge the wireless battery. She is grateful for the company of her dogs, Jo and Dina. Soon, they are completely cut off, like thousands of other villagers, in an Arctic siege, with little hope of coal or replenishing food or other supplies. The telephone is often down and, as the weeks progress with no let-up, animal feed and hay run low.

All field work stops, with efforts bent on the never ending task of thawing, floundering through snow with buckets of hot water, lighting fires under troughs and keeping the animals alive. The icy blast finds every paper-thin nook and gap in every accommodation. The cattle, pig and horse sheds and stables are deep littered with straw banked high against draughts and strawy muck is spread over the yard for purchase. The summer's golden harvested straw spills from the animals' outbuildings, making a lamplight glow onto the wintry whiteness without. It is a cold, wretched and lonely time for Julia. The house is an icebox and the temperature plummets, even across southern Britain, to as low as -20°C. In the mornings, under the hedgerows, there are the sad, frozen bodies of birds – redwing, fieldfare, blackbirds, yellowhammers, goldcrests. During the snow event of February 2018, caused by the Polar air mass and dubbed the 'Beast from the East', I found a barn owl on the hill, frozen and sad, like a wounded airman in a hospital gown, his hands behind his back. It seems the saddest, most pitiful thing to see the birds of the air, frozen upon the ground.

The gang find work in Wergs Barn, between expeditions to outlying yards and animals, under thatch weighted with icicles like swords, amid the warmth of cow's breath, body, dung and straw. They sort potatoes into sacks, split and point fence piles and cut thatching spars. They tell stories and sing. Julia loves this part of the day. Bert entertains them with his axe skills. He makes a light cut in a log, puts a sixpence in and splits it into two thin halves, lengthways. No one else can do it. They all try. Julia has to supply the sixpences.

Across the country, animals die of the cold: two million sheep and lambs, thirty thousand cattle, thousands of chickens. Vegetables are frozen in ground like iron and, for the first time, potatoes are rationed. The severe weather worsens into March and on the sixth, one of the worst blizzards of the twentieth century lasts forty-eight hours, powered by a gale force easterly. The deepest ever recorded depth of lying snow in an inhabited area in Britain (and not drifts) was two inches shy of seven feet, in Forest-in-Teesdale, County Durham.

Julia pauses at the kitchen window one morning, her breath suspended on the air and the rooms dimmed with a William Morris-patterning of frost ferns etched on every window. She casts a tall, rather melancholy pre-Raphaelite figure in the chilly lemon-and-blue light, her little dogs weaving around her legs. Her shoulders slope elegantly. Hands on hips, she stretches her neck and shoulders; a Mariana in the Moated Grange in Millais' painting, only in breeches and long brown boots, two jumpers (one American) and an overcoat, instead of a blue velvet gown.

There has been such a bustle in the house for so long, and she is lonely. Her short hair is covered with the most fantastic black beret that I've never noticed before, worn at a jaunty angle. Rather Greta Garbo, very chic. She scrapes out a square from the frosted ferns with a wooden spatula to see the great, white down looming close and disappearing into the sky. A blank white page. Uncountable flocks of birds move across the hill and sky like notebook prompts or subtitles in different fonts; rooks and jackdaws in an Arial Black, lapwings in a Broadway Poster, the gulls in a simple Segoe; golden plover in her own hand, which I am trying to decipher in her Day Book and Cultivations Record in the warmth of the Berkshire Records Office. The numbers and flocks of birds through her window astound me, so very many and such variety, and yet, even now, over her shoulder, are fewer than last year, fewer than the year before, though not enough to be noticeable.

Seventy-seven years later, I get to stand in the same spot, looking out onto Bumpy Field and the big down, as the snow falls and covers the green. A handful of rooks and jackdaws fly across, six goldfinches; nothing more. A rubbing out. Richard and Jackie, who own Manor Farm now (beautifully renovated and still a farm), have kindly invited me round. We chat over a cup of tea, our wellies at the door, and I enjoy the warmth of their ground-sourced underfloor heating, their retriever's head resting on my knee. We discuss how hard it is to farm on this ground and the extent of the farm, which was much larger when Julia had it. It is wonderful to be here and to see the place loved. Steve Cordery, who farms for them and knew the place as a boy, says it has always been a 'happy place'. We find a sad, dead hen sparrow in the Granary, now partly a cottage, partly a games room, and are both moved. It must've flown in unnoticed and got locked in, Richard reasons. There are a few here, which is a rarity in itself, but not the chirpy thousands regarded as grain-stealing pests in Julia's time. Richard, Jackie and Steve want to see the farmland birds back. We delight that there is still a barn owl here, which I see regularly on my back-and-forths to Mum's house and on my walks through the farm.

Back at her window, Julia watches her barn owl come past on its way back to the Granary, only distinguishable from the Canadian-style white-out by the warm toast of its breast. That is how she'd describe it, the colour of lightly browned toast. Now she is hungry and nostalgic for the white bread they all miss, not the brown, gritty National Loaf they all eat now. Julia brushes herself down. This is a low, and uncharacteristic. Her men will be waiting for instruction in the yard. She is worried about losing the unthreshed oats in the ricks off Bell Lane. The sheen and baler have been caught the other side of Parson's Hill where the snow is deepest, and threshing has proved impossible. She decides then to abandon those ricks for now and somehow get the tackle up to Grains, where the wind has kept the snow moving. She thinks of Canada, and Joe Eggleston with his levers and perseverance, claps her hands to the dogs and says to them, 'Well, give it a try Julia, you might do it.'

With all hands, they try everything, but the Allis's tracks can't grip the frozen road. Eventually, Miss White hires a lorry with a winch from the village and the threshing tackle is pulled slowly up the hill to the Rogation Beech and the ricks at Grains. It takes a whole day. She feels despair creeping in again. There are wheat ricks to do at Champions Field too and the cold won't leave her bones, it is all a bit much. Then comes Bert, comes Dick, Charlie, Bill Watts, Billy Edwards and Jack Hitchens: 'Don't you worry, Miss White; we'll do it. At least we're not being shot upon. We'll get him done.' And they do. Neighbours are kind too, offering hot food and friendship.

The thaw comes with a vengeance and for almost a month, heavy rain falls on impenetrable, deep-frozen ground. The Thames rises a foot in an hour and spreads her skirts a mile wide at Maidenhead, near Reading. There is terrible, widespread flooding across the country with six thousand homes affected in the Thames Valley alone. Sewage contaminates water supplies and food shortages are now acute. A Commonwealth Disaster Fund is set up, Canada sends food parcels to Suffolk and the Australian Red Cross assist Gloucestershire. In flooded streets, bread is thrown through upper windows from relief dinghies and milk is delivered only if a baby is shown at the window. Around two hundred thousand acres of corn is lost.

Though it is so terribly wet and sticky, the green grass is a relief to see, after months of Siberian whiteness. And, at last, a nice new couple, Fred and Mary, move into the house as tractor driver and housekeeper and things begin to look up. A short, intense spring, where everything seems to flower at once, relaxes into a sunny, warm summer. They make good hay from Hayes Piece and get it all on the trailers and the carts behind Dolly and Sylvie. As they finish 'aycrut', Miss White glances at the hill where a few wispy white clouds are travelling across the blue above. Early signs a thunderstorm is building. They remind her of white horses ahead of a rough sea, sailing. She can feel the tack and physicality of it, the saltwater sticky on her lips. She smiles at the memory, satisfied that this is who she is now, a farmer, weathering storms. She nods to the clouds. 'Weather breeders, Bert.' Without looking up, Bert says, 'Weather breeders, Miss. I felt them on my neck.'

Over the following years, and with her ARP responsibilities left off, Miss White throws herself fully into community life; a necessary part and parcel of a vibrant village, and a kind of responsibility, especially, it seems, if you are a woman of resource and you run a farm in the centre of it. You are always being called upon for something but often in need of help too. Miss White is put up as a candidate in a Parish Council election and is elected, quite quickly becoming chairman. From keeping footpaths open and unobstructed, to addressing and interrogating the apparently unfair allocation of new council houses by the District Council, Julia is a force to be reckoned with. The people of Inkpen are too; as in many rural parishes, they are not shy about airing their views and she must take their 'spirited criticisms', listen, and act upon them. There are plenty of good rows in the village hall, and she often feels like a bone between dogs, but things do get sorted. Julia supplies Christmas trees for the school and church, and sheaves for the harvest festival. After one particularly wet year, the wheat sheaves drip in the chancel. During a hearty rendition of 'We Plough the Fields and Scatter', she watches a wood mouse run along the aisle and up into the sheaf. She keeps this little delight to herself, wondering if, by the time Rector has the sheaf for his chickens, the mice will have eaten all the corn. The rector has not liked the wet sheaves, to which Miss White retorts, 'Well, the Almighty must like wet sheaves as he has made so very many of them this year.' This harvest, in her Day Book and Cultivations Record, she has written, 'This is a mug's game.'

I get, perhaps, the most insight into Miss White's character through her myriad and extensive community work. Like Doris Mason, like Marguerite de Beaumont, she does an awful lot and humbly so. A kind of civic duty, or a Scouting one that is of course immensely rewarding. But sometimes, she has to be tough and unpopular for the greater end. She stands up to the rector, when he makes an underhand application to route a sewage pipe over the new churchyard, upsetting villagers who are all for digging up and reburying their loved ones elsewhere. She campaigns for a new rectory, as the old one is damp and crumbling, and donates a corner of Champions Field for it, understanding that 'the Church' is really the people and a centre of this scattered place. When Tom Ward, the 'People's Warden', retires, the village campaigns for her to accept the post and to look out for their interests within the parish.

She organises a blood transfusion service in the village hall with the WI and is on the Flower and Produce Show Committee. She also becomes a school governor for the village school where the most pressing need, even as late as 1949, is water. The headmistress lives in the Victorian school building and sanitary arrangements for her, the schoolchildren and staff are primitive, to say the least: a rainwater tank from which water must be bucketed indoors and boiled. It runs dry in summer and three times a week, Billy or Miss White fill and take the water cart with Boxer to empty it into the school rain tank. It is a strain on all, especially Boxer, as he must go both down and uphill with it, although he thoroughly enjoys the children's attentions when he gets there. The nearest mains water supply is less than a mile up the road but, despite the urgency, neither District Council nor water company will sort the pipes. In frustration, Julia organises a campaign and goes 'on strike'. With apologies to Winnie the headmistress, also Julia's friend, she gets all the neighbours to refuse to supply water to the school, and resists, herself. Nobody dares break the strike. She invites Winnie to the farmhouse for baths, to cook and wash as much as she likes, in subterfuge. Julia is supported at first, but then, when neither Council nor water company give in, there are protests and persuasions. She remains firm. By 1950, a few months later, the school and their headmistress have piped, safe water.

Like Miss White, Land Girl Enid/John Barraud was also active in their community; joyfully, with some trepidation and great success, they voluntarily re-opened and ran the village library – a rural librarian after my own heart. And, like Miss White, Lady Eve Balfour was the ARP for her village and chair of Haughley Parish Council. Prior to this and between the wars, she was instrumental in leading a campaign and protests to abolish Agricultural Tithes – a remnant of a medieval tax whereby farmers still had to give 10 per cent of their produce or earnings directly to their rector and the Church of England. Lady Balfour was indomitable. As far as the US, she is described in the *Niagara Falls Gazette* of 1933 as 'no play farmeret [she is] mostly garbed in semi-masculine clothes ... and leads the militant famers'. For a short time, the British Union of Fascists seized an opportunity to gain support from some farmers by defending them, sometimes literally and bodily from the bailiffs, capitalising on a feeling of unfair treatment and oppression. They were no doubt encouraged by some of the founders of the organic movement, such as Henry Williamson, Rolf Gardiner and Jorian Jenks who were also fascists. On 24 June 1936, many farmers and their families went to London to protest, arriving in trains, coaches and by horse and cart. Present-day protests, against government policy and support, supermarket monopolies and, most recently, changes to inheritance tax on farms, have seen farmers drive into London in tractors. Some of these protests have also been co-opted by radical right-wing and climate-sceptic groups, and have also been largely rejected by the farmers.

In 1949, Oxford student John Schlesinger returns to his parents' house at Mount Pleasant in the village to make his first narrative film, having already made films on the front line. Engaging locals from the dramatic society, and friends Alan Cooke, Robert Hardy and Raymond Leppard, his short noir *The Black Legend* tells the dramatised story of the double gibbet on the hill: of an adulterous murderous couple whose bodies were hung there in 1676. It is filmed on location during harvest at Manor Farm, on Parson's Hill and Gallows Down. The farmworkers get on with their work, but in period dress. In the film, which I've watched several times in the village hall, I can see Bert, yelming ricks in the field in a smock. The gibbet itself is a sturdy replica. Miss White lends the character of Robert Broomham the treasured ploughman's smock given to her by Jack Tucker, as well as Sylvie and the green tip cart. The lovers stand in the tip cart with nooses round their necks, Jack's smock fluttering in the breeze, while Sylvie stands as patiently as she does at haycart. Just as well. The rural summer scene falls away giddyingly beneath them. John Schlesinger and his friends went on to become Oscar-winning directors, producers, conductors and actors, and it is funny to think of them making their debut in the Manor Farm fields, while harvest takes place around them.

In this year, Miss White manages to bring electricity to the farm. She must pay for the poles and wiring herself and, due to a curious piece of legislation, it must first go into the farm. The improvements are worth it, allowing them to install a little Benthall mill for grinding corn in the granary, light in the stables and cow sheds and a bucket heater for Jack, so he can heat calf gruel and wash buckets without trailing to the house. The year after, the cottages, then the farmhouse are done, and as a result of the wiring and lifting of ancient floorboards, the rats are finally eliminated from the farmhouse. But the house has one last challenge for her; one last need, and lets her know in dramatic fashion. Julia lights a fire one afternoon with some rather smoky wood, and Charlie Wright spots smoke pouring through the tiles around the chimney stack outside. She and Charlie put the fire out in the grate and venture up a ladder into the roof space. Walking over the joist, Julia finds a big hole in the chimney's brickwork, right next to some rather scorched rafters, the brickwork crumbling. On inspection, each chimney is found to be in a similar state of disrepair. Scaffolding is erected and Frank Carter begins this extensive work. The beautiful old oak beams are found to be sound, but all have a very near miss when one of the chimneys crumbles and comes crashing down through the upper floor and onto the coke boiler below. Incredibly, the old house kills no one, and with the four chimneys completely rebuilt, is in a good state of repair. It has all taken rather a long time. To set a seal on it perhaps, the War Ag make a visit and declare Manor Farm a model one, tough as it is to farm, and her grading goes from B to the treasured A. At Newbury Agricultural Show, in 1952, there are celebrations when Manor Farm wins third prize for 'Best Farmed Farm' among many much larger entrants.

As Julia enters her fifth decade, still fit, strong and healthy, the 1950s seem flooded with a new and sunny warmth, with the war years receding and a little more comfort, ease and confidence in her abilities and judgement. She buys a lovely herd of Blue Grey beef cattle, bred out of Aberdeen Angus cows by a white Shorthorn bull. They are lovely, hardy animals of a salt-and-pepper, blue-roan colour. With their bull, sweet Timid Ivan, they live out all winter and calve outside, with good thick hedges for shelter and a good ration of oat straw and hay. But nothing stays still in farming. The weather is ever a challenge and new innovations, markets and demands must be met. Miss White and her farm community move through that strange, misty portal, the paradox of the rural, where things are at once timeless and unchanging, but at the same time must often react to the winds of change first. It's through this portal that I see them, and can pull together the threads of our connections. Those we make in a community, whether we are quite newly arrived and bringing something fresh, or have been here for centuries. Either way, we are enriched by each other and find, in one another's stories of farming, food, community and the land, memories and, ultimately, ourselves.

CHAPTER EIGHTEEN

Miss Ambrose, Fetes and Junketings

May 1950–August 1954

Sometime in around 1950 or 1951, Miss Ambrose arrives in the village, like a blush on the roses, like warmth spreading across the hayfield at sunrise. She is friend of the rector's, in want of a job, and Miss White is need of a secretary. Miss Ambrose moves into the farmhouse and becomes a splendid addition to the staff, proficient at farm accounts, letter writing, form filling and wages, but has also relished being a Land Girl during the war. She can drive the car, the tractors, is good with livestock and immensely practical. When the men go to dinner, they leave the tractors running and the women hop to it, Julia driving the Allis and Miss Ambrose on the Fordson. She is also very fond of the cows and horses. Tommy and Dolly are particular favourites. Fred and Mary leave in 1952 to be closer to family and Miss Ambrose's capable, kind and friendly mother joins the party to do the housekeeping. Miss Ambrose spends her evenings with Julia, listening to the wireless, playing a game of cards or such like. They enjoy each other's company immensely. It is a happy household. Miss Ambrose is always called 'Amber'.

Julia has many friends in the village and elsewhere. Good friends, too, including Doris and Marguerite, and Miss Jo Denny, with whom she runs a dozen Scout and Guide camps each year – not to mention the grown-up Scouts and Guides who return to visit, sometimes bringing partners or children of their own; but she never mentions family. Her father, Arthur Frederick White, a successful insurance broker, dies aged forty in Paris on business when Julia is just nine. He leaves the family very well provided for, and Julia's mother, Helen White, née Lazenby, puts a substantial amount of their wealth to good charitable use early on in the First World War, fitting out their former rather grand home The Gorse, within Manor Park in Chislehurst, Kent, for refugee families, while living in another, nearby. My author friend and fellow *Guardian* Country Diarist, Nic Wilson, helps fill in some other details when she is on an ancestry site one evening, and a rapid volley of exciting messages follows. Julia's mother, Helen, dies fifteen years after her father does, when Julia is twenty-four and in Canada, visiting her brother, Freddie. Julia sails to Toronto and is in Vermont by 1928, then Durban, South Africa, in 1936. She speaks French and some German (vastly improved when working alongside her party of amicable German POWs) and she is the second of four siblings.

I find a photograph of her sister and sister-in-law online, in the *Bystander*, 1934, photographed in the gardens of the Golf Hotel at the luxury society sports resort of Le Touquet-Paris-Plage in northern France.* The caption utterly defines the two women through a proprietorial male gaze, though the magazine would have been read by more women. It later went on to merge with *Tatler*. The women's married names are used as you'd expect, but not only are their first names supplanted by the intended formality of their husbands', still fairly common up until recently, they are also shortened in an informal, matey way, reducing the independence and individuality of the women further. Who even are they, without husbands, fathers, brothers? It is hard to work out who is who, their own names erased by marriage. But here is 'Mrs Freddie White [Lois Olive Russell, Countess of Brandon, Australia] and Mrs Nicky Kasterine

* 'Le Toqs' was destroyed in the war, and became the most mined town in France, with around 130,000 explosive devices planted there, before then being heavily bombed by Allied forces.

[Alice Katherine White]. Mrs Kasterine's husband is Roumanian [actually, he was Russian] and a Monte Carlo summer regular. She is Mr Freddie White's sister.' I can recognise Julia in Alice's face and tall, slim frame. The women are cool and elegant in their white, sporty skirt-and-blazer suits. Even in black-and-white print, their silk stockings gleam.

It seems odd to align the glamorous-seeming life of her sisters in this photo with the image I have of Julia's manual work in the fields, in the rain perhaps, with sacking over her old clothes; or sitting by the fire with her dogs in a freezing, damp, unlit house riddled with rats, as it was. It is evident that she had the private financial means to be independent, was well educated and well travelled, almost always had a housekeeper and enjoyed a life before the Second World War, riding, sailing and travelling. But looking at the society photo of her sister and sister-in-law in 1934, I wonder how she, a single, unmarried woman in her thirties then, fitted into that scene. How (un) desirable and (in) accessible? Ultimately, she was able to truly do what she wanted and, though very hard at times, it is a happy, fulfilled and purposeful life, lived on her own terms. More texts come in from Nic. The farming seems to have skipped a generation or two, and landed with Julia. Her great-grandfather William White, born 1807, is a Cheshunt farmer with 270 acres and twenty labourers. Her Aunt Gwendoline married a 'keen agriculturalist'.

Julia's younger sister, Alice, divorced a year after the photograph was taken and died in 1947, aged just forty-two. Julia then lost both her brother and older sister in 1952, aged just fifty-one and fifty-four respectively. Very young.

I can't help wondering about Amber. Or a partner. I am prying, aren't I? Sometimes, I wonder, actually, who is haunting who. Because so much about Miss White remains elusive and misted, and why shouldn't it? Why should I impose my idea of a happy ending, when she might be an entirely happy single woman with wonderful friends, by design? Or was she gay in a difficult time to be out or, more to the point, was it harder to be gay and out in the mid 1980s, when she wrote up her diaries? Because I remember the '80s. In a decade of radical, social, political, economic and cultural change, I also remember friends' and teachers' fear and anger over Section 28, the Local Government Act banning schools, libraries, certain arts projects and local authorities from promoting or discussing homosexuality or 'pretended family relationships'. We protested together and I hope I've been an active lifelong ally. The curation I manage in my school library now is full of wonderful diverse fiction and texts, featuring all kinds of families and relationships. But I can see why someone might not want to expose themselves. In the introduction to Little Toller's edition of Enid Barraud's *Set My Hand upon the Plough*, Luke Turner urges caution around 'outing' the past through a modern prism of understanding sexual and gender identity, so I want to be careful. But Enid/ John refers to themselves as an invert and Lady Balfour, with her short hair and breeches, delighted in being mistaken for a man. I ask Betty, our very dear next-door neighbour for twenty years, what she remembers of Miss White. She knew her as a child, and into her teens, and recalls her as kind and always doing something for others, always involved in village life. And, she says emphatically, with a wink, 'She dressed as a *man*. She wore a smock sometimes or breeches and a waistcoat and a beret. And she always stood her ground!'

I wonder how well Julia, Doris or Marguerite knew Frances or Ralph Partridge. They would have been acquaintances, certainly, and their influence and renown felt, but two of the original Ham Spray Bloomsbury trio, Lytton Strachey and Dora Carrington, died weeks apart there in 1932, three years before Doris and Marguerite came to neighbouring Shalbourne Manor. Frances walks through Manor Farm regularly on her way to pick up her son, Burgo, from friends in Inkpen or to visit friends themselves, such as the Padels, an intriguing and talented musical couple, both pacifists and an 'admirable family'. Mrs Padel teaches Burgo for a while in a small school, though she is 'against schools, meat-eating and water closets'. Mr Padel teaches Frances the violin. They are the grandparents of Ruth Padel, a wonderfully warm, eclectic writer and award-winning poet of great range and depth, as well as a fellow of both the Royal Society of Literature and Zoological Society of London, and Charles Darwin's great-great-granddaughter. Ruth chairs an event I do at New Networks for Nature in Bath in 2021 and shows me an old photograph of her grandparents' Inkpen bungalow – I recognise it instantly.

There are two photographs of Julia in *The Inkpen Saga* – and I've found no other. On the back cover flap, there is a portrait of her as a younger woman. She is thoughtful, elegant and rather uncomfortable, with the look of a more pensive Mary Pickford about her, or a non-smiling Jean Arthur, both film actresses of the day. Her hair is bobbed short with a marcel wave and she wears a square-cut, simple loose shift with a long string of beads, flapper-girl style. In the other photo, she is in her fifties and sits on a bench outside the farmhouse with her dogs on her lap, looking down at them. In jodhpurs, and spats worn over hobnailed boots, a large, androgynous jacket over a shirt, with her hair bobbed short under a beret, and a pair of round glasses, she could be Vita Sackville-West in her garden. I rub a gloved hand over the film of the barn window between us, to try to get a clearer picture, my hand poised to knock at the glass. Anyone there?

Another older neighbour, Bob May, who has recently died, remembers her too. He is a keen naturalist and plantsman at his own conifer tree nursery that borders Manor Farm. He once showed me a cuckoo chick in a dunnock's nest at his place, and a pair of roosting barn owls. I meet him on a run one day when he is feeding his flock of geese and ask him what he remembers of her. Bob is a bit of a renegade. 'Stood for no nonsense. Firm but kind and,' he pauses for dramatic effect, 'I think she liked the other sex.' This seems to tickle him. He laughs and gives me a goose egg, knowing I'll have to try to run home with it. And I do, trying to hold on to an enormous, chalky-white warm goose egg down my top like an idiot – I can still hear him laughing as I jog off, and get the giggles myself. One day after Bob has died, I creep into his paddock to look at the caravan behind his parents' derelict Box Cottage. He was always going to show me the caravan, but couldn't remember where his parents had got it from. Miss White writes that she sold the little apple-green Cheltenham she towed across Salisbury Plain in the midst of a tank convoy, to a neighbour. But she also leaves with one that she and Amber use for mini-breaks in the New Forest. Did she buy another? I'm wondering if this is her first caravan.

I push through brambles to peer through the glassless back window and meet the eyes of a fox, scarfed by its own tail. It slips off the mossy foam of a torn cushion and is gone in a tangle of ivy, as if someone reached in and snatched back a stole through the window. I grin. There is the musky, singed-fur smell of fox. A coat hung from a hook swings slightly, disturbed by the fox's exit, and a comma butterfly flutters out. Like the ending in *A Canterbury Tale*, I think, when Alison the Land Girl ends her pilgrimage to a badly bombed Canterbury to find the caravan she shared with her missing-in-action fiancé, intact but moth-eaten and dusty in a lock-up garage. I'm sure it's a little (possibly apple-green) Cheltenham too. The original colour on this one is hard to decipher, faded as it is. Definitely stained green and of an old shape. I lay my hand on it for a moment, then leave it to the foxes. I google vintage caravans endlessly when I get home, not really sure what I want to prove. That she was here? That I am? Some kind of proof of Miss White's existence in the landscape that I can touch. She also describes giving her beautiful old smock to a museum for safe keeping. I try West Berkshire Museum in Newbury: thirteen smocks, but none with J.T. on the collar; none that fluttered eerily from a dummy on the gibbet high above the fields. I try Winchester Museum, the Richard Jefferies Museum in Swindon, the Museum of English Rural Life in Reading. No smock. I keep searching.

After the war, village fetes have a resurgence, fulfilling a need, perhaps, to dress up and parade and have a day off. When we think of village fetes now, when we organise and picture them in our own village, we hark back to their heyday in the 1950s. But reading Julia's account as well as records from the local Women's Institute, I find many wry similarities with now; the same few volunteers pulling everything together, takings sometimes covering expenses and raising funds for whatever cause is due, and sometimes not. That, if it is to be truly for everyone, among the motley collection of gazebos, hay bale arenas and bunting, the wonderful artisanal food, craft beers and expensive hog roasts, there must be provision for those of lesser means; usually the people that have been here the longest. Lucky dips and hook-a-ducks for the little ones, squash and homemade cake, so everyone can eat, a plastic bin of iced water full of cans. The economic diversity of a village can be apparent in the cast-off wellies lining up to be wanged: children's frog-eyed boots and near-transparent sparkly numbers stand beside colourful pairs of festival-wear, and high-end neoprene-lined Le Chameaus jostle in odd pairs with Dunlops, their soles lacerated by flints.

But this is the work, isn't it? The things you get to do in a community; the volunteering of time, of commitment, from which everyone benefits. Some of our best memories have been wrapped up in that. The school and village fetes, fundraising quizzes at the village hall, playgroups, book clubs and wildlife clubs at the school, firework nights. All three of our children have been Cubs, Scouts and Explorer Scouts, with my husband, Martin, a Scout leader for many years now. We are, or have been, school governors; Martin for the little village primary school Miss White sorted the water for and was a governor for herself, and me at the rural secondary school in Hungerford. Bert 'Jailer' Annetts spoke of 180 children at the primary school at one time, though it's usually been around the 50–60 mark, including when our three were there. But the numbers are falling. Many newer parents coming into the village opt to drive their children out of the village to bigger schools or, more often than not, private ones, rather than walk across the fields and through woods, joining up with their friends along the way, to their local one. Shalbourne Primary School closed last year with just five pupils on its roll, and the pub followed. Yet all the houses are occupied, as they always have been. Shalbourne recently featured in an article in the *Telegraph* on 'the poshest villages to move to'. The photo illustrating it was of a pheasant shoot. These, apparently, are the villages 'lined with chocolate-box, thatched cottages, with Range Rovers parked on the driveways'. Driveways?

'There's a bougie gastropub in the centre [nope], a well-stocked Waitrose [no...] and a fancy private school just around the corner.' Few of those things say village to me. Come for the cosy country pubs, the small schools, the fetes; and don't support any of them.

Miss White and Amber are on the committee of the annual Flower and Produce Show, held most years in Pigeon House Meadow opposite the farmyard. It is a lot of hard work. They raise money for instruments or new uniforms for the Inkpen Band, of which several of her men and their families are part. As well as the flower, fruit and vegetable competitions, there are a number of side shows: Bowling for a Pig, a handicraft section, lucky dip for the children and a beer tent. Julia and her neighbour from Pink's Farm have a fruit and vegetable stall they call Pink and White's. There is also a Baby Show, judged by Nurse Jordan, who has delivered all the babies and ends up completely unable to make a decision. We run the Dog Show at our village fete and decide, after the first year, to co-opt our neighbour Jenny from the Dogs Trust to actually judge it, for similar reasons. Between us, we know almost all of the dogs and owners, and she lends her authority. For the first fete after the war, Miss White decides to wear a summer dress and hat – but no one can find her when she is needed; no one recognises her. She goes home to change amid much fond and mutual hilarity and returns in her usual shirt, jacket and trousers so that then, 'Everybody knew who I was!' She is herself.

In May 1953, the village celebrates the Queen's Coronation with the usual junketings and a fancy dress parade of vehicles and attendants. By now, Miss White has a treasured Land Rover, and Amber drives it, pulling the green horse-drawn tip cart behind it. Their theme, poignantly, as these things often unexpectedly are, is 'Farming Then and Now'. The Land Rover is decorated with paper streamers and flowers, and two of Jack Hitchens' girls sit in the back with hay bales and very modern dresses. Miss White, Billy and three Scouts are dressed in old, borrowed smocks with floppy hats and kerchiefs around their necks. They ride in the tip cart with some of last year's sheaves, the two dogs and the oldest tools they have, including Bert's fiddle broadcaster. Afterwards, the villagers make their way up the hill to the Beacon on the top, as we have so often done for other celebrations, and it is lit as the band play into a stiff and disorganising breeze.

After the harvest of 1953, it becomes clear to Miss White that a labour shortage is critical. While more modern equipment has reduced the need for quite so many workers, the POWs and Land Girls have gone home, the school harvest camps disbanded and there is no more casual labour. Seven men is simply not enough. She makes enquiries into a combine harvester. She rides Tommy along the boundary track at Inglebutts, between Manor Farm and Major Huth's Wansdyke Farm, to see if such a machine might manage. She has right of way over the track and it is the only way a combine harvester can be got down there. The old track down Parson's Hill is too rough and steep and the new one already too narrow; things are moving at such a pace. She is surprised to see several big haystacks built right across the track. Before she has the chance to think about going to see Major Huth about this, a letter arrives in the post that is obviously not meant for her. Someone has blundered. Likely, the Major's unfortunate secretary. It is a letter from Major Huth to his solicitor. He would like to cancel the right of way and prevent the Manor Farm people from using it. Pure spite. Probably over the pheasant-shooting issue. Julia looks out the farm deeds and finds not only her copy of the agreement, made with Mr Lawrence, his heirs and successors some time ago, but also Major Huth's copy, which he should be in possession of, agreeing legal access to a right of way. She decides to deliver it herself.

She takes care to change into 'more respectable clothes': a smart tweed jacket and riding breeches with two front pockets. She is received politely enough into his study and asked to sit down. She prefers, she says, to remain standing – feeling more in possession of the situation. She is taller than he and feels she needs every advantage. She puts her hands in her pockets, which visibly angers his military mind, but it is too late to do anything about that now. She widens her stance. First, she asks him if he would kindly remove the haystacks that are blocking the right of way and cannot be got round with a combine harvester. He begins to tell her, quite firmly, that she has presumed a right of way, when there isn't one. She produces first the letter he has written to his solicitor but sent in error to her – he is furious, claiming some kind of skulduggery – and then she gives him the copy of his own agreement. With this last shot, he is apoplectic, but her right of access is sealed. As, in effect, is ours, as the route is a public right of way now. They part eventually after the row and not exactly friends. She chuckles all the way home. Tells Amber and Mrs Ambrose with glee. She is still chuckling about it now. Julia will come up against him again, but they are often in agreement about other things, as is the rural way, and as he is with Ralph Partridge when they both agitate successfully together for more and better social housing for the villagers. But, right of way secured, with one last hurdle, she may be able to purchase a combine harvester. Bravo, Miss White.

Julia calls a meeting with her men about the prospect of them being too few to get the harvest in and the threshing done. This they know. 'It has been satisfactory up until now,' she says, 'but what if we were to get a combine harvester?' She gives them time to think and discuss the ramifications of this monumental change. 'Bert,' she says, 'I would like you to come to me with your answer, given you are Captain of the Threshing Machine and King of the Harvest.' Bert duly delivers their message to her, with his decision that afternoon, very soberly, cap in hand. They are understanding of the difficulties. There is not nearly enough of them, and no others that want to do the work, outside the farm. 'We must move with the times and be prepared for change,' says Bert, very formally. 'Thank you, Miss.' Bert then, has made his last haystack, thatched and yelmed his last rick, curried and courted, fed and shovelled his last beloved threshing machine, on the farm. He is not, he says, of the sentimental sort. Julia is sure he is not. But all that skill, the way the countryside looks; the steepled sheaves casting their long shadows, the golden-thatched and windowless 'houses' of stored summer, the shocking up, the followers and gleaners; the camaraderie and machine of the interlocking, working, singing rhythm of the harvest and threshing gangs, is over.

The second-hand, bright-red Massey Harris 'bagger' combine comes from Andover on a lorry and is delivered in the road outside the farm, with the minimum of instruction. Julia decides Bill Watts should be the regular driver with Bert on the sacks. She offers Bill the seat, and he hesitates. 'You do it first, Miss,' he says. So she does. Amber drives the Land Rover in front with Bill and Bert in it to warn road users and to help Julia steer the awkward thing over the little sleeper bridge and down Hollow Lane, past the church and down the Ham Spray road towards Inglebutts. Turning into the track off the narrow lane is tight and there is, as there is now, another set of sleepers over a deep, wide ditch that carries water off the Downs. Slowly and with guidance from them all, she manages it and drives the first combine harvester in the village onto the field below Gallows Down.

Bill and Bert both take to it and Bert resumes his role as Captain of the Combine. It gathers and scythes the corn with the big, rolling header and knives, then threshes, shakes and rolls it to separate the corn from the chaff and cavings, and delivers the threshed corn into sacks, held by one man, and the straw out the back to be baled later. It is noisy, dusty work without a cab, but they get the harvest in, with just the six of them, and Amber. I walk the route they take with my dog, thinking of the much bigger modern combines that also travel with an escort, but with their wide rolling headers so long, they have to be taken separately on trailers, lengthways. It is a surreal and exciting thing, to be sat with the farmer in an air-conditioned cab, as I have done sometimes, and watch the corn be gobbled greedily and so efficiently up. I take a detour through the churchyard, where there is a lovely view of its own former rickyard, past the old blue-and-orange-painted, oak-handled, single-furrow Bedford plough that stands against the wall, its shining mouldboard sunk into the grass. I look at the plough, that I love; whose handle I always touch as I go past, sweeping its elegant shape with my hand, suddenly, with new eyes. It's hers. Of course it is – how have I never realised before? It was restored, freshly painted and given to the church by a recent owner of Manor Farm, Mark Kary, then dedicated in a ceremony on

Plough Sunday, some years back. Its little silver plaque faces Manor Farm's former fields and says, 'This plough is a tribute to all who over the years have worked the land in the parish of Inkpen.' It is engraved with a drawing of the curve of Gallows Down behind two horses ploughing and a tall man behind the plough. It could be Sylvie and Dolly and Billy. It is the same plough Julia owned and handled, and that she and Doris pulled up the aisle of the church to be blessed. Before they all went up to the Rogation Beech tree, singing and following behind the band and Sylvie and Dolly's broad white rumps, plaited with ears of corn and ribbons, where I heard the bells above me go ringing by, in a pocket of air. I step behind it and set my own hands upon the plough handles.

CHAPTER NINETEEN

The Ghosts of the Fields

Michaelmas 1954–1955 and 2023–2025

I do not search for Miss White in the churchyard, because she is not there. In seeking permission to rewrite her story, to bring her into the light, I request a record of probate. She had no children, no surviving parents or siblings, and Amber died before her. Neither her solicitors nor the publisher of her book exist any more. Her last address is a village near Winchester, but I can find no reference to Julia Maud White among the church records. I apply and wait for a copy of her will, which, when it comes, has a few surprises. Her estate is distributed mostly to her niece, great-niece and nephew, and there is a request that the manuscript of *The Inkpen Saga* is kept in the oak trunk in St Michael and All Angels Church, Inkpen, being of historical interest. Also that she be cremated, and her ashes interred in the old churchyard there. So she was here all along, right under my feet! She came back and I feel it is deeply significant that she did. That it meant so much to her. I go at once.

There are so many familiar names on the headstones, but not hers. I try the church, where two ladies are flower arranging. The air is fresh and heady with chrysanthemum scent. Together we find and open the oak trunk, which is just full of embroidered kneelers. No Julia, no manuscript. Eventually I locate it, through the village history society website, at the Berkshire Records Office in Reading, not far from the Museum of English Rural Life. That's where

I find all the volumes of her Day Book and Cultivations Record. They are presented for me, one at a time, propped upon a pillow. Some are black and red, but most are a beautiful deep blue, with orange spines. Essex cart, Fordson tractor colours. And there is her handwriting, like a flock of birds across the page. As perfunctory as her diary, neat, but a little hard to decipher and peppered with little joyful or wry observations and frustrations. 'Geese are blissful … Billy's leg not yet healed ... US Army actions distressing to witness … mangolds drowned, situation serious.' There is a little reminder note come loose that I spot with a jolt, because it is identical to the aide-memoire I've written and stuck to my writing hut wall to remind me of the correct terminology: rick = corn ... stack = hay. I read until I cannot straighten and am famished. February 1947 is headed 'can do nothing beyond tending cattle' and is followed by pages of a white-out emptiness. While I'm there, Martin has been doing some research of his own and has found a plan of the churchyard. He thinks he knows where Julia's ashes are buried. One late summer evening, we wander down to look.

It is haymaking time and there is the whirr and clatter of someone tedding out the windrows in Champions Field – hay that we will later buy to feed the horses with. The air smells of meadowsweet and there are early moths abroad. We enter the churchyard and wander over to the little squares in the grass that mark a cremation. We count the rows and columns (really not very many) and note the names she is between and find nothing. Just the springy, close-cropped Downland grass. I wander away, disappointed, to watch a huge moon wobble up from above Bumpy Field and the chalk pit. It seems to pull the light up from the moon daisies that dance around the plough. Perhaps I'm just not meant to find her. Perhaps, she doesn't want to be found after all. A thumping sound makes me jump and turn round. I find to my chagrin I am easily spooked in churchyards.

Martin calls me over – he is *actually knocking on the ground, between the gravestones*. 'Don't do that!' I whisper theatrically.

'You'll…' 'I'll what?' He laughs. I'm not amused. But he is on his hands and knees in the now gold light of a full hay moon, poking his fingers into the earth. There is the screech-snore of the barn owl at Manor Farm, no doubt with owlets to feed and making the most of the haycut. I jump again, spooked as a horse. 'There's a stone: feel,' Martin says, and I join him on my knees. He tugs a piece of the turf and it comes away, then I pull a piece away too and there, in the moonlight, is the word 'Farm'. Between us, we gently peel away the square of turf, thyme, plantain and yarrow, and reveal her memorial stone. It looks almost new, unweathered. It reads:

JULIA MAUD WHITE
14TH APRIL 1900
24TH OCTOBER 1989
FARMED
THE MANOR FARM
1941–1955

We sit back on our heels, look at each other, grin. I'm a little bit teary and still half expecting a ghoulish hand on my shoulder, though I am certain any ghosts would be friendly ones, who would quickly tire of my questions. I brush off the crumbs of dirt and pick a few moon daisies, now bright in the moonlight by the wall, and set them on her stone. Hello Julia. The moon shines on her face for the first time in decades.

After the harvest of 1954, spells of bad weather coincide with illness among the farm men and animals. All very draining. Miss White is laid up for three weeks with the measles and Billy has a septic leg from a blackthorn spike. Influenza in the village catches them all. The calves get a husk worm and the heifers black leg; the hay harvest has been poor and much of the corn spoilt. After thirteen years of very hard farming with hardly a break, Miss White finds it tough and knows, from conversations with Doris, that she does too. She rallies. She loves the farm and the life there so much, and determines to take a few more breaks in the caravan with Amber. But by winter 1954, she really is beginning to feel exhausted. Both she and Doris foresee changes ahead that will need the kind of large capital outlay they don't have: innovations in machinery, techniques and the need to enlarge and modernise buildings.

Julia is fifty-four, the same age as I am now, and I recognise a time of change and shift in my own life, too.

There are still always horses, somehow. That gateway into so much else. Horses that have brought me everything, in a way, though I've never actually owned one. Jobs, connections, university, my husband, our children, my best friend, this writerly, bookish life – all reached or found through a five-bar gate with a horse. For a time, there is an abundance of horses, so that Martin, our eldest daughter and I can all ride together, exercising borrowed horses. They knit us into this community. We fetch them from three different yards or stables within whistling distance of each other and the house to tack up. I ride Shadow, a dapple-grey from the yard of the house once owned by Victor and Lady Violet Bonham Carter, who were friends of the Partridges. The house, with its stunning views of Gallows Down, has been rebuilt by the daughter of the woman who inspected the horses' plaits I made in my teens, on dark and freezing winter mornings. I groom and tack up Shadow in their old dairy, where the Mrs Cave I did not know milked her wonderful Jersey cows and later, her son Gabriel, whom I *did* know, laid the hedge with Mr Cordery in Village Hall Piece. We ride together over the Downs and back, Martin in front on Honey Bee, Evie on Storm or Bluey, and me on Shadow. Often, our son, Billy, comes too on his bike, and our youngest daughter, Rosie, with the dog, in a raggedy processional circus.

Honey Bee and Storm grow too old to ride and we give them a happy retirement and enjoy them still, renting a field on behalf of their different owners. The seasonal routines continue, but the markers are skewed. The weather misaligned, thrown off, the birds and insects vanishing. The meadow fills with butterflies in spring and we count them, too easily, for the Big Butterfly Count survey – Julia's Land Girls recall happy *millions* rising up from the grasses falling under the cutter, with its rhythmic *chatter, chatter, chatter*. I remember hundreds. It is hard to imagine thousands, let alone millions. The swallows come to nest in the stables still, though their numbers halve, then quarter, until there are only two left. In winter, I pull silver moons of ice out of the buckets and lay them on the grass in a line in an illustrated chart of moon phases; new moon, quarter moon, half-moon, full. A year passes without any snow at all. Then barely a frost.

With Elizabeth's blessing, we put up a barn owl nest box, made by my father-in-law, Roger, in the oak by her house, next to Nightingale Wood. There have always been barn owls and swallows wherever there are horses; but it's becoming an untruth, isn't it? They are still here, just about, and I do everything in my power to make it so. One evening in early spring, I am searching the field for the pony's fly mask and spot it underneath the old, stag-headed oak tree. He must have rubbed it off on the trunk and it has caught there, looking like a knight's mount, peering around the tree. As I reach for it, there is the subtlest of sounds above: the soft thump and click of claws landing on the nest box platform. It can only, surely, be a barn owl. I flatten myself against the tree and look up and he's standing on the platform of the box, knock-kneed, feather-fur legged, heart-shaped face glowing as the sun sets. He dips off into flight and rows away, light as a moth across the meadow. As I am standing there, heartful and mouth open, his mate pops out too and onto a branch. She looks right down at me, two arm's lengths away. She squeezes her feathered claws into the branch with the tiniest of sounds, shedding small flakes of pale green lichen into my hair, and then is off hunting, too.

I hear plans to fell and then replant the woods on the estate where we live. There are government grants available to regenerate them. It's been happening for years on the neighbouring estates, is completely legal and nothing new, but it often happens in spring, at the height of bird-nesting season. Shocking as it may seem, it is standard practice in these operations. Woods are too wet in winter for the heavy machinery and if there is a pheasant shoot, it risks disturbing the birds. Exceptions to the Wildlife and Countryside Act 1981 read: 'It is not illegal to destroy a nest, egg or bird if it can be shown that the act was the incidental result of a legal operation which could not reasonably have been avoided.'

An application has been applied for, and permission granted from the Forestry Commission and Natural England. One of the woods is a protected Site of Special Scientific Interest (SSSI), albeit in a poor state. Much of the woods is dying ash. None of the people involved are monsters, and the woods will eventually, probably, benefit from regeneration. But why does it have to happen all at once, and in spring? I speak to the foresters, who reassure me of course they'll leave a tree if they spot a bird nesting there and do. We have an emotive but good conversation, yet even so, the woodlark that have recently begun nesting in the edge of the woods' headlands aren't considered. Neither the bats nor the willow tits, for which we have one of the last tiny, remnant populations in the UK, and who nest in dead, standing trees, are considered. On my way to work one morning, the chainsaws begin in Nightingale Wood. I pull over and ring everyone I can: the Barn Owl Trust and local bird ringers, the forestry company, the farm manager and the farm itself, and I say to each one: '*You must not disturb the barn owl.*' I fret all day, but by the time I get home, there is silence, the chainsaws jarring elsewhere. Barn owls are a Schedule 1 protected species and by alerting all involved, they have stopped the work on the woods. The barn owl has saved this little bit of woods and the owl box saved the barn owl.

That summer, the barn owls raise a brood of three chicks. And I think again, this is the work: knowing and reporting that the birds are there. If a tree falls in a forest, if a thousand trees fall in a woods in spring, who notices? Who cares, who knows, without access to these privately owned places? If we are shut out of the woods and the work of the countryside, we are shut off from that knowledge, responsibility and connection – how can we begin to support it in the right way? I think back to Julia and Doris on the brink of all that change, on the brink of so much loss, when I wanted to know what we should do now. But there's a role, isn't there. One on the margins, on the just-outside perhaps, but with a foot in both worlds; the voluntary advisor-without-agency that I was has evolved. There *is* agency in cheerleading good practice, in callingout bad. In campaigning for support for the farming we want and need. I may have left my dreams of farming behind, but in so many ways I've never stopped. I think what farming needs, what wildlife, people and farmers need is a bridge; people that care and are passionate about a living countryside we can all know, with the imagination to bring all the other stuff to bear in farming. A community link – a community that includes nature, the planet and all of us in a positive way.

The felled trees from all the other woods build in great piles, and on the end of them, orange paint spells out their destination: h/wood, f/wood, bio. The 'bio' means this wood is destined for biofuels, to power stations such as Drax in North Yorkshire. Once the UK's largest coal-fired power plant, it now runs on so-called green, renewable energy, burning millions of tonnes of wood pellets each year. But cutting down and burning trees for power emits more carbon than fossil fuels, making Drax not only the UK's single largest carbon emitter but one that harms forests across the world. Of course, trees grow back to reabsorb carbon but, as Greenpeace puts it, 'Climate change is impacted by carbon levels in the present. The regrowth of trees happens over a period of 44 to 104 years … carbon absorption in the future is no help in dealing with the emergency we are facing in the present.' If the wood here is going to power plants like Drax, it will make up only a tiny percentage of the wood burnt, because 99 per cent comes from deforesting biodiverse-rich forests in

Estonia, Latvia, Lithuania, Portugal, the US and, particularly, old-growth forests in British Columbia, Canada. We are powered by fuel, sold to us as 'green', that actually, actively destroys Canadian rainforests. And here we are again. Indigenous land. A caribou, a lynx's habitat, a willow tit's.

The forestry work continues further away, the noise of the felling machines and bark stripper sounding eerily like the cries from men in the fields '*ha woop*', and I keep looking up as if someone is calling me. I open the curtains on the shortest day and it is a shock to see the big down so exposed, having lost its woodland skirts. It looms a whole field closer, like a challenge. I wonder what Julia would have done in the circumstance. Would she have instigated the work regardless of consequences that can be distanced from, to make much-needed revenue? I can't know. The farm is a business. But she always made her own informed decisions, second guessing everything, doing her own research. I like to think she wouldn't have.

Elizabeth dies the following spring after a long illness and, in an echo of the pony books I read as a child, and that she would absolutely have appreciated, she leaves her beloved old, retired horse to us. Rather than go tell the bees of their master's death, as is tradition, I go tell Honey Bee of her mistress's, but, standing like a statue for much of the morning, ears pricked towards the house, it seems she already knows. A few weeks later, we are asked by Elizabeth's carer if we can help her clear some of the old farmhouse – she has been tasked with the job. We tiptoe across the wonky old floors with their nonsensical steps up and down and peer uncomfortably, though fascinated, into rooms filled with the flotsam and accoutrements of another age. One room looks as if it has washed out of a luxury cabin on the *Titanic*. There are monogrammed hat boxes and travelling cases, a side-saddle, a woman's netted riding bowler, paintings of favourite hunters, fabulous, utterly moth-eaten society gowns, and faded photographs of dogs and of people riding horses at picnics. I imagine Miss White's life to have been a little like this, before the Second World War. A life she rejected or, perhaps, that rejected her.

We feel deeply awkward about being asked to help and excuse ourselves. But I do ask for a painting of Honey Bee. We gradually lose the place that has felt like an extension of home. Not the house, apart from the farmhouse kitchen, but the little yard and stables: the tack room where we shared so many Christmas and tack-room teas with Elizabeth, my friend Sarah and her girls; the pony and tractor shed where there is still bunting from my daughter's socially distanced, Covid-times sixteenth birthday party for just her and one friend among the hay bales. Elizabeth's childhood pony trap goes and the gate between our cottage corner across the paddock is nailed shut before we even get the horses moved. I have a final cup of tea from a flask in the tack room and look at the farmhouse through a familiarly broken pane of glass, for the last time. I take with me Horseman John's old two-grained pitchfork and the new scythe he taught me to use, with its whetting stone.

I imagine myself as Miss White now. How would I do things and what might be the credentials that get me there? Me as a half-horse, half-girl, a groom, a cowgirl, artist, a conservation worker, wife and mother, writer of rural things, conjuror of ghosts, community cheerleader – all these things might have equipped and schooled me to be a farmer of sorts. Yet that has remained out of reach. But what I can be instead is a farmer of the imagination. A farmer that does not own or run or even *do* the farming, but one that does everything around that. One that tries to understand, support and applaud farming that has wildlife and people as a central and joyous part of it. That is open and responds to curiosity, which in return, rewards it. Farming that is more resilient to climate change, that stops propelling it. We cannot form a solution, support, a community around anything until we understand, confront and share the problems, and imagine the future. There is agency in that, in imagination activism.

Meanwhile, the ghosts of the birds, the flowers and insects, the ghosts of *abundance*, haunt and haunt me in the silences, the annual reports and anecdotes from others that echo mine, which is in itself an echo chamber, because we never think of anything other than *us* as ghosts, do we? In our fatal anthropocentricity, the ghosts of the fields are always human. But all that abundance, all that loss. I see them, moving across the sky, erupting from the hedgerows as I pass down the lane. I can hear Bert saying, 'Plenty of briddes in the blackthorn at aycrut.' Ghosts of all the birds in the fields and woods; made transient, refugees pushed from one place to another until they are gone. Watching the last flocks or individuals of a species is, in my more devastated moments, like watching the glittering fireworks of a dying star, a beautiful imploding planet. Lapwing: delete. Linnet: delete. Spotted flycatcher: delete. Barn owl: delete. Willow tit, nightingale: delete, delete, delete.

I find myself on the precipice of giving up my beloved 'day job' as a rural school librarian. I write in the gaps, but find the gaps are no longer big enough for me to do the writing I've committed to – and also love. And as much as I talk to the students about books, studying, writing and politics (while remaining neutral, of course) and the environment, we talk a lot about farming and debate those subjects that are part of their everyday lives as country children or the children of rural workers (descendants of Miss White's employees among them): shooting, hunting, veganism, 'that Chris Packham, that Wild Justice, and don't even mention the Right to Roam', campaigning for responsible access to the countryside. Others step in with a defence of rewilding. This morning's topic was the ploughing match and the chance to listen to Scarlett's fantastic speech she has written and prepared for the National Federation of Young Farmers' Clubs public speaking national competition. Her subject is 'Farming is a Feminist Issue' and it's so powerfully spoken, so compelling, she has me in tears. She argues women are better placed to embrace new tech and lead the way in organic and wildlife-friendly farming, and to consider the climate. She states that the 80 per cent of farmworkers that are women around the world, who share knowledge and build communities, are often those suffering the worst effects of climate breakdown. I tell Scarlett of my attempts to get into agricultural college 'way back', and together we discover that female students now outnumber men almost 2:1 on agricultural and related courses. We high five. 'It's our time to take the lead, Miss!' she says. Yes, Scarlett! I make her laugh, telling her of recent comments from a farmer we both know, disgusted that his farm, which is looking for a second farmer, must interview women if they apply. 'What a farce!' he says. 'It's not as if they could do or would get the job!' And the gamekeeper who told me he'd only take on a married underkeeper, 'because it's a strenuous job, and you need hot meals to come home to.' We laugh and rage together, knowing full well, too, that by 'married' this gamekeeper wouldn't imagine a same-sex marriage.

The week after I hand in my notice, I have doubts. I reach into the back of a cupboard for some long-forgotten donated books and pull out one called *Shalbourne to the Millennium*, a local history project. There are photographs and accounts and, yes, there is Doris Mason, there is Marguerite, their faces and eyes crinkled with smiling. What an enormous part of their community they were! After the war, Doris and Marguerite are key in amalgamating all the various wartime clubs into The Shalbourne Club 'to foster and maintain the comradeship and team spirit so evident during wartime, and to harness that spirit … for the social well-being and the good of the village generally'. They are fondly remembered. There are pictures of Jack Tucker in his smock, driving his pony, Bess, to the village fair and photographs of Scouts and Guides. One includes the evacuee farm boy John Robinson, who Julia shared her early mornings with in the kitchen before milking, in a line-up of the village football team in 1950. I am ridiculously thrilled that he stayed. There are no photographs of Julia, though. She remains a little out of reach. But if I needed a sign it was time to go, perhaps this was it. I hear the door in the library open and someone says, 'Well, give it a try; you can probably do it.' I think she is right.

Julia leaves at the end of an era and is sorry to do so. But she has taken on a dilapidated farm at the end of the horse era, introduced tractors and is seeing it into the combine era, with more machinery and fewer workers. She does not think anyone is happier. The old way of working in gangs was enjoyable and profoundly friendly, but hard. And modernisation is what farming, what the country, demands of them all. She tells her 'dear and faithful staff, the very best' early, and makes sure every one of them has somewhere good and secure to go. Tall Billy Edwards with his horses, dear Jack Hitchens, Bill Watts, John Dymond, and Dick and Charlie Wright; Bert, Captain of the Threshing Team and skilled master of all. They give her a wonderful send off at the village hall. The Inkpen Band plays and lifts the roof, and there are wonderful presents, a beautiful collage painting of the farm and village, signed by all her friends, with the most affecting testimonials. She is rather emotional and teary, as am I.

Moving day at Michaelmas, 1955, comes all too soon. A lorry is loaded with her things. She packs her Rover car with her two little dogs in their baskets and the caravan is hitched on. Amber is to follow in the Land Rover with her mother, towing the green tip cart full of chickens and sacks of tail corn. Just as they are about to leave, a cry goes up 'the cows are out' and, sure enough, her leaving is delayed while much of the village and the men come out to round up the Blue Grey cows and calves, and Timid Ivan the bull, following apologetically behind. She has more people to wave her off than she ever thought possible.

In the evening, in the field next door, I am pulling armfuls of ragwort in golden light, as a requirement of the tenancy of the field, making sure to leave plenty where the horses can't reach. There is a ribbon of mist along Dagg's Gully, between Mum's place and ours. The horses' heads come up like springs under pressure, looking at something. And then I see her, coming towards me, and closer now. Julia. It's a favourite spot of hers, where the wildflowers grow and so many birds nest. All quite enchanting. She feels a sort of magic there, as if she might see the great god Pan, down by the sparkling, tea-coloured stream. I can see her so plainly. The laughter-crinkled lines around her eyes, her weathered face, her hair short and curled under. She looks around at the land she knows so well – the little frost pockets in Bumpy that fill with stone curlew and their wailing calls each spring, the place at Grains that suddenly pulls at the plough because there's a clay cap over the chalk. I want to go over, to walk back to the farm together, to chat, because I too am sensing a goodbye.

I'd tell her of the rise of brilliant women farming now and how long it's taken, that it missed me out, but that's OK, I'm doing other things around farming, because of and for it, for the birds, the wildlife, the flowers and insects in whichever way I can; and I'd find a way to blithely mention that some of these farmers are lesbian or queer and that's a brilliant thing too; I'd tell her that there is still so very much work to be done, and I am suddenly shy and wondering where would I begin, there is so much to tell. Then, of course, I know. We'd begin at an open gateway, with all the horses we've ever known and all their names, which we never forget. She looks down at the stitching in her spats, that has come away and needs repairing, and wonders with a jolt whether she'll need to bother. The Michaelmas moon rises like a big copper pan over Pigeon House Meadow and we turn to look at it, and when I look back, she is walking away, stirring up moths as she goes, and the cows come jostling to greet her. Do we project ghosts, like an old cine reel playing out, a pale hologram of woodbine smoke, or a rising column of midges, golden in the late last light? Or do they seek us out, in a quest to be heard, with fresh relevance?

From my writing hut on Rooksnest Lane, the rooks go daily from the fields to their roost at Manor Farm, like so many words, and I write and I write and I write, until Miss White and I are writing the same book, from the same fields in a different time. Her book, the village and its friendly ghosts possess my fingers and keyboard in a mad dance, a gallop over the typewriter and laptop keys, infiltrating my phone, breaking pencils and running out pens. I am like Moira Shearer in *The Red Shoes* in 1948. I have a fever and when it breaks, it will be a book for Julia and all our ghosts.

The barn owl flies between me and my vision of Miss White. Somewhere, a horse whinnies, scrapes a shod hoof on the floor of the old threshing barn. I put the characters in place, set the cows in their fields, shut the gate. Rise up over the fields like a lapwing, and go home.

THE END.

EPILOGUE

Doris and Julia sold Manor Farm on 30 June 1955. The sales catalogue describes a 'valuable Corn and Stock Farm on the borders of Berkshire, Wiltshire and Hampshire'; a farm that is either in, or touches each of those three counties. The catalogue outlines an 'excellent old world farmhouse', two cottages, several outbuildings and barns and states, 'The farm has been well managed and well maintained and will be found to be in good heart.' It is sold to Captain Douglas for £28,000, with the new owner to take vacant possession on 29 September 1955 at Michaelmas. Prior to the sale, Doris and Julia sold some of the fields to neighbours, including the farm we live on, and the one opposite. Major Huth bought Inglebutts and Black Butts under the down, complete with a newly designated public bridleway and footpath. Bravo, Miss White! Manor Farm has changed hands and been let several times since, but from the records of the evacuee children at the primary school in the 1940s to the Fenemore family who farmed it in the 1970s and '80s, right up till now, it is known to have been a very happy place.

Julia retired from farming and lived first in Brockenhurst in the New Forest with Amber and Mrs Ambrose, and then in the pretty Downland village of Martyr Worthy, on the outskirts of Winchester. She named her bungalow there 'Smockland' in honour of her farming life and the smock she was gifted as Jack Tucker's apprentice, when it all began. Julia remained very active, running Guide camps with Amber in the little meadow beside her home, as well as gardening and becoming quite an artist. She and Amber were together twenty-eight years, until Amber's death. Julia lived another six years, with a succession of Dandie Dinmont terriers, the last of which were Cobweb and Sibyl. She professed to never be lonely, writing up and revisiting the diaries that became *The Inkpen Saga* that inspired this book; her 'Inkpen of happy memories'. She enjoyed the company of many friends who visited often and continued to paint despite suffering from arthritis. As a postscript, she writes, 'My long and varied life has taught me to be philosophical and to accept things as they come along, which makes for contentment and a peaceful mind.'

Doris Mason was the daughter of Lady Evelyn Mason of Eynsham Hall, Witney, Oxfordshire, and the granddaughter of the Earl of Crawford and Balcarres. She bought Shalbourne Manor and adjoining Baverstock Farm in 1935. Marguerite de Beaumont, daughter of Kathleen Mary née O'Hagan and Louis Charles Leopold Martial de Beaumont-Klein, a Cambridge university lecturer, was Doris's lifelong partner, and came with her. They both actively farmed and, between them, employed most of the village, quickly winning the affection and regard of all those around them. Doris spent twenty-four years as first woman member of the Marlborough, Bedwyn and Ramsbury Rural Council. She was the first woman magistrate to sit on the Marlborough County Bench when Sir Francis Burdett's reign ended. Doris said of this that Burdett 'would not have a woman on the Bench to save his life'. She retired in 1964 as chairman of the Bench 'so that some of the boys can take office before their hair turns grey'. She worked in mental health and was on Pewsey Hospital Management Committee as well as president of Shalbourne Sports Club and chair of the school governors. She donated the village green in 1937 and a large field for the village recreation ground in 1945, on which fetes and 'junketings' are still held today.

Doris died unexpectedly, aged just sixty, in Shalbourne, in 1964. On the evening before her death, villagers recall her walking cheerily through the village and up to the top of Rivars Hill, where she sat under the big oak tree, looking down on the home she had enjoyed for thirty years, and Inkpen Manor Farm. According to *Shalbourne to the Millennium*, she was 'remembered with great fondness by all the folk who had the privilege of either working for or with her'. Doris bequeathed the estate to her partner, Marguerite, who continued to run her renowned stud and involve herself in the community. Marguerite died the same year as Julia, when they were both in their ninetieth years (1989). In turn, Marguerite left Shalbourne Manor and farm to her veterinarian, Pip Pocock, who rethatched the oldest of the barns and used it to hold a village party in celebration of the fiftieth anniversary of VJ Day in 1995.

Old Harry Tucker (with the living floral hat) survived the distress and depression brought on by foot-and-mouth on his farm in 1940 and continued to work on the land. He and his wife, Florrie, celebrated their golden wedding anniversary in 1950. They had eighteen children: ten boys and eight girls, with thirteen surviving into adulthood. Five of their sons fought in the First World War. 'Granny' Florrie Tucker was renowned for her halfpenny bottles of ginger beer,which she made and sold as 'Granny Tucker's Halfpenny Fizzers' on Shalbourne Club Days, when the Inkpen Band would come over and play.

The Inkpen Saga was written more than thirty years after Julia retired from farming, when she was in her mid-eighties. It is informed by her Day Book and Cultivations Record, which I spent many hours poring over and deciphering at the Berkshire Records Office in Reading, which is, lucky for me, close to the Museum of English Rural Life.

All of the events in this book are true; both mine and Julia's. In the case of Julia White's story, I've allowed historically based and researched imagination, and my knowledge of the place, to fill and colour in small gaps. This may have been putting one or two thoughts in Julia's head, introducing a little conversation here and there – or bringing in the weather. Bizarrely for a farmer, the weather is barely mentioned in her book and would have been the most important thing in dictating what she did. The wildlife, abundant as it was, isn't mentioned very much either – it was just gloriously *there* and thriving, of its own accord. But she did appreciate it and love it very much – which is apparent when she does mention it.

Using a little creative licence in this way brings, I hope, Julia White to more vivid life. She is naturally self-deprecating and very funny with a dry, quick wit and an enormous energy and zest for life – but she is not, perhaps, a practised or natural writer. I wanted to show her, humble as she was, in her best light, as others saw her.

I walked and poked around the village a lot, looked at maps and spoke to a lot of local people – almost all of whom I know anyway, from living in the same village for a long time. There are many more, just out of reach now by only a few years, that of course I wish I'd spoken to when they were alive. I hope readers, especially local ones, will forgive me if I've omitted certain details, dates or people. Our memories are unique to us and true, and we are all, in our own way, unreliable yet utterly truthful narrators.

To put myself in the time – I am already in the place – I read as many wartime rural and farming books as I could, particularly by women farmers and Land Girls. There were more of them than I ever imagined, and, particularly, queer women farmers. The more I found this, the more I wanted to know why there didn't seem to be any women farmers by the 1980s. Which might raise the question, how do you begin to write a story like this, that is part retelling, part memoir, part biography of someone you almost, but didn't quite, meet? How do you celebrate, but not sanctify that life? How do you interrogate, but not judge? And how do you relate the farming of the past, in such a time of threat and war, to a kind of farming in these times of existential crisis, almost unimaginable to someone eighty-odd years ago? A haunting is what this story is and ghosts, whether of the paths I didn't take, the wildlife gone, attitudes, buildings, actual people, barns, birds, horses, weather, airmail from Canada – are what I harnessed to my little farm-cart narrative, and drove it forwards.

Epilogue

Miss White writes, with just a glimmer of sentiment and a wry smile, on the last page of *The Inkpen Saga*:

> *This is an authentic account of my life at Inkpen from Michaelmas 1941 to Michaelmas 1955. Having kept all my diaries, wages books and other records I have had no need to invent. I had enjoyed my time there very much and my partnership with Doris Mason had been very happy, I was very sorry to leave.*

I am glad Julia had a long, happy and active retirement. I'm there with the gathered villagers on that dusty road, waving her off in her Rover car and caravan, with Amber and Mrs Ambrose following on with the Land Rover and the green tip cart full of chickens, a tear in all our eyes.

ACKNOWLEDGEMENTS

Heartfelt thanks to Anne Williams, who first heard this idea on a sunny walk through grazing cows and horses on Port Meadow and out to Binsey, Oxfordshire. A walk that began, appropriately, from a little housing development called Old Rickyard Piece.

I am profoundly grateful to the editorial skill and intuition of Muna Reyal, who encouraged me to bring the righteous passion when I might have been holding back and also to very gently set aside my darlings (there were so many more stories!) for another time. Thank you to the whole Chelsea Green 'village', who have indeed made good on their promise to nurture and support me as an author, given when they published my first book, *On Gallows Down*, also set in the village of Inkpen.

Much gratitude to the Inkpen History Society, the Hungerford Virtual Museum, the Royal Berkshire Archives, the West Berkshire Museum and the Museum of English Rural Life – especially to Ollie Douglas – and anyone that takes the time to listen and record old stories and old methods. They are too often out of reach by the time we realise we need and want them.

Thank you to Carmen James of Beech Farm and the pony girls of 'The Babes', Whitchurch-Upon-Thames. Thank you to Julia's great-nieces and nephew for permission to use her book and the Society of Authors for advice and guidance.

I owe a debt to many Inkpenners for their stories and memories, some of which I've shared with them, too. It was very much a collaboration on occasion. Particular thanks to Betty Grimsey,

Janet Taylor, Kate Edwards, Stephen Painting, Bob May, Sally Colquhoun, Steve Cordery and the Athertons.

Nic Wilson has been a great source of encouragement and help in finding a bit more of Miss White (much gratitude). In stolen writerly lunchtime chats in the school staffroom, Hoffi Robinson has listened to so much of this journey and helped me work around some fences with such clarity, and close a few gates too, which I value so much. Thank you to the wonderful students and student librarians at John O'Gaunt School – you make me think afresh. Particular thanks to Scarlett Slatter, who definitely brings the fierce passion and indignation on behalf of rural women.

Love and thanks to my incredibly lovely and supportive family; the one I'm from and the one I joined, especially my dearest mum, who has put up with so much procrastination and horsey silliness (love ya), and Sarah Evans, the bestest of friends, who continues to canter alongside me and who has lived this story with me – enjoy the horses! To my amazing, creative, funny and kind country kids, Billy, Evie and Rosie, who I look up to in all the ways. And to my dear husband, Martin, thank you profoundly for your support through this and belief in me. Yours is the community I always want to be part of.

SELECT BIBLIOGRAPHY

Allingham, Margery. *The Oaken Heart: The Story of an English Village at War*. Golden Duck, 2011. With an introduction by Ronald Blythe.

Barraud, Enid M. *Set My Hand upon the Plough*. Little Toller Books, 2024. With an introduction by Luke Turner.

Collis, John Stewart. *The Worm Forgives the Plough*. Vintage, 2009. With an introduction by Robert Macfarlane.

Crean, Patrick B. *Pictures on My Pillow: An Oceanographer's Exploration of the Symbols of Self-Transcendence*. Agio, 2011. In which Patrick recounts some of his childhood as an evacuee and Scout in Shalbourne, Wiltshire.

Deakin, Rose. *Frances Donaldson: A Woman's War – Letters to a Soldier in the Second World War*. Eden Valley Editions, 2017. A fantastic insight into the life and challenges of a woman farmer/owner.

Evans, Lissa. *Their Finest Hour and a Half*. Black Swan, 2009. Lissa writes so utterly beautifully and convincingly, and all her books are delicious masterpieces of the era.

Evans, Lissa. *Small Bomb at Dimperley*. Doubleday, 2024.

Ginn, Peter, Ruth Goodman and Alexander Langlands. *Wartime Farm: Rediscovering the Spirit of World War II*. Mitchell Beazley, 2012. The BBC series, *Wartime Farm*, to which this book is an accompaniment, is also a valuable source of information.

Huth, Angela. *Land Girls*. Constable, 1994. A vivid and rich characterisation of the era from a female perspective.

Leighton, Clare. *Clare Leighton's Rural Life*, edited by David Leighton. Bodleian Library, 2024. Art and writing of the era, from a rural working perspective, in England, Canada and the US.

Malik, Rachel. *Miss Boston and Miss Hargreaves*. Penguin, 2017. A poignant and gripping story based on Rachel's grandmother's story and set just a few miles from Inkpen.

Martin, E.A. *Inkpen Yesterday*. Edyvean Printers, 1993. A much-read, detailed local history.

Nicholson, Virginia. *Millions Like Us: Women's Lives During the Second World War*. Penguin, 2012. A deeply moving treasure trove of women's wartime experience.

Partridge, Frances. *A Pacifist's War*. Hogarth Press, 1978. Frances' diary, which covers 1939–1945, was an excellent cross-reference as she is writing about the same place at the same time. It does, however, include some racist words of that period and a racist observation.

Shalbourne History Project. *Shalbourne to the Millennium*. Shalbourne History Project, 1999. Contains such fond and detailed memories of a rural community.

Sheridan, Dorothy, ed. *Wartime Women: A Mass Observation Anthology, 1937–1945*. Heinemann, 1990. Wonderfully candid and intimate insights from a broad spectrum.

Street, A.G. *Farmer's Glory*. Little Toller Books, 2017. With an introduction by James Rebanks.

Tyrer, Nicola. *They Fought in the Fields: The Women's Land Army: The Story of a Forgotten Victory*. The History Press, 2007. How women also overcame male prejudice and hostility with grit, positivity, camaraderie and tenacity.

Whitton, Barbara. *Green Hands*. Imperial War Museum, 2020. Margaret Hazel Watson's (writing under a pseudonym) fictionalised account of her time as a Land Girl during the Second World War.

ABOUT THE AUTHOR

Jeremy Prout

Nicola is the author of the award-winning memoir *On Gallows Down: Place, Protest and Belonging*, which was Highly Commended for the Wainwright Prize for Nature Writing and winner of the Richard Jefferies. Her first book was *RSPB Spotlight: Otters*.

One of the early female pioneers of nature writing, Nicola has written a column for the *RSPB Magazine* since 2004 after winning *BBC Wildlife Magazine*'s Nature Writer of the Year Award, as well as a column for the *Newbury Weekly News*, 2003–2023. She is a *Guardian* country diarist and writes for the BBC's *Countryfile* magazine as well as other online and print publications. Nicola's writing also features in several anthologies, most recently *Wild Service: Why Nature Needs You*, *Under the Changing Skies: The Best of the Guardian's Country Diary, 2018–2024*, *KIN: An Anthology of Poetry, Story and Art by Women from Romani, Traveller and Nomadic Communities* and *Women on Nature: 100+ Voices on Place, Landscape and the Natural World*. She wrote for the RSPB's junior and youth magazines for many years, inspiring many of today's young wildlife campaigners.

A former school librarian, Nicola was a judge for the inaugural Climate Fiction Prize 2025, which was launched at the Hay Festival. She has been a guest speaker and taught sessions for undergraduate, post-graduate and MA Creative Writing students at Cambridge University, Bournemouth University, Sheffield University, and for the MA in Nature and Travel Writing at Bath Spa University. Nicola is a passionate campaigner and activist for nature, and she and her family are tenants in an estate-workers' cottage at the heart of the North Wessex Downs.